Bible Studies
Psalms

Second Edition

James Malm

ISBN: 978-1-989208-06-9

Copyright 2018 James David Malm
all rights reserved
Unless otherwise noted all scriptures
are quoted from the King James Version

Dedication

This work is dedicated to the Great God whose house is eternity; the Father and Sovereign of all that exists and the sum of all Truth, Wisdom, Love, Justice and Mercy.
May God's house be filled with children whose chief joy is to be like Him!

Visit Our Website
theshininglight.info

Table of Contents
Psalms 5

    Introduction 7

    Psalms 1 - 10 9

    Psalms 11 - 20 27

    Psalms 21 - 30 44

    Psalms 31 - 40 62

    Psalms 41 - 50 86

    Psalms 51 - 60 105

    Psalms 61 - 70 121

    Psalms 71 - 80 140

    Psalms 81 - 90 164

    Psalms 91 – 100 183

    Psalms 101 - 110 197

    Psalms 111 - 118 227

    Psalm 119 244

    Psalms 120 - 129 273

    Psalms 130 - 140 284

    Psalms 141 – 150 300

Psalms

Introduction

God has seen fit to preserve much of David's history as well as the Psalms. Why?

We need to read David's Psalms and the history of his battles with enemies and with sin, and then stand back and see them in the allegorical spiritual context of our own struggles with sin and our struggles with spiritual enemies, persecutions and spiritual struggles.

Like David fought the Philistines and Canaanites, we fight against the hosts of wickedness. God gave David victories when he was faithful and many sore trials to perfect his righteousness and we also have many trials and we will also have an ultimate victory over all wickedness and sin if we faint not.

There are tremendous spiritual lessons in the Psalms and the struggles of David about godliness and deliverance, about who we can always trust and rely on and about faithfulness and perseverance.

When we realize that our struggles are not against flesh and blood but against sin and wickedness (Eph 6:12), the spiritual meaning of the Psalms [and the rest of the Old Testament] becomes plain.

Psalms 1 - 10

Psalm 1

The blessings for faithfully and diligently living by every Word of God without compromise

Psalm 1:1 Blessed is the man that walketh not in the counsel of the ungodly, nor standeth in the way of sinners, nor sitteth in the seat of the scornful.

The man who does not compromise with the commandments of God; who does not follow the counsel of the ungodly, who does not encourage sin by teaching the lie that God will understand and forgive wilful sin: The person who does not live sinfully by the wilful breaking of any of the commandments of God and who rejects those who scorn passionate love and zeal for the law of the God of Jacob; the one who lives passionately with Christ-like zeal to live by EVERY WORD of God: Are the people who will be called "The Blessed of the Lord" at his coming!

1:2 But his delight is in the law of the Lord; and in his law doth he meditate day and night.

If we seek our God and think on his Word day and night; if we drink deeply of the waters of the Word and Spirit of our God to do them; we will bear much fruit in our spiritual lives.

As a tree drinks water from the earth and bears its fruit in season, if we deeply drink of the water of the Word of God, to live by EVERY WORD of God we shall bear much fruit in the proper season of God's will.

> **Matthew 13:8** But other [seed of God's Word] fell into good ground, and brought forth fruit, some an hundredfold, some sixtyfold, some thirtyfold.

Psalm 1:3 And he shall be like a tree planted by the rivers of water, that bringeth forth his fruit in his season; his leaf also shall not wither; and whatsoever he doeth shall prosper.

The ungodly who cling to the false traditions of men and exalt idols of men above any zeal to live by every Word of God will have no spiritual growth, they are spiritually DEAD and will be disappointed in that day. The ungodly who teach tolerance for the wilful breaking of ANY part of God's Word, who supplant the commandments of God with their own ways; they shall spiritually dry up and be driven away by every wind of false doctrine until they be destroyed.

1:4 The ungodly are not so: but are like the chaff which the wind driveth away. **1:5** Therefore the ungodly shall not stand in the judgment, nor sinners in the congregation of the righteous.

Those who are not passionately zealously diligent in internalizing the nature of God through the doing of his will and enthusiastically living by every Word of God; will NOT be resurrected to eternal life in the day of judgment nor will they stand in the resurrected congregation of the righteous first fruits on the heavenly Crystal Expanse before the throne of God (Rev 15).

1:6 For the Lord knoweth the way of the righteous: but the way of the ungodly shall perish.

The ungodly are those who compromise with a zealous and diligent, night and day internalizing of the Word God, and who refuse to live by every Word of God, preferring their own ways, idols of men and false traditions above the Word of God.

That includes the vast majority today, and unless they repent and regain their first love for God, to live by every Word of God; they shall in no wise enter the kingdom of heaven. Yet a loving God will soon correct us to save us, afflicting the flesh so that he may save the spirit.

Psalm 2

A Prophecy of Messiah

Psalm 2:1 Why do the heathen rage, and the people imagine a vain thing? **2:2** The kings of the earth set themselves, and the rulers take counsel together, against the LORD, and against his anointed, saying, **2:3** Let us break their bands asunder, and cast away their cords from us.

The wicked desire to rebel against God and cast off the bands and cords of restraint on wickedness which are provided by the Word of GOD!

God holds such rebels in high derision for they are like naughty children who know nothing and yet think that they know all things, not realizing that they are making fools of themselves in their rebellion against the Mighty One of Jacob.

The day of the Lord will come upon them and Christ with his faithful shall stand a King on Zion and Jerusalem shall be God's capital city over all the earth.

2:4 He that sitteth in the heavens shall laugh: the LORD shall have them in derision. **2:5** Then shall he speak unto them in his wrath, and vex them in his sore displeasure. **2:6** Yet have I set my king [Messiah the Christ and his Chosen] upon my holy hill of Zion.

An inset about the begettal and birth of Christ

2:7 I will declare the decree: the LORD hath said unto me, Thou art my Son; this day have I begotten thee.

The Being who made all things as the Implementing Creator would later give up his God-hood to become flesh and be placed in the womb of Mary by God the Father who by that act then became the Father and the Creator became the Son.

Then after the Son lived a perfect sinless life and gave himself as a perfect and efficacious sacrifice for his creation was resurrected by God the Father; the Son will be placed by God the Father as King of kings over all the earth.

2:8 Ask of me, and **I shall give thee the heathen for thine inheritance, and the uttermost parts of the earth for thy possession.** **2:9** Thou shalt break them [all of the wicked and rebellious including those faithless in the Ekklesia of God] with a rod of iron; thou shalt dash them in pieces like a potter's vessel.

Repent quickly you faithless compromisers with the Word of God, and seek the wisdom of our God to live by every Word of God (Mat 4:4).

2:10 Be wise now therefore, O ye kings: be instructed, ye judges of the earth. 2:11 Serve the LORD with fear, and rejoice with trembling.

Live by every Word of God and embrace the teachings and ways of the Son who faithfully obeyed God the Father in ALL things.

2:12 Kiss the Son [embrace and follow Messiah the Christ], lest he be angry, and ye perish from the way, when his wrath is kindled but a little. Blessed are all they that put their trust in him.

Psalm 3

I want to dedicate this psalm to all those who are facing persecution and strong condemnation for their zeal for God; including from their brethren who they have loved and trusted..

Many are the troubles, trials and enemies of those who are truly zealous to live by every Word of the Mighty Father God.

Psalm 3:1 Lord, how are they increased that trouble me! many are they that rise up against me. **3:2** Many there be which say of my soul, There is no help for him in God. Selah.

Trust in God and continually live by every Word of God and there will be much opposition; from the mocking of some, to outright persecution by others; but if we remain faithful and Run to God our Father and the Son our espoused Husband for help, instead of thinking to save ourselves by compromising with God's ways, laws and teachings: We will be lifted up on that Great Day of Deliverance, when death itself is made to give up the Beloved of God!

3:3 But **thou, O LORD, art a shield for me; my glory, and the lifter up of mine head**. **3:4** I cried unto the LORD with my voice, and he heard me out of his holy hill. Selah.

Though we sleep the sleep of death, our God will raise us up from the sleep of the grave; if we are zealous to live by his Word.

3:5 I laid me down and slept; I awaked; for the LORD sustained me.

Fear not, you who love God enough to live by his Word; for he will deliver us at the coming of Messiah the Christ.

3:6 I will not be afraid of ten thousands of people, that have set themselves against me round about. **3:7** Arise, O LORD; save me, O my God: for thou hast smitten all mine enemies upon the cheek bone; thou hast broken the teeth of the ungodly. **3:8 Salvation belongeth unto the LORD: thy blessing is upon thy people** [all those who love to live by every Word of God].

Selah.

Psalm 4

A Prayer for Deliverance

Psalm 4:1 Hear me when I call, O God of my righteousness [God is righteousness and we are to live according to God's righteousness]: thou hast enlarged [saved and delivered the godly faithful] me when I was in distress; have mercy upon me, and hear my prayer.

The commandments of God will make us righteous like God, if we diligently live by them.

4:2 O ye sons of men, how long will ye turn my glory into shame? how long will ye love vanity, and seek after leasing [falsehood]? Selah. **4:3** But know that the LORD hath set apart him that is godly for himself: the LORD will hear when I call unto him.

Those who are zealous for our God and his law are "Set Apart" and are holy to our God. They are separated out from among their brethren that mock and shame them for their zeal; and for their shame they shall have the reward of eternal life and kingship over the nations.

4:4 Stand in awe, and sin not: commune [think on the Word of God] with your own heart [mind, thoughts] upon your bed, and be still [be quiet from sin and every false way]. Selah.

Be in awe of God and tremble at his Word. Abhor and reject sin, which is compromising with, or breaking any part of the Word of God. Consider these things in your thoughts.

4:5 Offer the sacrifices of righteousness [obedience to EVERY Word of God], and put your trust in the Lord.

4:6 There be many that say, Who will shew us any good? Lord, lift thou up the light of thy countenance upon us. **4:7** Thou hast put gladness in my heart, more than in the time that their corn [grain] and their wine increased.

The Word and commandments of God are better than an increase of grain and wine; better than any physical riches or personal exaltation.

4:8 I will both lay me down in peace, and sleep: for thou, Lord, only makest me dwell in safety.

Keeping all of the commandments of God brings us into a close relationship with our God and fills us with a faith that brings peace of mind. We know that whatever our troubles, even if we must obey unto death; God will keep his promise and raise us up on that day.

Psalm 5

Like David we should seek God night and day

Psalm 5:1 Give ear to my words, O Lord, consider my meditation. **5:2** Hearken unto the voice of my cry, my King, and my God: for unto thee will I pray.

5:3 My voice shalt thou hear in the morning, O Lord; in the morning will I direct my prayer unto thee, and will look up [exalt God]. **5:4** For thou art not a God that hath pleasure in wickedness: neither shall evil dwell with thee **5:5** The foolish shall not stand in thy sight: thou hatest all workers of iniquity.

The foolish are those who do not respect and tremble in awe at the Word and commandments of God, for God hates any compromise with his Word; which compromise is iniquity.

5:6 Thou shalt destroy them that speak leasing [falsely]: the Lord will abhor the bloody and deceitful man.

The Eternal abhors the deliberate twisting of words to deceive, and he despises the teacher of false doctrine and the false prophecies of the unconverted. Any man who allows compromise with the Word of God is a bloody man, for he separates people from God and leads them to damnation; unless they find their way and repent, leaving off from following such men.

The Eternal will have mercy on the sincerely repentant who are full of Christ-like zeal to live by EVERY WORD of God.

5:7 But as for me, I will come into thy house in the multitude of thy mercy: and in thy fear will I worship toward thy holy temple. **5:8** Lead me, O Lord, in thy righteousness because of mine enemies; make thy way straight before my face.

Let us long for God to reveal to us the secret things of his Word, and for God to give us a good understanding of His ways so that we might become like Him. Like God, let us despise deceitfulness and all compromising and rebellion against any part of the Word of God.

The worldly described and their end revealed

5:9 For there is no faithfulness in their mouth; their inward part is very wickedness; their throat is an open sepulchre; they flatter with their tongue [they use flatteries and deceit to lead people away from their zeal for God and into the sin of idolizing men]. **5:10** Destroy thou them, O God; let them fall by their own counsels; cast them out in the multitude of their transgressions; for they have rebelled against thee.

The joy of the faithful who love God enough to live by every Word of God

5:11 But let all those that put their trust in thee rejoice: let them ever shout for joy, because thou defendest them: let them also that love thy name be joyful in thee. 5:13 For thou, Lord, wilt bless the righteous [the commandment keepers who love God enough to live by every Word of God]; **with favour wilt thou compass him as with a shield.**

Psalm 6

A prayer for deliverance

Psalm 6:1 O LORD, rebuke me not in thine anger, neither chasten me in thy hot displeasure.

6:2 Have mercy upon me, O LORD; for I am weak: O LORD, heal me [deliver us from the Adversary for we cannot deliver ourselves]; for my bones are vexed [by the enemies of righteousness]. **6:3** My soul [breath, life] is also sore vexed: but thou, O LORD, how long?

How long must we wait for your merciful deliverance?

6:4 Return, O LORD, deliver my soul [breath, life]: oh save me for thy mercies' sake.

David is faithful to God but feels overwhelmed by the adversaries of godliness; who refuse to live by God's Word and who persecute those who do.

The dead are like a machine with the power switch shut off, unable to do anything

6:5 For in death there is no remembrance of thee: in the grave who shall give thee thanks?

This is a call to be saved from physical death, as an allegory of being saved from the grave in the resurrection to spirit.

6:6 I am weary with my groaning; all the night make I my bed to swim [with my tears of sorrow]; I water my couch with my tears. **6:7** Mine eye is consumed because of grief; it waxeth old because of all mine enemies.

God will deliver all those who exalt and put their trust in him to live by God's Word; and all those who condemn them for their Christ-like zeal for God will be ashamed.

6:8 Depart from me, all ye workers of iniquity; for the LORD hath heard the voice of my weeping. 6:9 The LORD hath heard my supplication; the LORD will receive my prayer. 6:10 Let all mine enemies be ashamed and sore vexed: let them return and be ashamed suddenly.

Psalm 7

David's prayer for deliverance from the ungodly continues

Psalm 7:1 O LORD my God, in thee do I put my trust: save me from all them that persecute me, and deliver me: 7:2 Lest he tear my soul like a lion, rending it in pieces, while there is none to deliver.

The natural thing is to lash back at our tormentors but whenever we fall into trials we must first examine ourselves, asking God to reveal to us the reason for the trial and asking God to help everyone involved to learn from the situation, and we are to sincerely repent if we have done any sin ourselves.

7:3 O LORD my God, If I have done this; if there be iniquity in my hands; **7:4** If I have rewarded evil unto him that was at peace with me; (yea, I have delivered him that without cause is mine enemy:) **7:5** Let the enemy persecute my soul, and take it; yea, let him tread down my life upon the earth, and lay mine honour in the dust. Selah.

David set an example which is also a prophecy of the conduct of Christ, who would later also command his people to follow this example.

> **Matthew 5:44** But I say unto you, **Love your enemies, bless them that curse you, do good to them that hate you, and pray for them which despitefully use you, and persecute you;**

David calls for and prophesies of the coming of Messiah the Christ to deliver his people from their enemies.

Psalm 7:6 Arise, O LORD, in thine anger, lift up thyself because of the rage of mine enemies: and awake for me to the judgment that thou hast commanded. **7:7** So shall the congregation of the people compass thee about: for their sakes therefore return thou on high.

Messiah the Christ will judge the people according to whether they are righteous in living by every Word of God or not.

7:8 The LORD shall judge the people: judge me, O LORD, according to [whether we are righteous according to God's Word] my righteousness, and according to mine integrity [whether we live by God's Word or not] that is in me.

7:9 Oh let the wickedness of the wicked [who reject any zeal to live by every Word of God] come to an end; but establish the just [who do live by every Word of God]: for the righteous God trieth the hearts and reins [kidneys, tests our weaknesses].

7:10 My defence is of God, which saveth the upright in heart. **7:11** God judgeth [delivers] the righteous [who are those zealous to live by every Word of God], and God is angry with the wicked every day.

7:12 If he turn not [if we will not repent of our lack of zeal to live by every Word of God, we shall be corrected in tribulation], he will whet [sharpen] his sword; he hath bent his bow, and made it ready. **7:13** He hath also prepared for him [for the unrepentant who compromise with the Word of God] the instruments of death; he ordaineth his arrows against the persecutors.

7:14 Behold, he travaileth [see the end of the wicked who work to do evil and rebel against godliness] with iniquity, and hath conceived mischief, and brought forth falsehood. **7:15** He made a pit [the wicked are trapped in their own false imaginations], and digged it, and is fallen into the ditch which he made. **7:16** His mischief shall return upon his own head, and his violent dealing shall come down upon his own pate.

The Eternal delivers those who internalize the righteousness of God through living by every Word of God; and the Eternal corrects and rebukes all those who will not live by every Word of God.

7:17 I will praise the LORD according to his righteousness: and will sing praise to the name of the LORD most high.

Psalm 8

The Glory of God and His Kindness to Men

Psalm 8:1 O LORD, our Lord, how excellent is thy name [reputation] in all the earth! who hast set thy glory above the heavens.

God works through the weak of this world to confound the mighty, so that all may know that such weak persons did not do the work on their own, but that the work was done by the power of Almighty God.

8:2 Out of the mouth of babes and sucklings hast thou ordained strength because of thine enemies, that thou mightest still the enemy and the avenger.

The Father calls the childlike and the weak in the wisdom of this world, so that he might give them the wisdom of God which surpasses all human wisdom. In that way the wise and great of this world will be forced to admit that this is not a natural wisdom but the wisdom of God.

> **1 Corinthians 1:25** Because the foolishness of God is wiser than [much wiser than the understanding of carnal man] men; and the weakness of God is stronger than men.

1:26 For ye see your calling, brethren, how that not many wise men after the flesh, not many mighty, not many noble, [of this world] are called:

1:27 But God hath chosen the foolish things [those that are ignorant of worldly wisdom] of the world to confound the wise; and God hath chosen the weak things of the world to confound the things which are mighty; [so that no flesh should glory in itself; and so that all men would eventually understand that all glory belongs to God alone]

1:28 And base things of the world, and things which are despised, hath God chosen, yea, and things which are not [are nothing in the eyes of this society], to bring to nought things that are: **1:29** That no flesh should glory in his presence.

1:30 But of him are ye in Christ Jesus, who of God is made unto us wisdom, and righteousness, and sanctification, and redemption: **1:31** That, according as it is written, He that glorieth, let him glory in the Lord.

Those steeped in worldly knowledge will consider the wisdom of God to be foolishness and will not respond positively to it. Therefore God must call out those ignorant in worldly wisdom, who will respond positively to the wisdom of God.

No man can say that he understands the things of God by his own efforts. Understanding is the gift of the Holy Spirit which guides into all truth and provides us with understanding of the things of God.

God does not call many wise in this society lest they become vain and proudly self-righteous; falsely thinking that they have understood and become righteous by their own efforts. God calls the poor in spirit, the contrite of heart, the humble; because they will exalt their God and will not exalt themselves.

Those who exalt themselves will be abased, so that being humbled they too can be saved. It is the Spirit, the very mind and nature of God the Father and Jesus Christ dwelling in us; which gives us the wisdom, righteousness and sanctification of Christ; who is our redemption!

Jesus Christ dwelling in us through the Holy Spirit; will empower us to obey God the Father [as Christ did and does] and such obedience will be rewarded with the gift of even more understanding!

The wise of this society think that obeying God is foolishness and will not obey God's Word. Therefore they cannot receive the Holy Spirit which gives understanding; until they have been humbled.

The Spirit of God is the wisdom, truth and mind of God and the Word of God defines God's mind and nature; therefore if we reject any zeal to live by every Word of God, we are rejecting God and God's Spirit!

If we refuse to DO what is godly; we are rejecting the very nature and Spirit of God!

The leaders and elders of today's spiritual Ekklesia who reject Nehemiah because they want to pollute the Sabbath; are rejecting a part of the very mind of God! They are rejecting the Spirit of God!

When we Prove All Things, and hold fast only to what God has proclaimed in his Word; then we are building the nature of God within ourselves!

> When the brethren do as the men over these organizations tell them to do, contrary to any part of the whole the Word of God; we are exalting such men over God's Word; which is IDOLATRY and spiritual ADULTERY against our espoused Husband!

> Idolatry and adultery are forbidden by God's law, and if we do what men say instead of what God's commands; we are rejecting the very nature and mind of God! We are rejecting Almighty God and God's Spirit, for idols of men!

God will stop the mouths of the wisest rebels with his far greater wisdom.

What is man compared to God?

Psalm 8:3 When I consider thy heavens, the work of thy fingers, the moon and the stars, which thou hast ordained; **8:4** What is man, that thou art mindful of him? and the son of man, that thou visitest him?

What is man that the Great God has given men dominion over the earth and all things therein? Our dominion is a gift from God the Creator, and none of these things was created by men.

8:5 For thou hast made him a little lower than the angels, and hast crowned him with glory and honour. **8:6** Thou madest him to have dominion over the works of thy hands; thou hast put all things under his feet: **8:7** All sheep and oxen, yea, and the beasts of the field; **8:8** The fowl of the air, and the fish of the sea, and whatsoever passeth through the paths of the seas.

8:9 O LORD our Lord, how excellent is thy name in all the earth!

Psalm 9

David prophesies of the joy of the people at the coming of Christ

Psalm 9:1 I will praise thee, O LORD, with my whole heart; I will shew forth all thy marvellous works. **9:2** I will be glad and rejoice in thee: I will sing praise to thy name, O thou most High.

At his coming, Messiah shall reprove the enemies of God who refuse to serve the Eternal.

9:3 When mine enemies are turned back, they shall fall and perish at thy presence. **9:4** For thou hast maintained my right and my cause [**Christ shall deliver all those who live by every Word of God**]; thou satest in the throne judging right.

Messiah shall rebuke the wicked who spurn any part of the Word of God, until they are crushed into repentant contrition.

9:5 Thou hast rebuked the heathen [all those who are unwilling to live by every Word of God], thou hast destroyed the wicked, thou hast put out their name for ever and ever.

Satan the destroyer and death itself, shall come to an end; but the Eternal and the godly shall live forever!

9:6 O thou enemy, destructions are come to a perpetual end: and thou hast destroyed cities; their memorial is perished with them.

9:7 But **the LORD shall endure for ever: he hath prepared his throne for judgment** [to judge all nations righteously by every Word of God forever].

It is sound godly judgment that establishes a people. Compromising with God's Word and tolerating sin will only bring ultimate destruction and ignominy.

Encouragement for all those who make the Eternal their trust

9:8 And he shall judge the world in righteousness, he shall minister judgment to the people in uprightness. 9:9 The LORD also will be a refuge for the oppressed, a refuge in times of trouble.

God will not forsake those who put their trust in Him, and seek to live by every Word of God.

9:10 And they that know thy name [all those that know God] will put their trust in thee: for thou, LORD, hast not forsaken them that seek thee.

Praise and glorify God now and forever more!

9:11 Sing praises to the LORD, which dwelleth in Zion: declare among the people his doings.

9:12 When he maketh inquisition for blood [God judges between the faithful to give them eternal life, and the wicked to destroy them], he remembereth them [those who live by the Word of God]: he forgetteth not the cry of the humble.

God will remember and deliver those who have been afflicted for their love and loyalty to Him.

9:13 Have mercy upon me, O LORD; consider my trouble which I suffer of them that hate me, thou that liftest me up from the gates of death: **9:14** That I may shew forth all thy praise in the gates of the daughter of Zion: I will rejoice in thy salvation.

The wicked shall fall into the snares that they have laid for others; they seek to exalt themselves and they shall destroy themselves.

9:15 The heathen are sunk down in the pit that they made: in the net which they hid is their own foot taken. **9:16** The LORD is known by the judgment which he executeth: the wicked is snared in the work of his own hands. Higgaion. Selah. **9:17** The wicked shall be turned into hell [the grave], and all the nations that forget God [shall be rebuked with a rod of iron].

Physically the poor being cared for are an allegory that those who are poor in the carnal spirit of rebellion against God [and rich in godliness] shall be delivered by God.

9:18 For the needy shall not alway be forgotten: the expectation of the poor shall not perish for ever.

May Christ come quickly to deliver his faithful and to rebuke the wicked to sincere repentance.

9:19 Arise, O LORD; let not man prevail: let the heathen [those who reject living by every Word of God] be judged in thy sight.

9:20 Put them in fear, O LORD: that the nations may know themselves to be but men. Selah.

The religious leaders of this world who oppose the Word of God and all those who mock and persecute the zealous for God, will soon be taught that the Eternal is God, and that: Beside HIM there in NONE OTHER (Deu 4:35-40) !!!

The whole world will be taught this lesson in the very near future.

Psalm 10

The godly righteous will be delivered and the wicked will be corrected or destroyed.

10:1 Why standest thou afar off, O LORD? why hidest thou thyself in times of trouble?

The wicked are full of arrogance and pride in their own ways and persecute those who truly love and live by every Word of God.

10:2 The wicked in his pride doth persecute the poor: let them be taken in the devices that they have imagined. **10:3** For the wicked boasteth of his heart's desire, and blesseth the covetous, whom the LORD abhorreth. **10:4 The wicked, through the pride of his countenance, will not seek after God: God is not in all his thoughts.**

10:5 His ways [the ways of the wicked] are always grievous; thy [God's Word is beyond the understanding of the wicked] judgments are far above out of his sight: as for all his [God's] enemies, he puffeth [snuffs his nose] at them.

10:6 He hath said in his heart, I shall not be moved: for I shall never be in adversity.

10:7 His mouth is full of cursing [blasphemy claiming to be of God when he is not] and deceit and fraud: under his tongue is mischief and vanity.

Like a physical murderer hides himself; the spiritual murderer who murders by deceiving the brethren away from their zeal for God, loves secrecy and hates the light of exposure of his deeds.

10:8 He [the wicked conceals his evil, hating exposure of his intentions] sitteth in the lurking places of the villages: in the secret places doth he murder the innocent: his eyes are privily set against the poor. **10:9**

He lieth in wait secretly as a lion in his den: he lieth in wait to catch the poor: he doth catch the poor, when he draweth him into his net.

10:10 He croucheth, and humbleth [the wicked makes himself appear humble so as to deceive the unwary who are not grounded on the sound doctrine of the Word of God] himself, that the poor may fall by his strong ones.

> **2 Corinthians 11:14** And no marvel; for Satan himself is transformed into an angel of light. **11:15** Therefore it is no great thing if his ministers also be transformed as the ministers of righteousness; whose end shall be according to their works.

The wicked man has no pity on others but uses them as his own merchandise, destroying them in the physical and spiritual sense.

The wicked plunder the needy and hasten to enrich and exalt himself; and the spiritually wicked do this in the spiritual sense, neglecting any zeal to live by every Word of God and teaching others to follow them in doing likewise.

Psalm 10:11 He hath said in his heart, God hath forgotten: he hideth his face; he will never see it [thinking that God will not see or care what he does].

The spiritually wicked says that "I am God's servant and I have a right to do these things," forgetting the words of Christ.

> **Matthew 24:48** But and if that evil servant shall say in his heart, My lord delayeth his coming;
>
> **24:49** And shall begin to smite his fellowservants, and to eat and drink with the drunken; **24:50** The lord of that servant shall come in a day when he looketh not for him, and in an hour that he is not aware of, **24:51** And shall cut him asunder, and appoint him his portion with the hypocrites: there shall be weeping and gnashing of teeth.

Psalm 10:12 Arise, O Lord; O God, lift up thine hand: forget not the humble.

God will deliver his faithful from the wicked smiter who oppresses God's beloved.

The wicked do not believe that God will judge him as wicked or remember his deeds against God's Word and the Beloved Faithful of the Lord. The wicked man deceives himself saying that: "Jesus is love and will wink at and overlook our sins."

10:13 Wherefore doth the wicked contemn God? **he hath said in his heart, Thou wilt not require it.**

10:14 Thou hast seen it; for thou beholdest mischief and spite, to requite it with thy hand: the poor committeth himself unto thee; thou art the helper of the fatherless.

God shall root out every deed of wicked rebellion against his Word and end all persecution against God's zealous faithful.

> **Matthew 25:41** Then shall he say also unto them on the left hand, Depart from me, ye cursed, into everlasting fire, prepared for the devil and his angels:
>
> **25:42** For I was an hungred, and ye gave me no meat: I was thirsty, and ye gave me no drink: **25:43** I was a stranger, and ye took me not in: naked, and ye clothed me not: sick, and in prison, and ye visited me not.
>
> **25:44** Then shall they also answer him, saying, Lord, when saw we thee an hungred, or athirst, or a stranger, or naked, or sick, or in prison, and did not minister unto thee? **25:45** Then shall he answer them, saying, Verily I say unto you, Inasmuch as ye did it not to one of the least of these, ye did it not to me.
>
> **25:46** And these shall go away into everlasting punishment: but the righteous into life eternal.

If this is the end of those who did not help; how much more sore is the end of those wicked men who drive out the righteous who are full of Christ-like zeal to live by every Word of God?

Those who are zealous and under pressure; remember the words of our Lord:

> **2 Timothy 4:3** For the time will come when they will not endure sound doctrine; but after their own lusts shall they heap to themselves teachers, having itching ears; **4:4** And they shall turn away their ears from the truth, and shall be turned unto fables.

Psalm 10:15 Break thou the arm [break their power and strength to deceive] of the wicked and the evil man: seek out his wickedness till thou find none. **10:16** The LORD is King for ever and ever: the heathen [the wicked will be converted or destroyed] are perished out of his land.

When Messiah comes no more oppression will be allowed in the earth.

10:17 LORD, thou hast heard the desire of the humble [before God]: thou wilt prepare [circumcise our hearts by bringing people to sincere repentance (Jer 31)] their heart, thou wilt cause thine ear to hear: **10:18** To judge the fatherless and the oppressed, that the man of the earth may no more oppress.

Psalms 11 - 20

Psalm 11

The godly righteous will put their trust in the Eternal and they will live by every Word of God.

Psalm 11:1 In the LORD put I my trust: how say ye to my soul, Flee as a bird to your [Holy Temple] mountain [the dwelling place of God]?

Wicked men are ever keen to attack those who are zealous to live by every Word of God.

11:2 For, lo, the wicked bend their bow, they make ready their arrow upon the string, that they may privily shoot at the upright in heart.

11:3 If the foundations [the foundation of righteousness is trust in the Word of God] be destroyed, what can the righteous do?

What can the godly do when the bulk of the brethren are turned away from any zeal to live by the Word of God; to follow idols of men and false traditions?

11:4 The LORD is in his holy temple, the LORD's throne is in heaven: his eyes behold, his eyelids try [God sees and test the deeds of men], the children of men.

11:5 The LORD trieth [tests and builds up] the righteous: but the wicked [God despises those who exalt themselves above God's Word] and him that loveth violence his soul hateth.

The wicked are those who break and teach others to compromise with God's Word and tolerate sin.

The wicked will reap strong correction.

11:6 Upon the wicked he shall rain snares, fire and brimstone, and an horrible tempest: this shall be the portion of their cup.

Those who live by EVERY WORD of God will receive a blessing.

11:7 For the righteous LORD loveth righteousness; his countenance doth behold the upright.

Psalm 12

The godly person is perishing from today's spiritual Ekklesia; wickedness, deception, idolatry and abominations are overspreading the nations and the brotherhood, just as they did in the days of Noah.

Psalm 12:1 Help, LORD; for **the godly man ceaseth; for the faithful fail from among the children of men. 12:2** They speak vanity every one with his neighbour: with flattering lips and with a double heart do they speak.

Today most of the leaders and elders of the spiritual Ekklesia speak vanity, deceitfully teaching the brethren the lie that God will overlook and tolerate sin, and that the brethren must be zealous to obey idols of men instead of living by every Word of God.

The Eternal will reject all such deceivers into the strong correction of great tribulation.

12:3 The LORD shall cut off all flattering lips, and the tongue that speaketh proud things: **12:4** Who have said, With our tongue will we prevail; our lips are our own: who is lord over us? **12:5** For the oppression of the poor, for the sighing of the needy, now will I arise, saith the LORD; I will set him in safety from him that puffethat him.

God will deliver his people from the great swelling words of foolish vanity conceived by wicked, vain and arrogant men.

12:6 The words of the LORD are pure words: as silver tried [refined and purified] in a furnace of earth, purified seven times.

The Eternal will preserve all those who live by every Word of God

12:7 Thou shalt keep them, O LORD, thou shalt preserve them from this generation for ever.

Most brethren in today's spiritual Ekklesia have exalted men of apparent talent and charm many of who are secret deceivers, because they have no zeal to live by the Word of God and they strive to exalt themselves over God's household and make merchandise of God's flock.

12:8 The wicked walk on every side, when the vilest men are exalted.

Be careful who you follow.

> **Matthew 7:15** Beware of false prophets, which come to you in sheep's clothing, but inwardly they are ravening wolves.

Psalm 13

David wrote in this prophecy for our time and we should also ask: How long, oh LORD, will this situation of the exaltation of the wicked continue in today's spiritual Ekklesia?

Psalm 13:1 How long wilt thou forget me, O LORD? for ever? how long wilt thou hide thy face from me? **13:2** How long shall I take counsel in my soul, having sorrow in my heart daily? how long shall mine enemy be exalted over me?

13:3 Consider and hear me, O LORD my God: lighten mine eyes [May God quickly deliver his people from the wicked deceivers in the congregations, and open our eyes to the light of God's Word, lest we spiritually perish.] lest I sleep the sleep of death;

Oh, LORD our LORD; open the eyes of the brethren to a passionate Christ-like zeal to live by every Word of God; lest Satan prevail through his wicked deceivers subtly planted in the congregations.

13:4 Lest mine enemy say, I have prevailed against him; and those that trouble me rejoice when I am moved.

Let us very quickly and sincerely repent and place our trust in the mercy of our Mighty One; then we shall greatly rejoice and shout aloud for joy at his deliverance!

13:5 But I have trusted in thy mercy; my heart shall rejoice in thy salvation. **13:6** I will sing unto the LORD, because he hath dealt bountifully with me.

Psalm 14

Psalm 14:1 The fool hath said in his heart, There is no God. They are corrupt, they have done abominable works, there is none that doeth good.

The foolish of the world say there is no God and the foolish in today's spiritual Ekklesia foolishly say that "there is a God but I am the master in his house" [God is Master in his own House].

Instead of teaching zeal to live by every Word of God; the wicked elders and leaders in the Ekklesia condemn the zealous for God, and exalt themselves as idols above the House of God.

Today's spiritual Ekklesia is sound asleep and all have gone astray, except the few that the Eternal has aroused.

14:2 The LORD looked down from heaven upon the children of men, to see if there were any that did understand, and seek God. **14:3** They are all gone aside, they are all together become filthy: there is none that doeth good, no, not one.

Most of the leaders and elders in today's Ekklesia work iniquity, deceiving the brethren away from any zeal to live by every Word of God and exalting themselves as idols of men over the heritage of the LORD.

14:4 Have all the workers of iniquity no knowledge? who eat up my people as they eat bread, and call not upon the LORD.

The godly will fear [have a high respect for] the Eternal and will love God enough to live by every Word of God.

14:5 There were they in great fear: for God is in the generation of the righteous. **14:6** Ye have shamed the counsel of the poor, because the LORD is his refuge.

The wicked have hated the zealous for God whose refuge is the LORD; and because they want followers after themselves, the wicked deceivers have hated the example of the zealous who live by every Word of God, casting them out of the congregations lest their zeal for God spread throughout the Assembly and the people be turned away from idolizing men back to God.

Oh how the zealous long for the coming of the salvation of the Lord; when he comes to deliver the zealous for every Word of God!

14:7 Oh that the salvation of Israel were come out of Zion! when the LORD bringeth back the captivity of his people, Jacob shall rejoice, and Israel shall be glad.

Psalm 15

What kind of person will the Eternal respect and deliver?

Psalm 15:1 Lord, who shall abide in thy tabernacle? who shall dwell in thy holy hill? **15:2** He that walketh uprightly, and worketh righteousness, and speaketh the truth in his heart.

The person who refrains from any sin and lives by every Word of God will have a heart full of the truth (God is truth); and will be in the resurrection of the first fruits and shall be a part of the government of God on the earth.

15:3 He that backbiteth not with his tongue, nor doeth evil to his neighbour, nor taketh up a reproach against his neighbour.

Backbiting means to falsely speak evil of others in their absence so that they cannot defend themselves from the verbal attack and slander.

Slanderers who bear deliberate false witness, will NOT be in the resurrection to spirit.

15:4 In whose eyes [the godly would never justify the wicked (Pro 17:15)] a vile person is contemned; but he [God and the godly] honoureth them that fear [respect and obey] the Lord. He [the man that] that sweareth to his own hurt, and changeth not [the godly will keep his word even to his own cost]. **15:5** He that putteth not out his money to usury, nor taketh reward [advantage] against the innocent. He that doeth these things shall never be moved.

> **Proverbs 17:15** He that justifieth the wicked, and he that condemneth the just, even they both are abomination to the Lord.

Psalm 16

Psalm 16:1 Preserve me, O God: for in thee do I put my trust.

The goodness of men is as nothing compared to the goodness of God.

16:2 O my soul, thou hast said unto the Lord, Thou art my Lord: my [own] goodness extendeth [does not reach to God] not to thee; **16:3** But to the saints that are in the earth, and to the excellent, in whom is all my delight.

Seeking out knowledge of false gods and the teachings of the unconverted to believe in them is an abomination to the Great God, and is spiritual adultery against the espoused Husband of our calling. All those who do this will be confounded and made ashamed.

16:4 Their sorrows shall be multiplied that hasten after another god: their drink offerings of blood [false teachings bring death] will I not offer, nor take up their names into my lips.

Let the children of God stay upon God their Father in heaven and on our espoused Husband, and not follow idols of men.

16:5 The Lord is the portion of mine inheritance and of my cup: thou [God] maintainest my lot [God gives the lot of eternal life and many blessings to his faithful].

16:6 The lines [borders] are fallen unto me in pleasant places; yea, I have a goodly heritage. **16:7** I will bless the Lord, who hath given me counsel: my reins [kidneys, symbolic of sensitivity to God] also instruct me in the night seasons [as we think on the things of God in the night].

A prophecy of the resurrection of Christ who would never be moved from living by every Word of God and who was therefore exalted by God the Father back to the glory he had before the foundation of the world.

> **John 17:5** And now, O Father, **glorify thou me with thine own self with the glory which I had with thee before the world was.**

Psalm 16:8 I have set the LORD always before me: because he is at my right hand, I shall not be moved. **16:9** Therefore my heart is glad, and my glory rejoiceth: my flesh also shall rest in hope. **16:10** For thou wilt not leave my soul in hell; neither wilt thou suffer thine Holy One to see corruption. **16:11 Thou wilt shew me the path of life** [which is to live by every Word of God (Mat 4:4)]**: in thy presence is fulness of joy; at thy right hand there are pleasures for evermore.**

Psalm 17

The Eternal hears the righteous who live by every Word of God, and his judgments are equitable and just.

Psalm 17:1 Hear the right[eous], O LORD, attend unto my cry, give ear unto my prayer, that goeth not out of feigned lips [but comes from sincerity of heart]. **17:2** Let my sentence come forth from thy presence; let thine eyes behold the things that are equal.

17:3 Thou hast proved mine heart [God tests us to prove our sincerity and faithfulness]; thou hast visited me in the night; thou hast tried me, and shalt find nothing [no sin is imputed to those who live by every Word of God and have been justified by Christ]; I am purposed that my mouth shall not transgress.

Those who live by every Word of God are kept from destruction.

17:4 Concerning the works of men, **by the word of thy lips I have kept me from the paths of the destroyer. 17:5** Hold up my goings [keep me in every Word of God] in thy paths, that my footsteps slip not.

A prayer for mercy and deliverance

17:6 I have called upon thee, for thou wilt hear me, O God: incline thine ear unto me, and hear my speech. **17:7** Shew thy marvellous lovingkindness, O thou that savest by thy right hand them which put their trust in thee from those that rise up against them. **17:8** Keep me as the apple of the eye, hide me under the shadow of thy wings,

17:9 [Save me from] From the wicked that oppress me, from my deadly enemies [a figure of Satan and sin], who compass me about.

17:10 They are inclosed in their own fat [caught by their pride]: with their mouth they speak proudly.

17:11 They have now compassed [the wicked stalk the godly to take them in their snares] us in our steps: they have set their eyes bowing down to the earth [the wicked hunt the godly like an animal seeks spoor when hunting prey]; **17:12** Like as a lion that is greedy of his prey, and as it were a young lion lurking in secret places. **17:13** Arise, O LORD, disappoint him [disappoint the wicked by saving us from the spiritual predator who would devour us], cast him down: deliver my soul from the wicked, which is [by the sword of truth, the Word of God] thy sword:

The righteous are not to seek the riches of this world; they are to be satisfied with the acceptance of God the Father through Christ. The joy of the zealous is to see the coming of Christ and godly righteousness spread like a flood over all humanity

17:14 From men which are thy hand, O LORD, from men of the world, which have their portion in this life, and whose belly thou fillest with thy hid treasure: they are full of children, and leave the rest of their substance to their babes.

17:15 As for me, I will behold thy face in righteousness: I shall be satisfied, when I awake [when we are resurrected from death we will see God] **with thy likeness.**

Psalm 18

God is the salvation of all those who live by every Word of God. Make this personal; When David uses the word "I" do not think of David; think of "I" as meaning ourselves.

Psalm 18:1 I will love thee, O LORD, my strength. **18:2** The LORD is my rock, and my fortress, and my deliverer; my God, my strength, in whom I will trust; my buckler, and the horn of my salvation, and my high tower. **18:3 I will call upon the LORD, who is worthy to be praised: so shall I be saved from mine enemies** [Satan and sin].

If we run away from God by compromising with his Word; we are running towards our own destruction. If we run to God and redouble our zeal when we face trials; we are going to the True and Only source of our Deliverance and Salvation!

18:4 The sorrows of death compassed me, and the floods of ungodly men made me afraid. **18:5** The sorrows of hell [the grave] compassed me about: the snares of death prevented [stops our fight] me.

WHO shall we call upon when we face trials? Who shall deliver us? Our own compromising with the ONLY thing that will save us, our zeal for God's law? Or the Fashioner and Giver of the Word of God which brings life eternal?

18:6 In my distress I called upon the Lord, and cried unto my God: he heard my voice out of his temple, and my cry came before him, even into his ears.

Be diligent to please God, and to live by every Word of God; then we will be on God's side and when the enemy attacks, Almighty God will be our Defender and will work everything out.

Even if we suffer to the death in this life; God will keep his promise and raise us up in that Day! It is better to die in worldly poverty and ignominy, being hated and destroyed for our zeal for our God; than to live grandly in this life by compromising with God's ways and receive eternal condemnation.

> **Luke 9:23** And he said to them all, If any man will come after me, let him deny himself, and take up his cross [burdens] daily, and follow me.
>
> **9:24** For whosoever will save his [physical] life shall lose it: but whosoever will lose his [physical] life for my sake, the same shall save it [shall save his spiritual life, be raised up and have life eternal].
>
> **9:25** For **what is a man advantaged, if he gain the whole world, and lose himself, or be cast away [by God]?**
>
> **9:26** For **whosoever shall be ashamed of me and of my words, of him shall the Son of man be ashamed, when he shall come in his own glory, and in his Father's, and of the holy angels.**

A prophecy of the Lord's deliverance of the godly, and the discomfiture of the wicked at the coming of Messiah the Christ

Psalm 18:7 Then the earth shook and trembled; the foundations also of the hills moved and were shaken, because he was wroth. **18:8** There went up a smoke out of his nostrils, and fire out of his mouth devoured: coals were kindled by it. **18:9** He bowed the heavens also, and came down: and darkness was under his feet. **18:10** And he rode upon a cherub [God's amgelic white horse], and did fly: yea, he did fly upon the wings of the wind. **18:11** He made darkness his secret place; his pavilion round about him were dark waters [clouds] and thick clouds of the skies. **18:12** At the brightness that was before him his thick clouds passed, hail stones and coals of fire.

> **Revelation 19:11** And I saw heaven opened, and **behold a white horse; and he that sat upon him was called Faithful and True, and in righteousness he doth judge and make war.**

The Mighty One will destroy the powers of darkness and deliver all those who love him enough to follow his leadership and live by every Word of God.

Psalm 18:13 The LORD also thundered in the heavens, and the Highest gave his voice; hail stones and coals of fire. **18:14** Yea, he sent out his arrows, and scattered them; and he shot out lightnings, and discomfited them.

The crossing of the Red Sea and rising up out of the waters is used as an allegory of the godly being raised up from the grave of death.

18:15 Then the channels of waters were seen, and the foundations of the world [the dry land under the sea was revealed by God's deliverance of Israel from Egypt, as an allegory of the resurrection of the godly at the coming of Christ] were discovered at thy rebuke, O LORD, at the blast of the breath of thy nostrils.

Just as God delivered Israel from the god-king of Egypt; God will deliver his zealous from the hands of Satan the god-king of this world and from the grave of death pictured by the sea.

18:16 He sent from above, he took me, he drew me out of many waters. **18:17** He delivered me from my strong enemy, and from them which hated me: for they were too strong for me. **18:18** They prevented me [sought the destruction of the godly] in the day of my calamity: but the LORD was my stay [powerful deliverance].

The Almighty will deliver all those who are zealous to live by every Word of God. The Eternal will deliver his beloved and set them with a good reward of eternal life and rulership as priests and teachers over the whole earth.

Revelation 5:10 And hast made us unto our God kings and priests: and we shall reign on the earth.

Psalm 18:19 He brought me forth also into a large place [as kings and priests over the whole earth]; he delivered me, because he delighted in me.

Those who delight to live by every Word of God will be delivered to eternal life.

18:20 The Lord rewarded me according to my righteousness [zeal to live by every Word of God]; according to the cleanness [sinlessness] of my hands hath he recompensed me. **18:21** For **I have kept the ways of the LORD, and have not wickedly departed from my God.**

18:22 For all his judgments were before me, and I did not put away his statutes from me. **18:23** I was also upright before him, and I kept myself from mine iniquity. **18:24** Therefore hath the LORD recompensed me according to my righteousness, according to the cleanness of my hands in his eyesight.

18:25 With the merciful thou wilt shew thyself merciful; with an upright man thou wilt shew thyself upright; **18:26** With the pure thou wilt shew thyself pure; and with the froward thou wilt shew thyself forward. [self-willed].

God will destroy the proud, the conceited, the arrogant; and he will bring down the haughty. God WILL SAVE those who endure all things to live by every Word of God and please him.

18:27 For thou wilt save the afflicted people; but wilt bring down high looks [abase the proud]. **18:28** For thou wilt light my candle [resurrect the faithful to eternal life]: the LORD my God will enlighten my darkness

God will raise up his faithful from the grave and open their eyes in eternal life.

Through diligent obedience to every Word of God we shall receive enlightenment into God's true ways. By God's Word we learn wisdom and by his power he will deliver us. By God's power we overcome all wickedness and even the grave itself.

18:29 For by thee I have run through a troop; and by my God have I leaped over a wall.

The commandments, statutes, precepts and judgments of God are perfect and not to be neglected or compromised with.

18:30 As for God, his way is perfect: the word of the Lord is tried: he is a buckler to all those that trust in him.

Dear brethren, if we are persecuted or punished for our diligent zeal and obedience to the Word of God; Fear Not, Stand Fast and wait on God's deliverance!

18:31 For who is God save the Lord? or who is a rock save our God?

God is our strength and our salvation; let us rely on HIM; and RUN to HIM all our lives, forever and ever. It is God's Word which will make us perfect before him.

18:32 It is God that girdeth me with strength, and maketh my way perfect. **8:34** He maketh my feet like hinds' [deer's feet, to leap gracefully] feet, and setteth me upon my high places.

18:34 He teacheth my hands to war [to wield the two edged sword of truth], so that a bow of steel is broken by mine arms.

The battles and wars of the Psalms and of David are allegories of our spiritual battles against the forces of evil. All the power of the enemy is broken by the power of truth. God's Word is truth, therefore God is truth and God cannot lie.

>**Titus 1:2** In hope of eternal life, **which God, that cannot lie**, promised before the world began;

Psalm 18:35 Thou hast also given me the **shield of thy salvation**: and thy right hand hath holden me up, and thy gentleness [love and mercy for those who live by every Word of God] hath made me great.

18:36 Thou hast enlarged my steps [God increases our understanding so that we may avoid sin and not perish] under me, that my feet did not slip [into sin].

We are to resist the enemy of sin and Satan and the sin and compromise which so easily besets us, and by the POWER OF GOD, we are to overcome all sin and become united with our God in mind, action and spirit through diligently living by every Word of God.

>**1 John 3:2** Beloved, now are we the [called] sons of God, and it doth not yet appear what we shall be [look like]: but we know that, when he [Christ] shall appear, we shall be like him; for we shall see him as he is. **3:3** And everyman that hath this hope in him purifieth himself, even as he is pure.

Brethren, EVERYONE is to purify himself from all sin, so that we may be pure as Christ was pure and sinned not!

We are to become pure from even the faintest trace of sin, which is the breaking or compromising with even the least part of God's Word. We are to avoid even the appearance of sin!

> **James 3:4 Whosoever committeth sin transgresseth also the law: for sin is the transgression of the law.**

Psalm 18:37 I have pursued mine enemies, and overtaken them [David's enemies were a type of Satan and sin to be overcome by us]: neither did I turn again [let us not turn aside from godliness; let us demolish and totally destroy all sin] till they were consumed.

18:38 I have wounded them [destroyed Satan and sin] that they were not able to rise [that no sin will ever again rise up in us]: they are fallen under my feet [by God's power and our diligence all sin shall be as ashes under the feet of the godly].

We are to fight the good fight and destroy the enemy of sin which oppresses us.

If we are valiant and depend on the power of our God to deliver us and enable us to overcome; instead of giving up the struggle for the pottage of an easy life; God shall deliver us with his Mighty Deeds like He delivered Israel out of Egypt!

18:39 For thou hast girded me with strength unto the battle [If we will only be faithful to live by every Word of God, God will provide the power to fight sin]: thou [God] hast subdued under me those [subdued Satan and the sin that afflicts us] that rose up against me.

18:40 Thou hast also given me the necks of mine enemies [God gives us power over the sin that assaults us, and all sin is destroyed in us through sincere repentance and the atonement of Christ; and the Spirit of God is given to us to enable us to keep all of God's Word]; that I might destroy them that hate me [Satan and sin, for sin works in us to destroy us].

Any person who teaches that we may overlook and tolerate sin and doctrinal heresy in our midst for the sake of [a false] organizational unity; is a FALSE TEACHER and should be cast out! Indeed, he is either foolish or a liar, for he is saying that doctrinal DIS-unity somehow brings unity

18:41 They [God's enemies and sinful commandment breakers] cried, but there was none to save them: even unto the Lord, but he answered them not.

Repentance means to STOP doing what we are doing and change our thoughts and actions, God will not respond positively to insincere repentance.

The lax and lukewarm for the Word of God will be beaten into the dust of contrition in the soon coming great tribulation. If they repent, they will still have to prove their repentance by suffering in the flesh to save the spirit.

God will NOT deliver those who sin against him! We must first sincerely repent of our sin and turn to God with passionate Christ-like love and zeal to live by every Word of God.

18:42 Then did I beat them [the enemy as a type of pride and sin] small as the dust before the wind: I did cast them out as the dirt in the streets.

The overcomer who loves and lives by every Word of God will achieve victory over sin and will be exalted to eternal life as rulers and priests by the power of God; to teach the paths of salvation to all the earth in the Kingdom of God.

18:43 Thou hast delivered me from the strivings of the people [the strivings of sin and Satan against us]; and thou hast made me the head of the heathen: a people whom I have not known shall serve me.

After the day of the Lord's coming is here, God's Spirit will be poured out on all flesh (Joel 2:28) and humanity will submit to the Eternal God the Father and to his High Priest and King of the earth Jesus Christ, and to the priests and kings of his government.

A prophecy of Christ and the resurrected Chosen

18:44 As soon as they hear of me, they shall obey me: the strangers [those who have not known God, shall come to God the Father through Christ] shall submit themselves unto me [Messiah the Christ]. **18:45** The strangers shall fade away, and be afraid out of their close [hiding] places.

Jesus Christ is the ROCK of our salvation and he does the will of God the Father: Delivering us to overcome Satan and all sin, and ultimately giving us a birthright inheritance of eternal life.

Why would anyone want to sell the birthright of this calling for a church catered meal on the Sabbath! or any other such sin of self-indulgence?

18:46 The LORD liveth; and blessed be my rock; and let the God of my salvation be exalted. **18:47** It is God that avengeth [delivers us] me, and subdueth the people under me.

18:48 He delivereth me from mine enemies: yea, thou liftest me up above those that rise up against me: thou hast delivered me from the violent [wicked] man.

18:49 Therefore will I give thanks unto thee, O LORD, among the heathen, and sing praises unto thy name. **18:50** Great deliverance giveth he to his king [God the Father delivered Christ in a resurrection to eternal spirit to become King of kings, and David and all God's faithful will also be resurrected to eternal life as spirit]; and sheweth mercy to his anointed, to David, and to his seed for evermore.

Psalm 19

The greatness of God is seen in the earth and the marvelous starry heavens.

Psalm 19:1 The heavens declare the glory of God; and the firmament sheweth his handywork. **19:2** Day unto day uttereth speech, and night unto night sheweth knowledge.

The glory of the creation is seen by all peoples and the glory of the Creator is much greater than the glory of His creation.

19:3 There is no speech nor language, where their voice [the creation is known by all] is not heard.

19:4 Their line is gone out through all the earth, and their words to the end of the world. In them hath he set a tabernacle for the sun, **19:5** Which is as a bridegroom coming out of his chamber, and rejoiceth as a strong man to run a race. **19:6** His going forth is from the end of the heaven, and his circuit unto the ends of it: and there is nothing hid from the heat thereof.

What is a man beside God? Who are we to question his Word? The Greatness of God is seen in his Magnificent Law.

19:7 The law of the LORD is perfect, converting the soul [men are converted from sin and saved from death through sincere repentance, the sacrifice of Christ and then living by the Word of God forever after]: **the testimony of the LORD is sure, making wise the simple.**

God's Word gives knowledge of the way to eternal life.

19:8 The statutes of the LORD are right, rejoicing the heart: the commandment of the LORD is pure, enlightening the eyes. 19:9 The fear of the LORD is clean, enduring for ever: the judgments of the LORD are true and righteous altogether. 19:10 More to be desired are they than gold, yea, than much fine gold: sweeter also than honey and the honeycomb.

Why do we desire gold and the perishable things of this world, shamefully going to uncontroverted law for judgment against our brothers? Why have we not cleaved with all our hearts and all our strength, to every Word of God?

19:11 Moreover by them is thy servant warned [God's Word warns us away from sin and the death which sin brings.]: and **in keeping of them there is great reward.**

There is no error in God

19:12 Who can understand his errors? cleanse thou me from secret [May God cleanse us from every hidden sin which we may not see.] faults.

19:13 Keep back thy servant also from presumptuous [brazen, impudent, pride and self-will] sins; let them not have dominion over me: then shall I be upright, and I shall be innocent from the great transgression.

19:14 Let the words of my mouth, and the meditation of my heart, be acceptable in thy sight, O LORD, my strength, and my redeemer.

Psalm 20

A blessing on the zealous that live by EVERY WORD of GOD

Psalm 20:1 The LORD hear thee in the day of trouble; the name of the God of Jacob defend thee; **20:2** Send thee help from the sanctuary, and strengthen thee out of Zion; **20:3** Remember all thy offerings, and accept thy burnt sacrifice; Selah. **20:4** Grant thee according to thine own heart, and fulfil all thy counsel.

Those who are filled with the righteousness of God through the keeping of every Word of God, will be delivered and blessed and they will greatly rejoice

20:5 We will rejoice in thy salvation, and in the name of our God we will set up our banners: the LORD fulfil all thy petitions.

When we are delivered from the grave, all people will know that the LORD delivers those who exalt him.

20:6 Now know I that the LORD saveth his anointed; he will hear him from his holy heaven with the saving strength of his right hand.

20:7 Some trust in chariots, and some in horses: but we [the godly who put their trust in the Eternal and live by his Word] will remember the name of the LORD our God.

Jesus Christ will deliver God's faithful and will strongly rebuke and destroy the proud who exalt their own ways above the any zeal to live by the Word of God.

20:8 They are brought down and fallen: but we are risen, and stand upright.

20:9 Save, LORD: let the king [King of kings] hear us when we call.

Psalms 21 - 30

Psalm 21

Rejoicing over the blessings of God for his faithful

God will resurrect his faithful from the pit of death and will make the resurrected David king over all Israel; and God's faithful will be resurrected to become kings and priests over all the earth (Rev 5:10)!

Psalm 21:1 The king shall joy in thy strength, O LORD; and in thy salvation how greatly shall he rejoice! **21:2** Thou hast given him his heart's desire, and hast not withholden the request of his lips. Selah. **21:3** For thou preventest [God will bless his faithful in a resurrection to eternal life.] him with the blessings of goodness: thou settest a crown of pure gold on his head.

21:4 He asked life of thee, and thou gavest it him [God gives eternal life to his faithful], even length of days **for ever and ever**.

A prophecy of Christ the King of kings, David and all the resurrected persons who will rule under Christ and God the Father

21:5 His [all those faithful to God] glory is great in thy salvation: honour and majesty hast thou laid upon him. **21:6** For thou hast made him most blessed for ever: thou hast made him exceeding glad with thy countenance.

All who put their trust in God the Father to live by his Word will be established in eternal life and shall never be moved.

21:7 For the king trusteth in the LORD, and through the mercy of the most High he shall not be moved.

God the Father and Jesus Christ will strongly correct all those who will not live by every Word of God, and if they will not repent they shall ultimately be destroyed!

21:8 Thine hand shall find out all thine enemies: thy right hand shall find out those that hate thee. 21:9 Thou shalt make them as a fiery oven in the time of thine anger: the LORD shall swallow them up in his wrath, and the fire shall devour them.

All wickedness and the fruit of wickedness will be destroyed from off the earth.

21:10 Their fruit shalt thou destroy from the earth, and their seed from among the children of men. **21:11** For they intended evil against thee: they imagined a mischievous device, which they are not able to perform.

The attempts of the wicked one to destroy Christ and to deceive the flock of God away from any zeal to live by EVERY WORD of God, will be overturned and in the long term will utterly fail.

21:12 Therefore shalt thou make them turn their back [wicked men will be corrected from their evil purposes], when thou shalt [reveal the wicked and correct them] make ready thine arrows upon thy strings against the face of them.

21:13 Be thou exalted, LORD, in thine own strength: so will we sing and praise thy power.

Psalm 22

A prophecy of Jesus Christ the Passover Lamb of God

Psalm 22:1 My God, my God, why hast thou forsaken me? why art thou so far from helping me, and from the words of my roaring? **22:2** O my God, I cry in the day time, but thou hearest not; and in the night season, and am not silent.

The cry for God's attention to his plight as quoted by Christ on the stake as he died

How many of us feel this way in the time of our trials? Let us not fall away when deliverance seems to be delayed but let us stand firm in faith towards God and his promises and endure all things for our Awesome God just as Jesus Christ did.

This Psalm is a prophecy of Jesus Christ; and as he suffered we will also be persecuted (Heb 11).

Trust in God, he WILL deliver according to his promises in his own way and in his own good time. Perhaps allowing us to suffer and die like God the Father allowed his only begotten son to suffer and die so that he could keep his promise to raise up faithful sons from corruption to incorruption for eternity!

> **1 Corinthians 15:42** So also is the resurrection of the dead. It is sown in corruption; it is raised in incorruption: **15:43** It is sown in dishonour; it is raised in glory: it is sown in weakness; it is raised in power: **15:44** It is sown a natural body; it is raised a spiritual body. There is a natural body, and there is a spiritual body.

We are sown in physical death, to be reaped in a resurrection to a new spirit body; even as baptism shows a person being buried under the waters with a physical carnal nature, to be raised up a new person with a new spiritual nature! We must then continue in the spiritual nature of God and not seek to turn back to the carnal physical nature that we are being delivered from.

> **15:45** And so it is written, The first man Adam was made a living soul [physical creature]; the last Adam was made a [Jesus Christ was changed from flesh to spirit.] quickening spirit.
>
> **15:46** Howbeit **that was not first which is spiritual, but that which is natural; and afterward that which is spiritual**. **15:47** The first man is of the earth, earthy [physical]: the second man is the Lord from heaven [spiritual].

15:48 As is the earthy, such are they also that are earthy: and as is the heavenly, such are they also that are heavenly. **15:49** And as we have borne the image of the earthy, we shall also bear the image of the heavenly.

If we sincerely repent of breaking God's law and then continue in living by EVERY WORD of GOD; we shall be raised up to eternal life.

15:50 Now this I say, brethren, that **flesh and blood cannot inherit the kingdom of God; neither doth corruption inherit incorruption**.

If we remain carnal and not subject to every Word of God; we shall NOT enter the resurrection to spirit.

15:51 Behold, I shew you a mystery; We shall not all sleep, but we [the faithful and chosen] shall all be changed, **15:52** In a moment, in the twinkling of an eye, at the last trump: for the trumpet shall sound, and the dead shall be raised incorruptible, and we shall be changed. **15:53** For this corruptible must put on incorruption, and this mortal must put on immortality.

15:54 So when this corruptible shall have put on incorruption, [the physical will be changed to spirit] and this mortal shall have put on immortality, then shall be brought to pass the saying that is written, Death is swallowed up in victory.

The faithful who live by every Word of God in Christ-like zeal, will be heard by God and they will be delivered by God in that day.

Psalm 22:3 But thou art holy, O thou that inhabitest the praises of Israel.

22:4 Our fathers [the godly of Hebrews 11] trusted in thee: they trusted, and thou [they will be delivered from the grave] didst deliver them. **22:5** They cried unto thee, and were delivered: they trusted in thee, and were not confounded.

The wicked scorn the godly, as contemptible; but God will deliver his faithful.

22:6 But I am a worm, [the wicked laugh to scorn those who love and live by every Word of God], and no man; a reproach of men, and despised of the people. **22:7** All they that see me laugh me to scorn: they shoot out the lip, they shake the head, saying, **22:8** He trusted on the LORD that he would deliver him: let him deliver him, seeing he delighted in him.

The wicked see the physical troubles and death of the godly righteous and judge that there is no profit in serving God; not understanding that God is trying us to perfect his people's zeal and loyalty and that God will yet deliver us from the grave to eternal life.

This is a prophecy of Jesus Christ, who knew God the Father from the beginning

22:9 But thou art he that took me out of the womb: thou didst make me hope when I was upon my mother's breasts. **22:10** I was cast upon thee from the womb: **thou art my God from my mother's belly.**

God the Father was always close to Christ and is always near those who love him and live by his Word.

22:11 Be not far from me; for trouble is near; for there is none to help. **22:12** Many bulls have compassed me: strong bulls of Bashan have beset me round. **22:13** They gaped upon me with their mouths, as a ravening and a roaring lion.

Jesus died as the Lamb of God for us, so that just like he was resurrected, we might also be resurrected to spirit and eternal life.

22:14 I am poured out like water, and all my bones are out of joint: my heart is like wax; it is melted in the midst of my bowels. **22:15** My strength is dried up like a potsherd; and my tongue cleaveth to my jaws; and thou hast brought me into the dust of death.

22:16 For dogs [packs of vicious attackers] have compassed me: the assembly of the wicked have inclosed me: **they pierced my hands and my feet. 22:17** I may tell all my bones: they look and stare upon me. **22:18 They part my garments among them, and cast lots upon my vesture.**

Jesus calls on God for deliverance

22:19 But be not thou far from me, O LORD: O my strength, haste thee to help me. **22:20** Deliver my soul from the sword; my darling [life] from the power of the dog. **22:21** Save me from the lion's mouth: for thou hast heard me from the horns of the unicorns.

Jesus the Lamb of God declared the existence of God the Father and taught that we should all live by every Word of God (Mat 4:4), and that we all should continually praise and glorify God the Father in words and in our deeds of doing God's will like Christ did and does.

22:22 I will declare thy name unto my brethren: in the midst of the congregation will I praise thee. **22:23** Ye that fear the LORD, praise him; all ye the seed of Jacob, glorify him; and fear him, all ye the seed of Israel.

God the Father heard the cry for deliverance from Jesus Christ the Passover lamb of God, and raised him up from the grave to eternal life; and if we faint not in pleasing God and living by God's Word, we shall also be raised up to eternal life.

22:24 For he hath not despised nor abhorred the affliction of the afflicted; neither hath he hid his face from him; but when he cried unto him, he [God the Father] heard.

22:25 My praise shall be of thee in the great congregation: I will pay my vows [Jesus Christ sacrificed himself as the Lamb of God, as he had committed himself to do from the foundations of the world, Rev 13:8] before them that fear him.

22:26 The meek [the humble before God to live by God's Word; shall be delivered from the grave] shall eat [shall internalize the Word of God] and be satisfied [the humble shall be full of the Word of God]: they shall praise the LORD that seek him: your heart [those that seek God in humility and zeal to live by God's Word shall live forever] shall live for ever.

22:27 All the ends of the world shall remember and [in the Kingdom of God all people shall turn to God] **turn unto the LORD: and all the kindreds of the nations shall worship before thee. 22:28 For the kingdom is the LORD's: and he is the governor among the nations.**

22:29 All they that be fat [those that flourish] upon earth shall eat and worship: all they that go down to the dust [the dying] shall bow before him: and [everyone will know that only God gives eternal life] none can keep alive his own soul.

22:30 A seed [the descendants of the nation's] shall serve him; it shall be accounted to the Lord for a generation [the resurrected generation].

22:31 They [the resurrected chosen] shall come, and shall declare his righteousness unto a people [to all the future generations] that shall be born, that he hath [that the Lamb of God was sacrificed for sin; and the way of Salvation will be declared open to all peoples] done this.

Psalm 23

David thanks God as he reminisces about his life

Psalm 23 is an allegory about the called out first fruits who are called to become kings in the Kingdom of God.

The called out first fruits of the New Covenant are to follow God and to live by every Word of God the Good Shepherd just like David did; and if they continue in doing so, they shall be filled with the spiritual meat of the Word of God and in the resurrection they will receive eternal life and all good things.

Psalm 23:1 The LORD is my shepherd; I shall not want. **23:2** He maketh me to lie down in green pastures: he leadeth me beside the still waters.

God leads us to the green pastures of the spiritual food and water of the Word of God, which brings life eternal.

23:3 He restoreth my soul: he leadeth me in the paths of righteousness for his name's sake.

God has promised that all who follow God and diligently live by every Word of the righteousness of God. will have their lives restored in the resurrection to eternal life from the dead.

23:4 Yea, though I walk through the valley of the shadow of death, I will fear no evil: for thou art with me; thy rod and thy staff they comfort me.

Even though we die physically, if we accept the rod of God's wise instructional correction and lean on the sure staff of God's Righteous Word we need not fear, for if we are faithful to live by every Word of God we have God's unshakable promise that he will raise us up from the valley of death to eternal life as a spirit.

23:5 Thou preparest a table before me in the presence of mine enemies: thou anointest my head with oil; my cup runneth over.

God has promised that if we are faithful to live by every Word of God, he will anoint us with his Holy Spirit and will raise up to eternal life and the anointing of kingship and priesthood in the sight of our enemies.

23:6 Surely goodness and mercy shall follow me all the days of my life: and I will dwell in the house of the LORD for ever.

We have God's unbreakable promise that if we are faithful to live by every Word of God, enduring and overcoming all things through the power of

God dwelling in us, God's mercy and blessings will pour down upon us like a river and we shall dwell for all eternity in the house [family] of God.

Psalm 24

All things were created by God [the YHVH family] and belong to God

Psalm 24:1 The earth is the LORD's, and the fulness thereof; the world, and they that dwell therein. **24:2** For he hath founded it upon the seas, and established it upon the floods.

The physical temple is an allegory of the heavenly Temple. This question is an allegorical question, asking who shall be in the resurrection to spirit and ascend to stand before God.

24:3 Who shall ascend into the hill [temple] of the LORD? or who shall stand in his holy place?

Only the person who is clean from any and all sin, being cleansed from all past sin by sincere repentance, the application of the blood sacrifice of the Lamb of God and going forward to live by and be filled full with every Word of God; will be filled with the righteousness of the Word of God and lifted up from the grave to eternal salvation.

24:4 He that hath clean hands, and a pure heart; who hath not lifted up his soul unto vanity, nor sworn deceitfully. **24:5** He shall receive the blessing from the LORD, and righteousness from the God of his salvation.

Only those who reject all sin and seek God with a whole heart to live by every Word of God; will be saved from death to eternal salvation.

24:6 This is the generation of them that seek him, that seek thy face, O Jacob. Selah.

If we open up the gates and doors of our hearts in sincere repentance and a wholehearted dedication to live by every Word of God, he shall enter and dwell within us through his Holy Spirit (Rev 3:19-22).

24:7 Lift up your heads, O ye gates; and be ye lift up, ye everlasting doors; and the King of glory shall come in. **24:8** Who is this King of glory? The LORD strong and mighty, the LORD mighty in battle.

If we are faithful to sincerely repent and turn away from all departure from the Word of God to live by every Word of God, the doors of our hearts will be opened eternally to the Holy Spirit of the King of Glory; and God shall dwell eternally within us through his Holy Spirit.

24:9 Lift up your heads, O ye gates; even lift them up, ye everlasting doors; and the King of glory shall come in. **24:10** Who is this King of glory? The LORD of hosts, he is the King of glory. Selah.

Psalm 25

A psalm of sincere trusting faithfulness to God, revealing the proper relationship between man and God

Psalm 25:1 Unto thee, O LORD, do I lift up my soul.

We are to give ourselves wholly to God in complete submissive humility.

25:2 O my God, I trust in thee: let me not be ashamed, let not mine enemies triumph over me. **25:3** Yea, let none that wait on thee be ashamed: let them be ashamed which transgress without cause.

If we put our trust in God to live by his every Word we shall never be ashamed, for God will lead us victorious over Satan, over bondage to sin and over the grave itself. Those who refuse to live by every Word of God shall surely be greatly ashamed when they see the godly exalted while they are sternly rebuked.

25:4 Shew me thy ways, O LORD; teach me thy paths. **25:5** Lead me in thy truth, and teach me: for thou art the God of my salvation; on thee do I wait all the day.

God's Word is Truth and brings eternal salvation to all those who live by it. Let us all repent and turn to live by every Word of God, and pray that Almighty God always remembers his merciful nature and forgive us for all our repented sins.

25:6 Remember, O LORD, thy tender mercies and thy lovingkindnesses; for they have been ever of old.

Let us sincerely repent of all our past sins and commit to "Go and sin no more" knowing that our merciful God will be gracious unto us to forgive and forget our past wickedness

25:7 Remember not the sins of my youth, nor my transgressions: according to thy mercy remember thou me for thy goodness' sake, O LORD.

Every Word of God is life, for God's Word teaches those who humble themselves to learn from him, how we may depart from all sin and live forever.

25:8 Good and upright is the LORD: therefore will he teach sinners in the way. **25:9** The meek will he guide in judgment: and the meek will he teach his way.

Those who walk in the paths laid out by the Word of God and keep their commitment to live by every Word of God, will live in Truth and will receive the mercy of the LORD.

25:10 All the paths [the whole Word of God] of the LORD are mercy and truth unto such as [diligently live by every Word of God] keep his covenant and his testimonies. **25:11** For thy name's sake, O LORD, pardon mine iniquity; for it is great.

The iniquity of men is great, but God is greater and will deliver men from their bondage to sin.

25:12 What man is he that feareth the LORD? him shall he teach in the way that he shall choose. **25:13** His soul shall dwell at ease; and his seed shall inherit the earth.

Those who are humbly submissive to live by every Word of God will be taught of God because they have chosen the ways of God; and those who live by every Word of God shall inherit the earth in the resurrection of the chosen.

25:14 The secret of the LORD is with them that fear him; and he will shew them his covenant.

God's salvation and the secret things of God shall be revealed in those who love God enough to live by every Word of God.

25:15 Mine eyes are ever toward the LORD; for he shall pluck my feet out of the net.

If our eyes and thoughts are ever focused on the Eternal to do his will, he shall surely deliver us.

25:16 Turn thee unto me, and have mercy upon me; for I am desolate and afflicted. **25:17** The troubles of my heart are enlarged: O bring thou me out of my distresses. **25:18** Look upon mine affliction and my pain; and forgive all my sins.

Let us cry out in sincere repentance to our Mighty One for his sure deliverance.

25:19 Consider mine enemies; for they are many; and they hate me with cruel hatred.

The enemies we struggle with are bondage to Satan, sin and death.

25:20 O keep my soul, and deliver me: let me not be ashamed; for I put my trust in thee.

God will deliver all those who put their trust in him, to follow him and live by God's every Word; delivering them from their bondage to Satan, sin and the grave.

25:21 Let integrity and uprightness preserve me; for I wait on thee.

If we are filled with the integrity and righteousness of the Word of God, through living by every Word of God, the Eternal will save us.

25:22 Redeem Israel, O God, out of all his troubles.

God the Father has redeemed the sincerely repentant with the blood and life of the Lamb of God.

Psalm 26

The reward of a resurrection to an eternal life in a leadership role is very great, therefore the faithful will be tested regarding our fidelity to God to prove our dedication to absolute faithfulness to live by every Word of God.

Psalm 26:1 Judge me, O LORD; for I have walked in mine integrity: I have trusted also in the LORD; therefore I shall not slide. **26:2** Examine me, O LORD, and prove me; try my reins [God examines our most secret thoughts and deeds and tests our loyalties to Him alone] and my heart.

God's Word which is righteousness and loving kindness; was ever in David's mind and should always be in our minds

26:3 For thy lovingkindness is before mine eyes: and I have walked in thy truth.

We are not to keep company [for social or religious purposes] with the wicked who are not zealous to live by every Word of God

26:4 I have not sat with vain persons, neither will I go in with dissemblers. **26:5** I have hated the congregation of evil doers; and will not sit with the wicked.

> **1 Corinthians 5:11** But now I have written unto you **not to keep company, if any man that is called a brother be a fornicator, or covetous, or an idolator, or a railer, or a drunkard, or an extortioner; with such an one no not to eat.**

Psalm 26:6 I will wash mine hands in innocency: so will I compass thine altar, O LORD:

David washed himself in innocency which is a poetic way of saying that the sincerely repentant who are immersed in godliness and washed clean through living by every Word of God [Ephesians 5:25-26] and the application of Christ's sacrifice for all sincerely repented PAST sins; will, because of our innocence in Christ be able to approach the throne of God the Father.

26:7 That I may publish with the voice of thanksgiving, and tell of all thy wondrous works.

Let us all witness to and publish the greatness of God, for God has done wonderful things for us.

26:8 LORD, I have loved the habitation of thy house, and the place where thine honour dwelleth. **26:9** Gather not my soul with sinners, nor my life with bloody men: **26:10** In whose hands is mischief, and their right hand is full of bribes.

God will account all those who live by every Word of God as faithful godly persons.

26:11 But as for me, I will walk in mine integrity: redeem me, and be merciful unto me. **26:12** My foot standeth in an even [permanent] place: in the congregations will I bless the LORD.

Those who walk [live] by every Word of God, and stand on the sure and solid foundation of the Rock of our Salvation, will receive the mercy of the LORD and are accounted among God's beloved faithful.

Psalm 27

The LORD and every Word of God is the light of righteousness, casting out the darkness of wickedness.

Psalm 27:1 The LORD is my light and my salvation; whom shall I fear? the LORD is the strength of my life; of whom shall I be afraid?

Those who walk in the light of living by every Word of God, need never fear, for whatever happens in this life they have a sure place in the resurrection to spirit and eternal life with God.

27:2 When the wicked, even mine enemies and my foes, came upon me to eat up my flesh, they stumbled and fell. **27:3** Though an host should encamp against me, my heart shall not fear: though war should rise against me, in this will I be confident.

The unrepentant wicked will ultimately fall into eternal death, while those who love truth and living by the Word of God shall live for eternity. The godly go down to the grave with the unshakable promise of the resurrection to spirit and eternal life with God.

27:4 One thing have I desired of the LORD, that will I seek after; that I may dwell in the house of the LORD all the days of my life [forever], to behold the beauty of the LORD, and to enquire [into the Word of God] in his temple.

The heart of the faithful is dedicated to live by the Word of God, FOREVER

27:5 For in the time of trouble he shall hide me in his pavilion: in the secret of his tabernacle shall he hide me; he shall set me up upon a rock.

When the godly die, they are preserved in the secret place of God, resting on the sure foundation of the Rock of Salvation

27:6 And now shall mine head be lifted up above mine enemies round about me: therefore will I offer in his tabernacle sacrifices of joy; I will sing, yea, I will sing praises unto the LORD.

In the resurrection of God's chosen called out first fruits, they shall be raised from the grave and exalted as kings and the priests of the order of Melchizedek above the nations (Rev 1:6 and 5:10).

27:7 Hear, O LORD, when I cry with my voice: have mercy also upon me, and answer me. **27:8** When thou saidst, Seek ye my face; my heart said unto thee, Thy face, LORD, will I seek.

27:9 Hide not thy face far from me; put not thy servant away in anger: thou hast been my help; leave me not, neither forsake me, O God of my salvation. **27:10** When my father and my mother forsake me, then the LORD will take me up.

What an incredible comfort to really KNOW that when the faithful who love God enough to live by his Word, cry out to God: He will deliver them! The love of God transcends the love of parents for their children, or the love of a bride and bridegroom; and even when our fathers and mothers forsake us, Almighty God our Father in heaven loves his children and will remember and deliver us from death and the grave, and all evil!

27:11 Teach me thy way, O LORD, and lead me in a plain path, because of mine enemies. **27:12** Deliver me not over unto the will of mine enemies: for false witnesses are risen up against me [including those witnessing falsely about God's Word to deceive us to fall away from our Beloved LORD], and such as breathe out cruelty.

Let us learn the ways of righteousness and salvation; which is to live by every Word of God. Pray diligently that God will give a good understanding and make the Word of God plain and easy to understand and save us from all deceivers!

27:13 I had fainted, unless I had believed to see the goodness of the LORD in the land of the living.

Remember that we would all surely faint, fall and fail, but for the mercy of our Great Deliverer who in his merciful love strengthens us to do his will and live by his Word

27:14 Wait on the LORD: be of good courage, and he shall strengthen thine heart: wait, I say, on the LORD.

Be patient, faithful and diligent to live by every Word of God and he will deliver us in the resurrection to eternal life

Psalm 28

A prayer for deliverance to the ONLY Deliverer who can deliver from all enemies including death itself

Psalm 28:1 Unto thee will I cry, O LORD my rock; be not silent to me: lest, if thou be silent to me, I become like them that go down into the pit [the grave]. **28:2** Hear the voice of my supplications, when I cry unto thee, when I lift up my hands toward thy holy oracle.

28:3 Draw me not away with the wicked, and with the workers of iniquity, which speak peace [deceitfully to gain advantage] to their neighbours, but mischief is in their hearts. **28:4** Give them [the unrepentant wicked] according to their deeds, and according to the wickedness of their endeavours: give them after the work of their hands; render to them their desert.

God will correct all those who reject living by every Word of God, and if they still adamantly refuse to repent they will be cast into eternal death

28:5 Because they regard not the works of the LORD, nor the operation of his hands, he shall destroy them, and not build them up.

Praises to Almighty God; the Deliverer of all those who faithfully live by every Word of God

28:6 Blessed be the LORD, because he hath heard the voice of my supplications.

The Eternal is the strength of all those who put their trust in him to live by his Word

28:7 The LORD is my strength and my shield; my heart trusted in him, and I am helped: therefore my heart greatly rejoiceth; and with my song will I praise him.

28:8 The LORD is their [the strength of the faithful] strength, and he is the saving strength of his anointed [the ones filled with the Spirit of God].

Messiah the Christ will come to save his creation and deliver them from bondage to Satan and sin, and in their appointed times he will resurrect and change to eternal spirit all those who turn to live by every Word of God

28:9 Save thy people, and bless thine inheritance: feed them also, and lift them up for ever.

Psalm 29

The faithful are mighty to overcome by the power of the Just and Mighty Deliverer, therefore let us rejoice and praise God, the Just and Holy!

Psalm 29:1 Give unto the LORD, O ye mighty, give unto the LORD glory and strength. **29:2** Give unto the LORD the glory due unto his name; worship the LORD in the beauty of holiness.

When Messiah the Christ comes, the voice of righteousness will ring forth through the whole earth and all nations shall flow to God.

> **Isaiah 2:2** And it shall come to pass in the last days, that the mountain of the Lord's house shall be established in the top of the mountains, and shall be exalted above the hills; and all nations shall flow unto it.

Psalm 29:3 The voice of the LORD is upon the waters [nations, peoples]: the God of glory thundereth: the LORD is upon many waters [will rule many [peoples].

The earth and heavens tremble at the voice [Word] of God, who is mighty to destroy the wicked and to deliver God's faithful who live by every Word of God

29:4 The voice of the LORD is powerful; the voice of the LORD is full of majesty. **29:5** The voice of the LORD breaketh the cedars [the strong and mighty men]; yea, the LORD breaketh the cedars of Lebanon [the great among the Gentiles].

29:6 He maketh them [the great nations] also to skip like a calf; Lebanon and Sirion [an ancient name for Mt Hermon] like a young unicorn.

29:7 The voice of the LORD divideth [saves the godly and separates the wicked into Gehenna] the flames of fire.

29:8 The voice of the LORD shaketh the wilderness [a figurative type of the ungodly]; the LORD shaketh the wilderness of Kadesh.

The voice [Word] of God created and sustains all things, and his faithful glorify and obey him

29:9 The voice of the LORD maketh the hinds [God created animals and enabled them to reproduce] to calve, and discovereth [God created the forests] the forests: and in his temple [spiritually God's faithful (spiritual Temple) glorify God] doth every one speak of his glory.

Messiah the King of kings shall rule all nations

29:10 The LORD sitteth upon the flood [many nations]; yea, the LORD sitteth King for ever.

29:11 The LORD will give strength unto his [the faithful who live by every Word of God] people; the LORD will bless his people [in the resurrection to spirit with eternal life and peace] with peace.

Psalm 30

Praises for God's deliverance

Psalm 30:1 I will extol thee, O LORD; for thou hast lifted me up, and hast not made my foes to rejoice over me. **30:2** O LORD my God, I cried unto thee, and thou hast healed me.

God spiritually heals his faithful from bondage to sin and from the wages of sin, which is death

30:3 O LORD, thou hast brought up my soul from the grave: thou hast kept me alive, that I should not go down to the pit [grave].

The faithful who live by every Word of God, will be raised up from death and the grave to eternal life

30:4 Sing unto the LORD, O ye saints of his, and give thanks at the remembrance of his holiness. **30:5** For his anger endureth but a moment; in his favour is life: weeping may endure for a night, but joy cometh in the morning.

Let us rejoice for the correction of the LORD is momentary and is for our good so that he might save us to eternal life

30:6 And in my prosperity [blessings of godliness] I said, I shall never be moved [away from godliness]. **30:7** LORD, by thy favour thou hast made my mountain [house, family or kingdom, government] to stand strong: thou didst hide thy face, and I was troubled.

God's eternal blessings come to those who will not be moved from living by every Word of God

30:8 I cried to thee, O LORD; and unto the LORD I made supplication.

Let us quickly sincerely repent and seek the mercy of the LORD with dedicated single mindedness when we fall astray and quickly turn back to live by every Word of God

30:9 What profit is there in my blood, when I go down to the pit [grave]? Shall the dust praise thee? shall it declare thy truth?

What does it profit us if we cleave to past sins, errors and false traditions and reject knowledge of the Word of God for our own ways? Far better to be humbled and sincerely repent, crying out to the Mighty One to deliver us and mercifully forgive us, for we can do nothing in the grave.

Holy Father, Mighty One; give us a repentant heart and be merciful making a New Covenant with us; write your Word and Law upon our hearts

> **Jeremiah 31:33** But this shall be the covenant that I will make with the house of Israel; After those days, saith the Lord, **I will put my law in their inward parts, and write it in their hearts; and will be their God, and they shall be my people.**

Psalm 30:10 Hear, O LORD, and have mercy upon me: LORD, be thou my helper.

Forgive us, oh Lord, and turn our sadness over our sins into rejoicing for your merciful deliverance.

30:11 Thou hast turned for me my mourning into dancing: thou hast put off my sackcloth, and girded me with gladness; **30:12** To the end that my glory [in my forgiveness and resurrection] may sing praise to thee, and not be silent. **O LORD my God, I will give thanks unto thee for ever.**

Psalms 31 - 40

Psalm 31

A prayer for the deliverance of all those who put their trust in the LORD God: May God deliver all those who live by his Word, no one will ever be ashamed for trusting and living by every Word of God.

Psalm 31:1 In thee, O LORD, do I put my trust; let me never be ashamed: deliver me in thy righteousness.

God hears the prayers of those who follow and live by his Word, and he will deliver us from bondage to Satan, sin and death.

31:2 Bow down thine ear to me; deliver me speedily: be thou my strong rock, for an house of defence to save me [from bondage to sin and the grave]. **31:3** For thou art my rock [of salvation] and my fortress [of defense against the Adversary]; therefore for thy name's sake [not for any merit of mine but for your glorious reputation] lead me, and guide me. **31:4** Pull me out of the net [deliver the faithful from the deceitful words intended to lead us astray to destruction] that they have laid privily for me: for thou art my strength.

The faithful who commit themselves to live by every Word of God and all truth shall never be ashamed, for they have been redeemed by the sacrifice of the very Lamb of God. Those who reject any truth to maintain the false traditions and ways of men shall be greatly ashamed for the sacrifice of Christ shall not be applied to lovers of error.

31:5 Into thine hand I commit my spirit: thou hast redeemed me, O LORD God of truth. **31:6** I have hated them that regard [teach deceitful lies] lying vanities: but I trust in the [the Word of God] LORD.

Those who trust in God to live by every Word of God shall be given victory over Satan and sin and death itself; they shall rejoice in God's merciful forgiveness and acceptance in the resurrection to spirit.

31:7 I will be glad and rejoice in thy mercy: for thou hast considered my trouble; thou hast known my soul in adversities; **31:8** And hast not shut me up into the hand of the enemy: thou hast set my feet in a large room.

God will not leave his faithful in the embrace of death, but will deliver them and give them offices in his kingdom. Those who put their trust in God submitting to and living by his Word, are consumed with grief over their past sins and cry out to him in sincere humble wholehearted repentance

31:9 Have mercy upon me, O LORD, for I am in trouble: mine eye is consumed with grief, yea, my soul and my belly. **31:10** For my life is spent with grief, and my years with sighing: my strength faileth because of mine iniquity, and my bones are consumed.

Because of our trust to live by every Word of God, we are slandered and forsaken of men: Therefore Holy Father in heaven; lift us up and deliver us for we put our trust in thee

31:11 I was a reproach among all mine enemies, but especially among my neighbours, and a fear to mine acquaintance: they that did see me without fled from me. **31:12** I am forgotten as a dead man out of mind [far from their thoughts]: I am [cast aside by men] like a broken vessel. **31:13** For I have heard the slander of many: fear was on every side: while they took counsel together against me, they devised to take away my life.

The wicked hate those who chose to live by every Word of God and seek to deceive them away from God or to attack and destroy them; yet the godly will be steadfast to trust in the Mighty One of Moses

31:14 But I trusted in thee, O LORD: I said, Thou art my God.

The lives of men are in the hands of God and although the faithful may suffer in this life to better learn godliness, God will bless those who put their trust in him by raising them up to eternal life and many blessings

31:15 My times are in thy hand: deliver me from the hand of mine enemies, and from them that persecute me. **31:16** Make thy face to shine upon thy servant: save me for thy mercies' sake.

The wicked will be ashamed and the godly shall greatly rejoice in the day of their change

31:17 Let me not be ashamed, O LORD; for I have called upon thee: let the wicked be ashamed, and let them be silent in the grave.

The slanderers will be silenced by the manifestation of the truth, when all things are fulfilled

31:18 Let the lying lips be put to silence; which speak grievous things proudly and contemptuously against the righteous.

God will hide his chosen faithful Spring Harvest in the grave for a short time before he lifts them up to eternal life as kings and priests of the Most High, forever

31:19 Oh how great is thy goodness, which thou hast laid up for them that fear thee; which thou hast wrought for them that trust in thee before [served God openly in the sight of men] the sons of men! **31:20** Thou shalt hide them in the secret of thy presence from the pride of man: thou shalt keep them secretly in a pavilion from the strife of tongues [the godly will be delivered from the lies and slanders of deceitful men].

The faithful may be cut off from the land of the living, but the Eternal will raise them up to the reward of eternal life for faithfully living by every Word of God through great adversity

31:21 Blessed be the LORD: for he hath shewed me his marvellous kindness in a strong city. **31:22** For I said in my haste, I am cut off from before thine eyes: nevertheless thou heardest the voice of my supplications when I cried unto thee.

Be strong, be faithful, all His children; for our Great God will deliver and strengthen us in that day!

31:23 O love the LORD, all ye his saints: for the LORD preserveth the faithful, and plentifully rewardeth the proud [properly: God rewards the faithful doer and keeper of the Word of God] doer.

31:24 Be of good courage, and he shall strengthen your heart, all ye that hope in the LORD.

Psalm 32

A Psalm about the blessing of forgiveness for the sincerely repentant

Psalm 32:1 Blessed is he whose transgression is forgiven, whose sin is covered. **32:2** Blessed is the man unto whom the LORD imputeth not iniquity, and in whose spirit there is no guile.

To be forgiven one must sincerely repent from all past sin and STOP sinning [stop transgressing the Word of God] in future, committing to go forward and sin no more. Only then will the sinner be forgiven and justified by the application of the sacrifice of Jesus Christ. the Atoning sacrifice.

> **Romans 2:13** (For not the hearers of the law are just before God, but **the doers of the law shall be justified.**

When we keep silent and fail to sincerely repent of our past sins and we refuse to commit to STOP sinning, we begin to die spiritually and such people will not be forgiven nor raised up from the grave to eternal life.

Psalm 32:3 When I kept silence [did not sincerely repent], my bones waxed old [all hope of lasting life failed and my body judged for destruction] through my roaring [proud self-will] all the day long. **32:4** For day and night thy hand [chastening and rebuke] was heavy upon me: my moisture [my life strength dried up as moisture in a drought] is turned into the drought of summer. Selah.

Because we will surely die in our sin, let us quickly acknowledge our iniquity and sincerely repent to turn to live by every Word of God; so that we might be saved from eternal death.

If we confess our sins against God and we sincerely repent, committing ourselves to go forward and live by every Word of God; we shall be forgiven, justified by the application of the sacrifice of the Lamb of God and saved from damnation.

32:5 I acknowledge my sin unto thee, and mine iniquity have I not hid. I said, I will confess my transgressions unto the LORD; and thou forgavest the iniquity of my sin. Selah.

Every godly person prays for forgiveness from sins and the godly strength to live by every Word of God.

32:6 For this shall every one that is godly pray unto thee in a time when thou mayest be found: surely in the floods of great waters [the godly shall be delivered from the grave as pictured by Israel being delivered from the waters of the Red Sea] they shall not come nigh unto him.

The godly put their trust in God and live by every Word of God, quickly repenting when any sin or error is discovered.

32:7 Thou art my hiding place; thou shalt preserve me from trouble [God's Word teaches us the way to peace and life]; thou shalt compass me about [God will ultimately surround those who are zealous to follow him with eternal blessings] with songs of deliverance. Selah.

God's Word instructs his faithful in the ways of peace and eternal life.

32:8 I will instruct thee and teach thee in the way which thou shalt go: I will guide thee with mine eye.

Let us not be self-willed so that we must be forced to obey God's Word, but let us obey willingly and enthusiastically because God's Word is for our good.

32:9 Be ye not as the horse, or as the mule, which have no understanding: whose mouth must be held in with bit and bridle, lest they [if we are self-willed like the stubborn mule, we shall be corrected] come near unto thee.

The unrepentant refuse to live by God's Word to their own hurt; while those who are zealous to live by every Word of God are greatly blessed in learning the way to peace, blessings and eternal life.

32:10 Many sorrows shall be to the wicked: but he that trusteth in the LORD, mercy shall compass him about.

Those who sincerely repent of their failure to live by every Word of God and who dedicate themselves to live by every Word of God in Christ-like zeal; shall surely Greatly Rejoice and Shout for Joy at their resurrection and change to eternal spirit.

32:11 Be glad in the LORD, and rejoice, ye righteous [true righteousness is to live by EVERY WORD of GOD]: and shout for joy, all ye that are upright in heart.

Psalm 33

Praise God for his Holy Righteous Word

Psalm 33:1 Rejoice in the LORD, O ye righteous [God is righteousness, and living by every Word of God is righteousness]: for praise [God is worthy of praise] is comely for the upright. **33:2** Praise the LORD with harp: sing unto him with the psaltery and an instrument of ten strings. **33:3** Sing unto him a new song [of praise]; play [music] skilfully with a loud noise.

Every Word of God is righteousness and truth

33:4 For the word of the LORD is right; and all his works are done in truth. **33:5** He loveth righteousness and judgment [justice]: the earth is full of the goodness of the LORD.

Jesus Christ taught that we are to live by every Word of God (Mat 4:4) and Paul taught that:

> **Romans 7:12** Wherefore **the law is holy, and the commandment holy, and just, and good.**

Psalm 33:6 By the word of the LORD were the heavens made; and all the host of them by the breath of his mouth [the words coming from God's mouth].

By God's command the waters were gathered and the land raised up above the waters in Genesis 1:6-10.

33:7 He gathereth the waters of the sea together as an heap: he layeth up the depth in storehouses.

Let every person respect, glorify and stand in awe of the Great Creator God the Father and the Son.

33:8 Let all the earth fear the LORD: let all the inhabitants of the world stand in awe of him. **33:9** For he spake, and it was done; he commanded, and it stood fast.

God will bring the stratagems of deceivers to nothing; and God's purpose will be accomplished

33:10 The LORD bringeth the counsel of the heathen to nought: he maketh the devices of the people of none effect.

The Will and Word of God will stand forever, blessed are those who are called to God and who faithfully live by every Word of God and exalt the Eternal above all else

33:11 The counsel of the LORD standeth for ever, the thoughts of his heart to all generations. **33:12** Blessed is the nation whose God is the LORD; and the people whom he hath chosen for his own inheritance.

God knows the hearts of all men and no person may hide anything from God

33:13 The LORD looketh from heaven; he beholdeth all the sons of men. **33:14** From the place of his habitation he looketh upon all the inhabitants of the earth. **33:15** He fashioneth their hearts alike; he considereth all their works.

There is no place to hide from God's judgment and no power in men to resist the will and judgment of God

33:16 There is no king saved by the multitude of an host: a mighty man is not delivered by much strength. **33:17** An horse is a vain thing for safety: neither shall he deliver any by his great strength.

God is just and he will deliver all those who love him enough to live by his Word and put their hope and trust in HIM, to raise them up to eternal life

33:18 Behold, the eye of the LORD is upon them that fear him, upon them that hope in his mercy; **33:19** To deliver their soul from death, and to keep them alive in famine.

The LORD is the Deliverer of all those who put their trust in him to follow him whithersoever he goeth (Rev 14:3) in living by every Word of God.

33:20 Our soul waiteth for the LORD: he is our help and our shield. **33:21** For our heart shall rejoice in him, because we have trusted in his holy name. **33:22** Let thy mercy, O LORD, be upon us, according as we hope [let us put our trust in, and live by God's Word] in thee.

Psalm 34

Rejoicing over God's deliverance from the grave, in a resurrection to spirit

A prophecy of Messiah the Christ and his resurrection as the first of many to also be delivered from the grave

Psalm 34:1 I will bless the LORD at all times: his praise shall continually be in my mouth. **34:2** My soul shall make her boast in the LORD: the humble shall hear thereof, and be glad. **34:3** O magnify the LORD with me, and let us exalt his name together.

When we live by every Word of God the Father in Christ-like zeal; God will deliver us from fear of death and the grave

34:4 I sought the LORD, and he heard me, and delivered me from all my fears. **34:5** They [the faithful] looked [put their trust in God to live by every Word of God.] unto him, and were lightened [enlightened with truth and encouraged]: and their faces were not ashamed [because God keeps his promises].

34:6 This poor [God will hear the humble and poor in the spirit of self-will] man cried, and the LORD heard him, and saved him out of all his troubles. **34:7** The angel of the LORD encampeth round about them that fear him [God delivers those who love and respect him enough to live by his Word], and delivereth them.

God is good and full of mercy and deliverance for all those who put their trust in him to live by every Word of God

34:8 O taste and see that the LORD is good: blessed is the man that trusteth in him. **34:9** O fear [greatly respect and hold in awe] the LORD, ye his saints: for there is no want [no lack of deliverance from sin and death] to them that fear him.

Even though the mighty perish, God's faithful will be preserved

34:10 The young lions do lack, and suffer hunger: but they that seek the LORD shall not want any good thing.

34:11 Come, ye children, hearken unto me: I will teach you the fear [love, faithful obedience and respect] of the LORD.

If we desire victory over bondage to Satan and sin, and the gift of eternal life then we must learn to live by every Word of God

34:12 What man is he that desireth life, and loveth many days, that he may see good? **34:13** Keep thy tongue from evil, and thy lips from speaking guile. **34:14** Depart from evil, and do good; seek peace, and pursue [godliness, for only God is good] it.

God the Father watches over and will deliver from death and the grave all those who love him enough to live by every Word of God

34:15 The eyes of the LORD are upon the righteous, and his ears are open unto their cry.

God the Father will destroy all those who refuse to live by every Word of God, rejecting God and the truth of his Word

34:16 The face of the LORD is against them that do evil, to cut off the remembrance of them from the earth.

God's Word is righteousness and the righteous will live by every Word of God, God will deliver all those who passionately live by every Word of God in the resurrection to spirit

34:17 The righteous cry, and the LORD heareth, and delivereth them out of all their troubles. **34:18** The LORD is nigh unto them that are of a broken heart [are sincerely repentant abhorring their sins]; and saveth such as be of a contrite spirit.

The proud stubborn spirit of self-will will be crushed to powder and submissive humility before God.

God will deliver those who live by every Word of God but the wicked shall perish in their unrepentant wickedness

34:19 Many are the afflictions of the righteous: but the LORD delivereth him out of them all. **34:20** He keepeth all his bones: not one of them is broken [a prophecy of the death and resurrection of Christ the righteous].

34:21 Evil shall slay the wicked: and they that hate the righteous [Those who despise God's faithful who are zealous to live by every Word of God, and who do not sincerely repent; will NOT be in the resurrection to spirit, even if they have been baptized and attend some corporate assembly.] shall be desolate. **34:22** The LORD redeemeth the soul [lives] of his servants [by the blood sacrifice of the Lamb of God]: and none of them that trust in him shall be desolate.

Psalm 35

A prayer for the deliverance of the godly who live by the Word of God, and a prophecy of the crucifixion of Jesus Christ

God our Father WILL hear the prayer of all those who love him enough to live by every Word of God, and he will deliver us from death and the grave just like he delivered the Lamb of God, the first born of many brethren!

The day will come when God the Father will send Messiah the Christ the Deliverer, to take up his instruments of war and return to the earth to deliver his faithful and destroy Babylon the Wicked (Rev 15 - Rev 19)!

Psalm 35:1 Plead my cause, O LORD, with them that strive with me: fight against them that fight against me. **35:2** Take hold of shield and buckler, and stand up for mine help. **35:3** Draw out also the spear, and stop the way against them that persecute me: say unto my soul, I am thy salvation.

Almighty God will crush the wicked, which persecute the righteous who live by the Word of God, in his zeal for his beloved

35:4 Let them [the wicked] be confounded and put to shame that seek after my soul: let them be turned back and brought to confusion that devise my hurt. **35:5** Let them be as chaff before the wind: and let the angel of the LORD chase them. **35:6** Let their way be dark and slippery: and let the angel of the LORD persecute them.

35:7 For without cause have they hid for me their net in a pit, which without cause they have digged [a grave] for my soul [life]. **35:8** Let destruction come upon him [the wicked] at unawares; and let his net that he hath hid [let the wicked fall into their own trap] catch himself: into that very destruction [let the wicked fall into the trap he had planned for the godly] let him fall.

35:9 And my soul shall be joyful in the LORD: it shall rejoice in his salvation. **35:10** All my bones shall say, LORD, who is like unto thee, which deliverest the poor [the poor in the spirit of pride and stubborn self-will] from him that is too strong for him, yea, the poor [deliver the humble] and the needy [who know they need and therefore hunger and thirst for the Word of God] from him that spoileth him?

A prophecy of the trial and crucifixion of Christ, and a complaint of the righteous against the lies and deeds of the wicked

35:11 False witnesses did rise up; they laid to my charge things that I knew not. **35:12** They rewarded me evil for good to the spoiling of my soul. **35:13** But as for me, when they were sick, my clothing was sackcloth: I humbled my soul with fasting; and my prayer returned into mine own bosom [answered by God].

The godly mourn for the wicked, and their desire is that the wicked would sincerely repent and be saved. Jesus healed even the unconverted in his physical ministry as an example that he will heal mankind from all evil when he comes.

35:14 I behaved myself as though he [the wicked persons] had been my friend or brother: I bowed [Jesus and the faithful deeply desire the sincere repentance and saving of the wicked, as David mourned for Absalom] down heavily, as one that mourneth for his mother.

35:15 But in mine adversity they rejoiced, and gathered themselves together: yea, the abjects gathered themselves together against me, and I knew it not; they did tear me, and ceased not:

Although Jesus Christ loved them, the wicked rejoiced over his death; even so the wicked rejoice over the trials of the righteous to this day.

35:16 With hypocritical mockers in feasts, they gnashed upon me with their teeth [their abusive words].

The wicked who observe the Feasts in hypocrisy, not living by every Word of God; mock and persecute those who are zealous to live by every Word of God

David asks, as every righteous man has asked through the ages: When will God's deliverance come?

35:17 Lord, how long wilt thou look on? rescue my soul from their destructions, my darling from the lions.

The day will come when the righteous will greatly rejoice over their deliverance from all evil, including death itself. Then when all nations are gathered at the Feasts of the LORD the delivered will teach them the greatness of God

35:18 I will give thee thanks in the great congregation: I will praise thee among much people. **35:19** Let not them that are mine enemies wrongfully rejoice over me: neither let them wink with the eye [in derision] that hate me without a cause. **35:20** For they speak not peace: but they devise deceitful matters against them that are quiet in the land.

The wicked rejoiced over the crucifixion of Messiah and they still rejoice at the calamities of the righteous. Let not the wicked rejoice over the apparent fall of those who live by the righteousness of every Word of God

35:21 Yea, they opened their mouth wide against me, and said, Aha, aha, our eye hath seen it.

The wicked rejoice saying that they have seem the fall of those who love God enough to live by his every Word; they rejoice for they feel vindicated by the calamity of the righteous, thinking that they are right and the zealous for God are wrong

35:22 This thou hast seen, O LORD: keep not silence: O Lord, be not far from me. **35:23** Stir up thyself, and awake to my judgment, even unto my cause, my God and my Lord. **35:24** Judge me, O LORD my God, according to thy righteousness [which is every Word of God] ; and let them not rejoice over me.

35:25 Let them not say in their hearts, Ah, so would we have it: let them not say, We have swallowed him [thinking they have destroyed Christ in the crucifixion, and also his servants] up.

When Christ comes the wicked will see him and they will hear his words commanding that all men live by every Word of God the Father. The rejoicing of the wicked over the calamity of all those who live by every Word of God shall be turned to terrible correction and mourning.

35:26 Let them be ashamed and brought to confusion together that rejoice at mine hurt: let them be clothed with shame and dishonour that magnify themselves against me.

When the righteous are delivered, they will rejoice and praise God the Father and his Christ forever

35:27 Let them shout for joy, and be glad, that favour my righteous cause: yea, let them say continually, Let the LORD be magnified, which hath pleasure in the prosperity of his servant. **35:28** And my tongue shall speak of thy righteousness and of thy praise all the day long.

Psalm 36

David's inspired opinion of the wicked; they are proud, loving themselves and having no regard for God to live by the Word of God

Psalm 36:1 The transgression of the wicked saith within my heart [David is inspired to understand the wicked], that there is no fear of God before his eyes.

The wicked are proud, self-willed and full of themselves, having no humility to submit to the Word of God.

36:2 For he flattereth himself in his own eyes [the wicked are always right in their own eyes], until [until God rejects the evil and corrects them for their hateful wickedness] his iniquity be found to be hateful [wickedness is abhorrent to God and will be corrected by God's righteous rebuke].

The wicked lay awake at night scheming how to deceive others and gain advantage for themselves; their words are deceitful for they have no love for truth and no love to live by the Word of God.

The wicked can be very impressive slick talkers who can con a dove out of its feathers. They claim to be full of love as they deceitfully steal your spiritual crowns and your physical means. They love their own ways and abhor to live by every Word of God.

36:3 The words of his mouth are iniquity and deceit: he hath left off to be wise, and to do good. **36:4** He deviseth mischief upon his bed; he setteth himself in a way that is not good; he abhorreth not evil.

The power, wisdom, judgments and justice of God are far greater than the power of the wicked, and God's mercy is everlasting to all those who love him and live by every Word of God.

36:5 Thy mercy, O LORD, is in the heavens; and thy faithfulness reacheth unto the clouds. **36:6** Thy righteousness is like the great mountains; thy judgments are a great deep: O LORD, thou preservest man and beast.

36:7 How excellent is thy lovingkindness, O God! therefore the children of men put their trust under the shadow of thy wings. **36:8** They shall be abundantly satisfied with the fatness [the wealth] of thy house [family, kingdom]; and thou shalt make them drink of the river [the river of Living Waters of the Word and Spirit of God] of thy pleasures.

The chief pleasure of the faithful is to please God by fulfilling his Word.

Water is essential for life and this is most clearly evident in a desert land; therefore the scriptures refer to God's Word and Spirit as the Fountain or River of Living Waters which is essential for eternal spiritual life.

36:9 For with thee is the fountain of life: in thy light shall we see light.

Let us plead along with David, that God will not allow the spirit of pride to find a place in us or come near to us, and that we will always cleave to the righteousness of the Word of God.

Pray that we, by clinging to every Word of God, will never be deceived by the wicked who seek to turn us away from our LORD

36:10 O continue thy lovingkindness unto them that know thee; and thy righteousness to the upright in heart [upright in wholehearted faithfulness to live by every Word of God]. **36:11** Let not the foot of pride come against me, and let not the hand of the wicked remove me. **36:12** There are the workers of iniquity fallen: they are cast down, and shall not be able to rise.

Psalm 37

Encouragement to trust in God and to neither envy the apparent physical prosperity nor fear the deeds of the wicked; for the wicked will soon perish and their deeds with them

Psalm 37:1 Fret not thyself because of evildoers, neither be thou envious against the workers of iniquity. **37:2** For they shall soon be cut down like the grass, and wither as the green herb.

Always be absolutely faithful to trust in the LORD and to live by every Word of God, and we shall be raised up to eternal life

37:3 Trust in the LORD, and do good [live by every Word of God]; so shalt thou dwell in the land, and verily thou shalt be fed. **37:4** Delight thyself also in the LORD: and he shall give thee the desires of thine heart. **37:5** Commit thy way unto the LORD; trust also in him; and he shall bring it to pass.

When the righteous of God are raised from their graves they shall shine brightly forever

> **Daniel 12:3** And they that be wise [live by every Word of God] shall shine as the brightness of the firmament [heavens]; and they that turn many to righteousness as the stars for ever and ever.

Psalm 37:6 And he shall bring forth thy righteousness as the light, and thy judgment [justice] as the noonday.

Do not be concerned over the prosperity of the wicked for this is Satan's world and he gives to those who follow him. These physical things will perish with the wicked, while those who put their trust in the LORD to live by God's every Word shall live forever and partake of eternal riches.

Avoid anger and envy of the wicked who will quickly perish, and remain dedicated in Christ-like zeal to live by every Word of God, and we shall be raised up to eternal life like Jesus was.

37:7 Rest in the LORD, and wait patiently for him: fret not thyself because of him who prospereth in his way, because of the man who bringeth wicked devices to pass. **37:8** Cease from anger, and forsake wrath: fret not thyself in any wise to do evil.

37:9 For **evildoers shall be cut off: but those that wait upon the LORD, they shall inherit the earth. 37:10** For yet a little while, and the wicked shall not be: yea, thou shalt diligently consider his place [we shall look for them and they will not be found, because the unrepentant wicked will perish forever], and it shall not be.

Those who are meek and submissive to the Word of God shall inherit the earth.

    Matthew 5:5 Blessed are the meek: for they shall inherit the earth.

Psalm 37:11 But the meek shall inherit the earth; and shall delight themselves in the abundance of peace.

37:12 The wicked plotteth against the just, and gnasheth upon him with his teeth.

The wicked attack godliness with deceitful words and lies

37:13 The LORD shall laugh at him: for he seeth that his day is coming.

God and his faithful, laugh at the devises of the wicked; knowing that they are doomed to destruction if they will not sincerely repent; while those who love and live by every Word of God shall be delivered and sanctified forever

37:14 The wicked have drawn out the sword, and have bent their bow, to cast down the poor and needy, and to slay such as be of upright conversation.

The wicked seek to destroy the godly righteous away from living by every Word of God.

37:15 Their sword shall enter into their own heart, and their bows shall be broken.

The devices of the wicked will be turned back against them and they shall fall by their own actions

37:16 A little that a righteous man hath is better than the riches of many wicked. **37:17** For the arms [strength, wealth] of the wicked shall be broken: but **the LORD upholdeth the righteous.**

The Eternal upholds those who love him and live by his Word, but the unrepentant wicked will surely perish

37:18 The LORD **knoweth the days of the upright: and their inheritance shall be for ever. 37:19** They shall not be ashamed in the evil time: and in the days of famine they shall be satisfied.

The Eternal delivers his faithful in the day of trouble, raising them up from the very grave and death itself; to eternal life with God and every good thing

In the ultimate end the unrepentant wicked shall be consumed in the fires of eternal death in Gehenna

37:20 But the wicked shall perish, and the enemies of the LORD shall be as the fat of lambs: they shall consume; into smoke shall they consume away.

The wicked take selfishly and then laugh at the righteous for their honesty, while the godly are a merciful people like their Father in heaven

37:21 The wicked borroweth, and payeth not again: but the righteous sheweth mercy, and giveth.

37:22 For such as be blessed of him shall inherit the earth; and they that be cursed of him shall be cut off [destroyed].

37:23 The steps of a good man are ordered by the LORD [a good man conducts himself according to the Word of God]: and he delighteth in his [God's] way [every Word of God and in all truth]. **37:24** Though he fall, he shall not be utterly cast down: for the LORD upholdeth him [will teach him and lift him up] with his hand.

The measure of a person is not whether they have problems, for all have sinned and everyone has problems; the true measure of a person is in how he handles his troubles.

A godly man will acknowledge his errors and turn to God in sincere repentance getting back up and continuing in the godly way, having learned from his mistakes.

The wicked will justify themselves and continue in their errors and sins, defending falsehood in their great pride and preferring to cleave to sin rather than to admit error and accept truth.

> **Proverbs 24:16** For a just man falleth **seven times**, and riseth up again: but the wicked shall fall into mischief.

Those who live by every Word of God will be filled with the unleavened Bread of Life, Jesus Christ the Passover Lamb of God

Psalm 37:25 I have been young, and now am old; yet have I not seen the righteous forsaken, nor his seed begging bread.

Spiritually this refers to the Bread of Eternal Life, which is the Word of God, Jesus Christ; who will dwell in the godly through the Holy Spirit. God will never forsake those who diligently live by every Word of God; and even if they must suffer to learn important lessons in the present, if they are faithful they will be raised up to eternal life.

37:26 He is ever merciful, and lendeth; and his seed is blessed (Luk 8:5-15).

The godly, like their God; are merciful

37:27 Depart from evil, and do good [live by every Word of God]; and dwell for evermore [shall receive eternal life]. **37:28** For the LORD loveth judgment [justice], and forsaketh not his saints; they are preserved for ever: but the seed of the wicked shall be cut off.

The wicked shall come to their end, but those who live by every Word of God shall be established forever

37:29 The righteous shall inherit the land, and dwell therein for ever.

Righteousness is to live by every Word of God; the righteous of the Mosaic Covenant inherited the physical promised land, and the righteous of the New Covenant shall inherit the Promised Land of eternal life

37:30 The mouth of the righteous speaketh wisdom, and his tongue talketh of judgment [justice].

The Word of God is Wisdom and Justice

37:31 The law of his God is in his heart; none of his steps shall slide.

The Law and Word of God are written on the hearts of the righteous who have received the gift of God's Holy Spirit. God the Father has been calling out a few and offering them his Spirit since righteous Abel (Heb 11); writing the Word of God on their hearts (Jer 31). Ultimately God will call all humanity to his righteousness (Joel 2:28, Is 2:2)

37:32 The wicked watcheth the righteous, and seeketh to slay him. **37:33** The LORD will not leave [the righteous] him in his hand [in the hand of the wicked], nor [God will not condemn those who live by his Word] condemn him when he is judged.

The wicked seek to persecute and destroy the godly, but God will deliver those who live by his Word

37:34 Wait on the LORD, and keep his way, and he shall exalt thee to inherit the land: when the wicked are cut off [destroyed], thou [the righteous will see the unrepentant wicked perish] shalt see it.

Those first fruits who patiently endure and live by every Word of God will be changed to spirit and granted eternal life to inherit the earth as kings and priests of God forever (Rev 5:10). The unrepentant wicked shall be destroyed forever.

37:35 I have seen the wicked in great power, and spreading himself [growing strong] like a green bay tree. **37:36** Yet he passed away, and, lo, he was not: yea, I sought him, but he could not be found.

The strongest and greatest of the unrepentant wicked, including Satan himself; shall be destroyed never to be found again

37:37 Mark the perfect man, and behold the upright: for the end of that man is peace.

The final end of the person who lives by every Word of God is eternal life at peace with God

37:38 But the transgressors [of any part of the Word of God] shall be destroyed together: the end of the wicked shall be cut off.

The final end of the unrepentant wicked is eternal destruction (Rev 20:15, 21:8)

37:39 But the salvation of the righteous is of the LORD: he is their strength in the time of trouble. **37:40** And the LORD shall help them, and deliver them: he shall deliver them from the wicked, and save them, because they trust in him.

Those who live by every Word of God are precious in God's eyes and they shall be delivered to eternal life with God

Psalm 38

God will correct all those he loves when they go astray, so that by afflicting the flesh the spirit may be saved

Psalm 38:1 O lord, rebuke me not in thy wrath: neither chasten me in thy hot displeasure. **38:2** For thine arrows stick fast in me, and thy hand presseth me sore. **38:3** There is no soundness in my flesh because of thine anger; neither is there any rest in my bones because of my sin.

Our own stubborn self-will and insistence on living by our own ways instead of living by the Word of God will bring our eternal destruction. When we fall into such pride, a loving God corrects us afflicting the flesh to bring us to repentance and save the spirit.

38:4 For mine iniquities are gone over mine head: as an heavy burden they are too heavy for me. **38:5** My wounds [which have come as the result of sins] stink and are corrupt because of my foolishness.

38:6 I am troubled; I am bowed down greatly [greatly afflicted]; I go mourning [over the evils in the land, and repenting over my sins] all the day long. **38:7** For my loins are filled with a loathsome disease: and there is no soundness in my flesh. **38:8** I am feeble and sore broken: I have roared [cried out in anguish] by reason of the disquietness of my heart.

The godly are full of sorrow over the wickedness overspreading the earth.

If our desire is to live by every Word of God, God will correct us when we go astray and he will deliver us when we learn our lesson and turn back to him. Nothing can be hidden from God.

38:9 Lord, all my desire is before thee; and my groaning is not hid from thee.

Even though all the earth is against us because we live by every Word of God, the godly will be steadfast and will put their trust in the Eternal. Even if we must suffer many sorrows in this physical life our Mighty One will deliver us from the grave into an eternal life of blessings and rejoicing.

38:10 My heart panteth, my strength faileth me: as for the light of mine eyes, it also is gone from me. **38:11** My lovers and my friends stand aloof from my sore; and my kinsmen stand afar off. **38:12** They also that seek after my life lay snares for me: and they that seek my hurt speak mischievous things, and imagine deceits all the day long.

The righteous put their trust in God and the Word of God and not in men.

38:13 But I, as a deaf man, heard not; and I was as a dumb man that openeth not his mouth. **38:14** Thus I was as a man that heareth not, and in whose mouth are no reproofs. **38:15** For in thee, O LORD, do I hope: thou wilt hear, O Lord my God.

God will deliver his faithful and the enemy will not continue in rejoicing over the fall of the godly, but will be corrected.

38:16 For I said, Hear me, lest otherwise they should rejoice over me: when my foot slippeth, they magnify themselves against me. **38:17** For I am ready to halt [ready to perish] sorrow is continually before me.

When we are afflicted let us sincerely repent and RUN to the Eternal our Deliverer.

38:19 But mine enemies [spiritually our enemies are Satan and sin] they that hate me wrongfully are multiplied. **38:20** They also that render evil for good are mine adversaries; because I follow the thing that good is.

When we do well, the wicked hate us and attack us for living by God's Word.

38:21 Forsake me not, O LORD: O my God, be not far from me. **38:22** Make haste to help me, O Lord my salvation.

Ultimately God delivers those who live by every Word of God: May God's deliverance come quickly

Psalm 39

The faithful pay serious attention to their words and actions in order to live by and be consistent with every Word of God. David says that he often kept silent in order to be guiltless of speaking wrongfully.

Psalm 39:1 I said, I will take heed to my ways, that I sin not with my tongue: I will keep my mouth with a bridle, while the wicked is before me. **39:2** I was dumb with silence, I held my peace, even from good; and my sorrow was stirred.

After much deep thought David calls on God to give him an understanding of the transitory nature of the flesh, so that he could be humble before God and not full of the pride of the flesh.

God often teaches his people humility through sickness, trials and afflictions of the flesh.

39:3 My heart was hot within me, while I was musing the fire burned: then spake I with my tongue, **39:4** LORD, make me to know mine end, and the measure of my days, what it is: that I may know how frail I am.

Physical things are vanity, because all physical things are temporary and transitory in nature, with no lasting value except for the lessons to be learned, which lessons [if we are sincerely repentant] can last forever.

39:5 Behold, thou hast made my days as an handbreadth; and mine age is as nothing before thee: verily every man at his best state is altogether vanity. Selah.

All the efforts and sufferings of the flesh are pointless unless we learn to be humble before and learn to put our trust in the LORD to do his will.

39:6 Surely every man walketh in a vain shew: surely they are disquieted in vain: he heapeth up riches, and knoweth not who shall gather them.

Let us reject any departure from the Word of God and be silent in defense of our own ways, and let us place our trust in the LORD to be faithful for HIS ways

39:7 And now, Lord, what wait I for? my hope is in thee. **39:8** Deliver me from all my transgressions: make me not the reproach of the foolish.

Let us be speechless in trying to justify ourselves and let us be submissive to the Word and ways of God, who corrects us for our good.

39:9 I was dumb, I opened not my mouth [to complain against the correction of God]; because thou didst it. **39:10** Remove thy stroke [Father be merciful for I sincerely repent] away from me: I am consumed by the blow of thine hand.

God's merciful correction reveals to men the transitory nature of the beauties of the flesh and humbles men to put their trust in God, in order that through living by every Word of God they might receive the true lasting beauty of eternal life.

This same lesson of the transitory mature of the flesh is taught in the book of Ecclesiastes, and through living in temporary dwellings during the Feast of Tabernacles.

39:11 When thou with rebukes dost correct man for iniquity, thou makest his beauty to consume away like a moth: surely every man is vanity. Selah.

God's called out are strangers and travelers in this physical land of our flesh, because we serve God and not vain physical things

39:12 Hear my prayer, O LORD, and give ear unto my cry; hold not thy peace at my tears: for I am a stranger [we are strangers in this present world because we serve God and not the things of the flesh] with thee, and a sojourner, as all my fathers were.

God will save his chosen from the grave, but the wicked will perish forever

39:13 O spare me, that I may recover strength, before I go hence, and be no more.

Psalm 40

If we patiently continue in living by every Word of God, God will hear our prayers and he will deliver us out of the pit of the grave

Psalm 40:1 I waited patiently for the LORD; and he inclined unto me, and heard my cry. **40:2** He brought me up also out of an horrible pit [God will resurrect his chosen faithful from the grave], out of the miry clay [the grave], and set my feet upon a rock [the Rock of Salvation, Jesus Christ], and established my goings.

Those who are resurrected will sing the praises of their Deliverer, and those who see the resurrection at the coming of Christ will begin to fear and glorify God and repent to live by every Word of God

40:3 And he hath put a new song in my mouth, even praise unto our God: **many shall see it, and fear, and shall trust in the LORD.**

The person who lives by every Word of God shall be blessed, for they will be delivered from the grave to eternal life

40:4 Blessed is that man that maketh the LORD his trust, and respecteth not the proud [do not respect impressive men more than God], nor such as turn aside to lies.

40:5 Many, O LORD my God, are thy wonderful works which thou hast done, and thy thoughts which are to us-ward: they cannot be reckoned up in order unto thee: if I would declare and speak of them, they are more than can be numbered.

The mercies and awesome deeds of our Mighty God to deliver his people, are beyond counting by men

40:6 Sacrifice and offering thou didst not desire; mine ears hast thou opened: burnt offering and sin offering hast thou not required.

God desires faithful obedience to his Word, more than sacrifices

A prayer of David as a prophecy of "That Prophet," Jesus Christ

40:7 Then said I, Lo, I come: in the volume of the book [the scriptures prophesied of Christ] it is written of me, **40:8** I delight to do thy will, O my God [God the Father]: yea, thy law is within my heart [having the Holy Spirit of God]. **40:9** I have preached righteousness in the great congregation: lo, I have not refrained my lips [from teaching the Word of God], O LORD, thou knowest. **40:10** I have not hid thy righteousness [Jesus taught God's Word] within my heart; I have declared thy faithfulness and thy salvation: I have not concealed thy lovingkindness and thy truth from the great congregation.

In his work in the flesh, Jesus Christ declared the righteousness and holiness of God the Father and commanded us to live by every Word of God (Mat 4:4).

40:11 Withhold not thou thy tender mercies from me, O LORD: let thy lovingkindness and thy truth [God's Word is truth] continually preserve me. **40:12** For innumerable evils have compassed me about: mine iniquities [David speaks of his sins as an allegory that Jesus Christ would bear the sins of the whole world] have taken hold upon me, so that I am not able to look up; they are more than the hairs of mine head: therefore my heart faileth me.

David was inspired to speak as if he were Christ, asking the Father to confound all those who had conspired to take his life and by resurrecting him from the grave

40:13 Be pleased, O LORD, to deliver me: O LORD, make haste to help me. **40:14** Let them be ashamed and confounded together that seek after my soul to destroy it; let them be driven backward and put to shame that wish me evil. **40:15** Let them be desolate for a reward of their shame that say unto me, Aha, aha.

40:16 Let all those that seek thee rejoice and be glad in thee: let such as love thy salvation say continually, The LORD be magnified.

All those who sincerely repent and seek to live by every Word of God accepting the sacrifice of Christ; will rejoice in the resurrection to eternal life

40:17 But I am poor and needy; yet the Lord thinketh upon me: thou art my help and my deliverer; make no tarrying, O my God.

The LORD thinks upon God's faithful, who are poor in the spirit of stubborn self-will and pride and are submissive and humble knowing, how much they need him.

Psalms 41 - 50

Psalm 41

God is compassionate and will deliver all the godly, who are merciful and compassionate; and who feed the spiritually poor with the Word of God

Psalm 41:1 Blessed is he that considereth the poor: the LORD will deliver him [God will deliver the godly compassionate who live by every Word of God] in time of trouble.

41:2 The LORD will preserve him [God will preserve the merciful because they are merciful and God is merciful], and keep him alive [with the gift of eternal life]; and he shall be blessed upon the earth: and thou wilt not deliver him unto the will of his enemies [Satan and sin].

Those who live by God's Word, which defines God's love; will not be given over to eternal destruction like the unrepentant wicked.

41:3 The LORD will strengthen him upon the bed of languishing: thou [God will deliver those who live by his Word, from the ultimate sickness which is sin and death] wilt make all his bed in his sickness

God will save the repentant from the sickness of sin

In his compassionate mercy God will heal the sins of all repentant sinners who choose to live by every Word of God

41:4 I said, LORD, be merciful unto me: **heal my soul; for I have sinned against thee**.

The wicked rejoice in the death of the righteous who live by God's Word, not understanding that the godly will be raised up and given the gift of eternal life and that the godly faithful will rule over those who have despised them.

41:5 Mine enemies speak evil of me, When shall he die, and his name perish? **41:6** And if he come to see me, he speaketh vanity: his heart gathereth iniquity to itself; when he goeth abroad, he telleth it. **41:7** All that hate me whisper together against me: against me do they devise my hurt.

The unrepentant person hates godliness and the godly, because the things of God make no sense to him.

41:8 An evil disease, say they, cleaveth fast unto him: and now that he lieth he shall rise up no more.

The wicked rejoice at every calamity of the righteous, not understanding that God has allowed trials for our own good to mold us into the people that the Master Potter wants us to be.

Even if our dearest friend or family member turns against us for our love of God to live by God's every Word; our Mighty One will deliver us, raising us up from death and the grave so that we may be forever with him

41:9 Yea, mine own familiar friend, in whom I trusted, which did eat of my bread, hath lifted up his heel against me. **41:10** But thou, O LORD, be merciful unto me, and raise me up, that I may requite them.

41:11 By this I know that thou favourest me, because mine enemy [Satan, sin and death] doth not triumph over me.

When we rise up from death and the grave, we will KNOW that we have pleased God through diligently loving him and living by his every Word;

and the wicked will also know that God has loved those who love godliness and are faithful to live by every Word of God

41:12 And as for me, thou upholdest me in mine integrity [the integrity of diligently living by every Word of God], and settest me before thy face for ever.

41:13Blessed be the LORD God of Israel [spiritually every faithful person is the Israel of God] **from everlasting, and to everlasting. Amen, and Amen.**

Psalm 42

If we hunger and thirst after every Word of God like a person dying of thirst or famine, then we will surely learn and internalize the Word of God to live by it and we shall be filled becoming like God in our thoughts and deeds, through thinking and living like God thinks and lives

Psalm 42:1 As the hart panteth after the water brooks, so panteth my soul after thee, O God. **42:2** My soul thirsteth for God, for the living God: when shall I come and appear before God?

The righteous continually hunger and thirst after God and his Word (Mat 5:5)

42:3 My tears have been my meat day and night, while they continually say unto me, Where is thy God?

The wicked mock the godly asking: "where is God?"

42:4 When I remember these things, I pour out my soul in me: for I had gone with the multitude, I went with them to the house of God, with the voice of joy and praise, with a multitude that kept holyday.

The righteous remember and live by every Word of God, and delight to come before God on God's Sabbath and true appointed Holy Days

Why should the righteous who love God and live by his Word be distressed? Let us rejoice despite our many trials, for the very King of the Universe loves us with a passionate enduring everlasting love, and has promised with unshakable promises to give us eternal life with him!

42:5 Why art thou cast down, O my soul? and why art thou disquieted in me? hope thou in God: for I shall yet praise him for the help of his countenance.

Wherever we are and whatever our trials, let us remember God our Father in heaven and put our trust on him, always living by every Word of God

42:6 O my God, my soul is cast down within me: therefore will I remember thee from [in our exile] the land of Jordan, and of the Hermonites, from the hill Mizar. **42:7** Deep calleth unto deep at the noise of thy waterspouts: all thy waves and thy billows are gone over me.

David is inspired to speak of his exile across Jordan from the rebellion of Absalom, as an allegory of the correction of Babylon in our days.

42:8 Yet the LORD will command his lovingkindness in the day time, and in the night his song shall be with me, and my prayer unto the God of my life.

When we find ourselves in distress and the great trials of God's correction, let us sincerely repent and cry out to God for our deliverance. If we love God enough to live by every Word of God, he will deliver us from all sorrows and from the terrors of sin, death and the grave; therefore let our thoughts always be on him and may songs of his praise be ever in our mouths.

42:9 I will say unto God my rock, Why hast thou forgotten me? why go I mourning because of the oppression of the enemy? **42:10** As with a sword in my bones, mine enemies reproach me; while they say daily unto me, Where is thy God?

God is the Hope and Deliverer of his faithful; let us put our trust in him and rejoice in his ultimate deliverance to eternal life, always

42:11 Why art thou cast down, O my soul? and why art thou disquieted within me? **hope thou in God: for I shall yet praise him, who is the health of my countenance, and my God.**

Psalm 43

God will judge every person by whether they have sincerely repented and lived by every Word of God or not

> **Revelation 20:12** And I saw the dead, small and great, stand before God; and the books were opened: and another book was opened, which is the book of life: and **the dead were judged out of those things which were written in the books, according to their works.**

David asks why he is oppressed when he has chosen to live by every Word of God. This is the question covered in the books of Job and Ecclesiastes

Psalm 43:1 Judge me, O God, and plead my cause against an ungodly nation: O deliver me from the deceitful and unjust man.

David in his oppressed state, feels that God has cast him away; but in truth the oppression has been allowed because God is working with him and is using that tool to teach him important lessons

43:2 For thou art the God of my strength: why dost thou cast me off? why go I mourning because of the oppression of the enemy?

David calls upon God to lead him to the Ark of God on the Holy Mount, which is a figurative way of saying that he wants to be in the presence of God always

43:3 O send out thy light and thy truth [every Word of God is truth]: let them lead me; let them [living by every Word of God will bring us into the presence of God in the resurrection to spirit] bring me unto thy holy hill, and to thy tabernacles. **43:4** Then will I go unto the altar of God, unto God my exceeding joy: yea, upon the harp will I praise thee, O God my God.

Whenever we are discouraged in this physical life, remember that the godly who live by every Word of God, have God's unbreakable promise of a resurrection to eternal life and a much better world.

43:5 Why art thou cast down, O my soul? and why art thou disquieted within me? **hope in God: for I shall yet praise him** [those who live by every Word of God, will SHOUT his praises after our resurrection to spirit and eternal life], **who is the health of my countenance** [God brings health and healing from sin, death and the grave], **and my God.**

Psalm 44

Through the Scriptural record we hear of the mighty deeds of God; including God's calling out and deliverance of Physical Israel, which is an allegory of God's calling out and deliverance of a Spiritual Israel.

Psalm 44:1 We have heard with our ears, O God, our fathers have told [and recorded for us] us, what work thou didst in their days, in the times of old. **44:2** How thou didst drive out the heathen [drive the wicked out] with thy hand, and plantedst them [established the Mosaic Covenant People]; how thou didst afflict the [wicked] people, and cast them out.

Physical Israel defeated the physical wicked and gained the physical promised land, not by their own strength but by the power of God; and spiritual Israel shall gain victory over the spiritual Pharaoh of this world, Satan and sin, and shall inherit the Promised Land of eternal life; not by their own strength, but by the power of God

44:3 For they got not the land in possession [of the physical promised land] by their own sword, neither did their own arm save them: but thy right hand, and thine arm, and the light of thy countenance, because thou hadst a favour [God was merciful] unto them.

David asks God to remember his past acts of deliverance and save the Covenant People in all their distresses. The deliverance of the Mosaic Covenant, being a type of spiritual deliverance from the spiritual enemy [Satan and sin] of the faithful New Covenant called out.

44:4 Thou art my King, O God: command deliverances for Jacob [Israel both physical and spiritual] . **44:5** Through thee will we push down our enemies [the physical enemies of the Mosaic Covenant People, being a type of the spiritual enemies of Satan and sin, of the New Covenant People]: through thy name will we tread them [wickedness and sin] under that rise up against us.

God's faithful will put their trust in him to deliver them, just as he delivered others by his mighty deeds in the past

44:6 For I will not trust in my bow, neither shall my sword save me. **44:7** But thou hast saved us from our enemies, and hast put them to shame that hated us.

44:8 In God we boast all the day long, and praise thy name for ever.

Selah.

A prophecy about the trials of the Godly

44:9 But thou hast cast off [we suffer and it seems that we have been rejected], and put us to shame; and goest not forth with our armies. **44:10** Thou makest us to turn back [run away] from the enemy: and they which hate us spoil for themselves. **44:11** Thou hast given us like sheep appointed for meat [slaughter]; and hast scattered us among the heathen. **44:12** Thou sellest thy people for nought [the faithful must often endure many trials and are given into the hand of their enemies], and dost not increase thy wealth by their price. **44:13** Thou makest us a reproach to our neighbours, a scorn and a derision to them that are round about us. **44:14** Thou makest us a byword among the heathen, a shaking of the head among the people.

Although the process may hurt for a short time, the perfecting of the faithful through their trials is a blessing from God.

> **Romans 5:3** And not only so, but we glory in tribulations also: knowing that tribulation worketh patience; **5:4** And patience, experience; and experience, hope:

Psalm 44:15 My confusion is continually before me, and the shame of my face hath covered me, **44:16** For the voice of him that reproacheth and blasphemeth; by reason of the enemy and avenger. **44:17** All this is come upon us; yet have we not forgotten thee, neither have we dealt falsely in thy covenant. **44:18** Our heart is not turned back, neither have our steps declined from thy way; **44:19** Though thou hast sore broken us in the place of dragons [a desolate wilderness], and covered us with the shadow of death.

When trials come upon us we will remember our God, and despite the hatred of others we shall continue to faithfully live by every Word of God in sincerity and truth.

44:20 If we have forgotten the name of our God, or stretched out our hands to a strange god; **44:21** Shall not God search this out? for he knoweth the secrets of the heart.

God knows who his zealously faithful are; and God knows who has departed from his Word turning aside to false ways

44:22 Yea, for thy sake are we killed all the day long; we are counted as sheep for the slaughter.

Those who seek to faithfully live by every Word of God will have many trials in this world

44:23 Awake, why sleepest thou, O Lord? arise, cast us not off for ever. **44:24** Wherefore hidest thou thy face, and forgettest our affliction and our oppression? **44:25** For our soul [lives] is bowed down to the dust [the grave]: our belly [bodies are in the grave] cleaveth unto the earth. **44:26 Arise for our help, and redeem us** [and resurrect us] **for thy mercies' sake.**

The above is a figurative call of the faithful dead, for God's deliverance and the resurrection to spirit

Psalm 45

A Prophecy of Jesus Christ

Psalm 45:1 My heart is inditing [considering] a good matter [the coming of Messiah]: I speak of the things which I have made touching the king [Messiah the King of kings]: my tongue is the pen of a ready writer.

45:2 Thou art fairer than the children of men: grace [the mercy of Christ for the sincerely repentant through his sacrifice as the Lamb of God and his teachings to repent and live by every Word of God] is poured into [pours out from the lips of Christ] thy lips: therefore God hath blessed thee for ever [God the Father shall (and did) raise him up to eternal life] .

45:3 Gird thy sword [the sword of Truth, which is every Word of God] upon thy thigh, O most mighty, with thy glory and thy majesty.

Messiah the Christ was spiritually prosperous because of Christ's humility and zeal to live by the truth of the Word (the righteousness) of God

45:4 And in thy majesty ride prosperously because of truth and meekness and righteousness; and thy right hand shall teach thee terrible [wonderful things] things.

45:5 Thine arrows [God's correction] are sharp in the heart of the king's [the correction of the King of kings destroys the unrepentant wicked] enemies; whereby the people fall under thee.

The correction of the wicked will cause the people to fall to, or turn to, Christ and God the Father

The throne of God the Father over the universe is eternal; and the throne of Messiah the Christ under God the Father over humanity shall last forever

45:6 Thy throne, O God, is for ever and ever: the sceptre of thy kingdom is a right [just and righteous] sceptre.

45:7 Thou [Jesus Christ and every godly person] lovest righteousness [every Word of God], and hatest wickedness [anything contrary to the Word of God]: therefore God, thy God [the Father] hath anointed thee with the oil of gladness [the Holy Spirit and the resurrected Christ's anointing as the High Priest of the priesthood of Melchizedek] above thy fellows. **45:8** All thy garments smell of myrrh, aloes, and cassia [the perfumed Holy Oil, a type of the Holy Spirit], out of the ivory palaces, whereby they have made thee glad.

The Ekklesia as the collective bride of Christ, is likened to the daughters of kings [i.e. royalty 1 Peter 2:9]

45:9 Kings' daughters were among thy honourable women: upon thy right hand did stand the queen in gold of Ophir [the bride of Christ].

The children of God the Father are admonished to forget the past things they were called out of, and to pay attention to live by every Word of God; so that they might be desired and accepted as the bride of the King of kings

45:10 Hearken, O daughter [the Spiritual Ekklesia, the called out children of God the Father], and consider, and incline thine ear; forget also thine own people, and thy father's house;

If we are faithful to live by every Word of God, we shall be a most desirable bride of great beauty to Jesus Christ the Messiah the Deliverer, our Royal Husband, our Lord.

Let those called out to be a part of the bride of Christ; worship [obey] God the Father, and Messiah, Jesus Christ their Husband.

45:11 So shall the king greatly desire thy beauty: for he is thy Lord; and worship thou him.

When Christ comes with his bride they will rule the nations under God the Father, and the nations will bring gifts to the bride who rules with her Husband.

45:12 And the daughter of Tyre shall be there with a gift; even the rich among the people shall intreat thy favour.

The faithful called out collective daughter of God the Father is full of the inward beauty of living by every Word of God and dressed in the purity of linen (Revelation 19:8) embroidered with fine gold, being pure in spirit

45:13 The king's daughter is all glorious within: her clothing is of wrought gold. **45:14** She shall be brought unto the king [the King of kings] in raiment of needlework: the virgins her companions that follow her [the pure holy angels shall bring her to Christ] shall be brought unto thee.

The bride will be brought to the throne of God in heaven, with great rejoicing for the marriage of the Lamb (Rev 15,19).

45:15 With gladness and rejoicing shall they be brought: they shall enter into the king's palace

The chosen will be resurrected to spirit and taken to the heavenly palace of God the Father, to be married to Christ the Lamb of God (Rev 15, 19)

The leaders of the nations will be replaced by Jesus Christ the King of kings

45:16 Instead of thy fathers [the leaders (figuratively fathers) of the nations, will be replaced with God's resurrected chosen] shall be thy children, whom thou mayest make princes [Christ will set up God's resurrected faithful to rule the nations] in all the earth.

45:17 I will make thy name [God the Father and Messiah the Christ] to be remembered in all generations: therefore shall the people praise thee for ever and ever.

Psalm 46

Jesus Christ is the LORD and refuge of the faithful who live by every Word of God

Psalm 46:1 God is our refuge and strength, a very present [God is always there to help the faithful; although he may allow trials to teach us important lessons, even during those trials he is there helping us to overcome] help in trouble.

Those who live by the righteous Word of God need never fear, for they shall be raised to eternal life on their day

46:2 Therefore will not we fear, though the earth be removed, and though the mountains be carried into the midst of the sea; **46:3** Though the waters thereof roar and be troubled, though the mountains shake with the swelling thereof. Selah.

There is a river of the Living Waters [the Holy Spirit] of eternal life for those who love and live by every Word of God

46:4 There is a river [of Living Waters of the Holy Spirit], the streams whereof shall make glad the city of God, the holy place of the tabernacles of the most High (John 7:37-39, Rev 22:1, 22:17).

Through his Holy Spirit God dwelt in his physical temple in Jerusalem, and through his Spirit God dwells within his faithful

46:5 God is in the midst of her; she shall not be moved: God shall help her [God the Father will send Messiah the Christ to save his people], and that right early [quickly].

During the tribulation the nations will rage, but Jesus Christ [Hebrew: Yeshua Mashiach] will come to deliver God's faithful and destroy evil from off the earth

46:6 The heathen raged, the kingdoms were moved: he uttered his voice, the earth melted. **46:7** The LORD of hosts is with us; the God of Jacob is our refuge. Selah. **46:8** Come, behold the works of the LORD, what desolations he hath made [destroying the wicked] in the earth.

Our Mighty One will destroy war and the implements of war, to bring peace to the earth

46:9 He maketh wars to cease unto the end of the earth; he breaketh the bow, and cutteth the spear in sunder; he burneth the chariot in the fire.

God the Father and Jesus Christ will be exalted over all things

46:10 Be still, and know that I am God: I will be exalted among the heathen, I will be exalted in the earth.

Why should we fear anything, even death? God the Father and Jesus Christ the LORD of hosts [armies] will deliver all God's faithful who trust in God and live by every Word of God

46:11 The LORD of hosts is with us; the God of Jacob is our refuge. Selah.

Psalm 47

Let us greatly rejoice over God's plan of spiritual eternal salvation; and the coming of Christ to deliver his faithful, destroy all wickedness and rule all nations; teaching all people the way to eternal life in peace with God and man

Psalm 47:1 O clap your hands, all ye people; shout unto God with the voice of triumph. **47:2** For the LORD most high is terrible [powerful and awesome]; he is **a great King over all the earth.**

47:3 He shall subdue the people under us [the resurrected bride will rule the nations with him], and the nations under our feet.

God distributed the physical promised land to physical Israel and he will distribute the nations and kingdoms of the earth to Spiritual Israel; the faithful collective resurrected bride of Christ

47:4 He shall choose our inheritance for us, the excellency of Jacob [Israel; physical and spiritual] whom he loved. Selah.

Messiah will come to resurrect his faithful with shouting and the blast of the seventh trumpet (Rev 10:7, 11:15); and after the Wedding Feast he will return to the earth WITH his bride (Jude 1:14) to destroy wickedness and rule all nations in the righteousness of every Word of God

47:5 God is gone up with a shout, the LORD with the sound of a trumpet.

Let everything that has breath, rejoice at the coming of the righteousness of God to the earth!

47:6 Sing praises to God, sing praises: sing praises unto our King, sing praises. **47:7** For God is the King of all the earth: sing ye praises with understanding. **47:8** God reigneth over the heathen: God sitteth upon the throne of his holiness.

After Christ comes the nations of Israel will continue to live in the lands they have today, but leaders and representatives of all the nations of Israel shall be gathered to their ancient physical promised land to live in the presence of their resurrected king David and in the presence of Messiah the King of kings.

47:9 The princes of the people are gathered together, even the people of the God of Abraham: for the shields of the earth belong unto God: he is greatly exalted.

Psalm 48

When Christ comes, Jerusalem will overflow with the Word and Wisdom of God, which will make her a thing of immense spiritual beauty; she shall be exalted above all nations and shall be called great; because the Ezekiel Temple of God the Father will be there and Messiah the Christ will rule the earth with the beautiful Wisdom, Word and Righteousness of God.

Psalm 48:1 Great is the LORD, and greatly to be praised in the city of our God, in the mountain [the temple mount] of his holiness. **48:2** Beautiful for situation [location], the [all nations shall flow to her to hear the Word of God (Isaiah 2:2)] joy of the whole earth, is mount Zion, on the sides of the north, the city of the great King.

Every dwelling in Jerusalem will be full of the knowledge and Spirit of God, and God will be the defense of the city, for it will be the city of God

48:3 God is known in her palaces for a refuge.

The rulers of the earth will see the coming of Christ and they shall fear to dispute Christ when he comes and destroys the wicked

48:4 For, lo, the kings were assembled, they passed by together. **48:5** They saw it [The earth's rulers will see the coming of Christ with his bride and the destruction of the vast armies of the wicked at Jerusalem. They shall be greatly astonished and afraid.], and so they marvelled; they were troubled, and hasted away [flee to hide]. **48:6** Fear took hold upon them there, and pain, as of a woman in travail.

Jesus Christ will destroy the wicked and establish his own authority under God the Father over all the earth forever. Jerusalem will first be the capital of the physical earth, and later the capital of the entire universe at the coming of God the Father and the New Jerusalem

48:7 Thou breakest the ships of Tarshish with an east wind. **48:8** As we have heard, so have we seen in the city of the LORD of hosts, in the city of our God: God will establish it for ever. Selah.

The faithful consider the mercy and kindness of God when they assemble before him to learn the Word of God, and to praise and glorify the Eternal for his righteous Word

48:9 We have thought of thy lovingkindness, O God, in the midst of thy temple.

The glorious righteousness and great reputation and mighty deeds of God to deliver humanity from bondage to Satan and sin will be known throughout the earth

48:10 According to thy name [deeds, reputation], O God, so is thy praise unto the ends of the earth: thy right hand is full of righteousness.

48:11 Let mount Zion rejoice, let the daughters [descendants of] of Judah be glad, because of thy judgments [God's laws and decisions are just].

48:12 Walk about Zion, and go round about her: tell the towers thereof. **48:13** Mark ye well her bulwarks [which are the Word of God] consider her palaces; that ye may tell it to the generation following.

David pledges loyalty to God forever even to the death, and he will be raised up from the grave to incorruptible spirit with all of God's faithful; to live forever with God

48:14 For this God is our God for ever and ever: he will be our guide even unto death [all our lives].

Psalm 49

> **Matthew 16:26** For what is a man profited, if he shall gain the whole world, and lose his own soul [lose his life forever]? or what shall a man give in exchange for his soul [pnuema, breath, life]?

Psalm 49:1 Hear this, all ye people; give ear, all ye inhabitants of the world: **49:2** Both low and high, rich and poor, together.

Let every person hear and understand that iniquity brings eternal death, but the Word of God is Light and Life eternal; and those who live by every Word of God need not fear anything, not even death itself, for God will raise them up to life eternal

49:3 My mouth shall speak of wisdom [God's Word is wisdom]; and the meditation of my heart [deep prayerful thought on God's Word, will bring understanding of the Word of God] shall be of understanding.

The godly will learn from the parables, object lessons and the teachings of Holy Scripture

49:4 I will incline mine ear to a parable: I will open my dark saying upon the harp.

Even when the wicked are snapping like dogs at our heels and we live in a world surrounded by evil; those who live by every Word of God need not fear, for they will be resurrected to eternal life in peace with God

49:5 Wherefore should I fear in the days of evil, when the iniquity of my heels shall compass me about?

Why set the heart on physical wealth when man cannot be redeemed by physical things, but must sincerely repent and have his past sins paid for and be redeemed by the sacrifice and life of the very Creator, the Lamb of God?

49:6 They that trust in their wealth, and boast themselves in the multitude of their riches; **49:7** None of them can by any means redeem his brother, nor give to God a ransom for him:

A prophecy of the sacrifice of the Lamb of God which redeems the sincerely repentant. Christ needed to die only once, never needing to die again; because his sacrifice is perfect; and he was then resurrected to spirit to live forever.

49:8 (For the redemption of their soul is precious [the life of the Creator, the Lamb of God is the redemptive sacrifice that saved the repentant], and it ceaseth [The Lamb of God died only once, never needing to die again; because his sacrifice was perfect and redeems all repentant humanity.] for ever:) **49:9** That he should still live [be resurrected] for ever, and not see corruption.

All flesh will die and all physical things shall perish; only God and those who live by every Word of God, whom God will raise up and change to spirit, will last forever

49:10 For he seeth that wise men die, likewise the fool and the brutish person perish, and leave their wealth to others.

Men think that through their descendants they will live on, but God offers something much better; a resurrection from the dead to eternal life for every person willing to live by every Word of God!

49:11 Their inward thought is, that their houses shall continue for ever, and their dwelling places to all generations; they call their lands after their own names.

Even great men will die like the brute beasts

49:12 Nevertheless man being in honour abideth not [still dies]: he is like the beasts that perish. **49:13** This their way is their folly: yet their posterity approve their sayings. Selah.

49:14 Like sheep they [all men die just like the beasts] are laid in the grave; death shall feed on them; and the upright [both the wicked and the upright will die] shall have dominion over them in the morning; and their beauty [even the most beautiful and powerful of physical persons will all rot in the grave] shall consume in the grave from their dwelling.

The life (spirit of man) dwells in the physical body; and the physical body which is the dwelling place of the spirit of man, will die and rot away in the grave.

God will apply the redemptive sacrifice of Christ to the sincerely repentant who live by every Word of God, and God will resurrect the faithful from physical death to eternal life as spirit.

49:15 But **God will redeem my soul from the power of the grave: for he shall receive me.** Selah.

49:16 Be not thou afraid [impressed] when one is made rich, when the glory of his house [of his physical things] is increased; **49:17** For when he dieth he shall carry nothing away: his glory shall not descend after him.

49:18 Though while he lived he blessed his soul: and men will praise thee, when thou [those who are prosperous in this world are praised of men] doest well to thyself. **49:19** He shall go to the generation [we shall go to the grave like our fathers] of his fathers; they [the unrepentant wicked shall perish eternally] shall never see light.

Although people may be prosperous and respected in this life, those who do not repent and go forward to live by every Word of God will die and perish forever like the brute beast

49:20 Man that is in honour, and understandeth not, is like the beasts that perish.

Psalm 50

Psalm 50:1 The mighty God, even the LORD, hath spoken, and called [to everyone on the earth all day long] the earth from the rising of the sun unto the going down thereof.

Jesus Christ the Messiah will come to Jerusalem which he will enter on the foal of a donkey from the Mount of Olives to become King of kings bringing peace to all nations as the prophets have said. Then the glory of Messiah will shine forth from the physical Jerusalem until the glory of God the Father also shines forth from the New Jerusalem

50:2 Out of Zion, the perfection of beauty, God hath shined.

Messiah the Christ who is also the very Creator God who was made flesh to die for and redeem repentant humanity from bondage to Satan and sin:

will resurrect the godly dead, delivering all those who have lived by every Word of God to life eternal; and he will destroy the armies of the wicked.

When he comes he will not keep silent, he will powerfully rebuke all sin and he will teach all humanity to live by every Word of God the Father.

50:3 Our God shall come, and shall not keep silence: a fire shall devour before him, and it shall be very tempestuous round about him.

Messiah the Christ will come from the heavens above, to judge the nations with the justice and wisdom of every Word of God the Father

50:4 He shall call to the heavens from above, and to the earth, that he may judge his people.

The chosen overcomers who have entered the New Covenant through sincere repentance and the application of the sacrifice of the Lamb of God will be resurrected to spirit.

50:5 Gather my saints together unto me; those that have made a covenant with me by sacrifice. **50:6** And the heavens [all the holy angels] shall declare his righteousness: for God is judge himself. Selah.

God testifies against physical and spiritual Israel because of their need for sacrifices to cover their continual sins; for all things belong to God and he desires that we obey him so that we would have no need of sacrifice.

In verse 8 the word "reprove" is properly translated "justify" Strong's lexicon H3198; verse 8 meaning "I will testify against thee - and I will NOT justify thee for all your sacrifices because you remain in sin."

50:7 Hear, O my people, and I will speak; O Israel, and **I will testify against thee**: I am God, even thy God. **50:8** I will **not** [God says "I will testify against thee - and I will NOT justify thee for all your sacrifices because you remain in sin."] reprove [properly "justify" Strong's lexicon H3198] thee for thy sacrifices or thy burnt offerings, to have been continually before me.

God does not want our sacrifices for our sins, rather God wants us to STOP sinning

50:9 I will take no bullock out of thy house, nor he goats out of thy folds. **50:10** For every beast of the forest is mine, and the cattle upon a thousand hills. **50:11** I know all the fowls of the mountains: and the wild beasts of the field are mine. **50:12** If I were hungry, I would not tell thee: for the world is mine, and the fulness thereof. **50:13** Will I [does God want to receive our sacrifices?] eat the flesh of bulls, or drink the blood of goats?

Trust in God and sin not: Offering many sacrifices for not living by every Word of God without any real repentance, is meaningless and is NOT acceptable to God

50:14 Offer unto God thanksgiving; and pay thy vows [including keeping our baptismal commitment to live by every Word of God] unto the most High:

50:15 And call upon me [let us trust in God to deliver his faithful] in the day of trouble: [God promises that he will deliver his faithful from death itself in a resurrection, and the dead raised to life will rejoice greatly] I will deliver thee, and thou shalt glorify me.

God will judge the wicked [especially religious leaders and teachers] who live by their own ways and refuse to live by every Word of God.

How is it and by what right do these false teachers claim to teach the Word of God, seeing that they despise to live by every Word of God and instead teach their own false traditions as if they were of God when they are an abomination to God?

50:16 But unto the wicked God saith, What hast thou to do to declare my statutes, or that thou shouldest take my covenant in thy mouth? **50:17** Seeing thou hatest instruction, and casteth my words behind thee.

Wicked false teachers teach the brethren to idolize false leaders and corporate entities above the Word of God, so that they might profit

50:18 When thou sawest a thief, then thou consentedst with him, and hast been partaker with adulterers. **50:19** Thou givest thy mouth to evil [to teach idolatry and many things contrary to the Word of God], and thy tongue frameth [teaches deceits] deceit.

The wicked speak evil of the righteous, even against the godly in their own families

50:20 Thou sittest and speakest against thy brother; thou slanderest thine own mother's son.

Because God was patient and did not immediately rebuke the wicked, they thought themselves godly in their wickedness. That time of patient forbearance is now past and the wicked shall be thoroughly corrected in the fiery furnace of great tribulation

50:21 These things hast thou done, and I kept silence; thou thoughtest that I was altogether such an one as thyself: but I will reprove thee, and set them in order before thine eyes.

God calls today's elders and religious leaders and teachers of the New Covenant to sincerely repent and to teach and live by every Word of God

50:22 Now consider this, ye that forget God, lest I tear you in pieces, and there be none to deliver. **50:23** Whoso offereth praise glorifieth me: and to him that ordereth his conversation [conduct] aright [to live by every Word of God] will I shew the salvation of God.

Psalms 51 - 60

Psalm 51

A Psalm of repentance and prayer for mercy

Psalm 51:1 Have mercy upon me, O God, according to thy lovingkindness: according unto the multitude of thy tender mercies blot out my transgressions. **51:2** Wash me throughly from mine iniquity, and cleanse me from my sin.

Only sincere repentance and a wholehearted commitment to live by every Word of God will bring cleansing from sin by the application of the sacrifice of Christ the Lamb of God (Rom 2:13).

51:3 For I acknowledge my transgressions: and my sin is ever before me [we are to be always alert to seek out and expunge our sins]. **51:4** Against thee, thee only, have I sinned, and done this evil in thy sight: [let us accept that our own ways and stubborn self-will are wrong, and that God's Word is right and the right way to live] that thou mightest be justified when thou speakest, and be clear when thou judgest. **51:5** Behold, I was shapen in iniquity; and in sin did my mother conceive me. **51:6** Behold, thou desirest truth in the inward parts: and in the hidden part thou shalt make me to know wisdom.

John 17:17 Sanctify them through thy truth: **thy word is truth.**

Psalm 51:7 Purge me with hyssop [Hyssop was used to sprinkle the blood of the lamb, this reference meaning: please purge my sins by the blood of the Lamb of God.], and I shall be clean [from all sin]: wash me, [with the water of the Word and Spirit of God (Eph 5:26)] and I shall be whiter than snow. **51:8** Make me to hear joy and gladness [when God tells us that we are forgiven we will delight in God's salvation]; that the bones which thou hast broken may rejoice. **51:9** Hide thy face from my sins, and blot out all mine iniquities.

51:10 Create in me a clean heart [God will purify the sincerely repentant from all sin and all proud self-will, to follow God] O God; and renew a right spirit [give us a proper godly attitude of love for God and loving zeal to live by every Word of God] within me. **51:11** Cast me not away from thy presence; and take not thy holy spirit from me. **51:12** Restore unto me the joy of thy salvation [deliver the repentant by thy tender mercies, for we abhor our sins against the Word of God]; and uphold me with thy free spirit.

When we live by every Word of God, we set an example for all who see us; and we learn by doing the ways of God so that we may teach others to do the same.

51:13 Then will I teach transgressors thy ways; and sinners shall be converted unto thee. **51:14** Deliver me from bloodguiltiness, O God, thou God of my salvation: and my tongue shall sing aloud of thy righteousness.

51:15 O Lord, open thou my lips; and my mouth shall shew forth thy praise. **51:16** For thou desirest not sacrifice; else would I give it: thou delightest not in burnt offering.

51:17 The sacrifices of God are a broken spirit [submissive humility before God, with all stubborn self-will and pride crushed to powder]: a broken and a contrite heart [the pride of sin crushed to powder], O God, thou wilt not despise.

51:18 Do good in thy good pleasure unto Zion [Messiah, come to Jerusalem and build the Kingdom of God]: build thou the walls of Jerusalem. **51:19 Then shalt thou be pleased with the sacrifices of righteousness, with burnt offering and whole burnt offering** [When Christ comes, God will convert Israel and Jerusalem to sincere repentance, and then their repentance (now sincere) and their sacrifices both physical and spiritual will be accepted.]: **then shall they offer bullocks upon thine altar.**

Sin and Trespass Offerings represent sin repented of, and Burnt Offerings represent the righteousness of wholehearted obedience, dedication and Christ-like zeal to live by every WORD of God.

Psalm 52

Why do the wicked boast of their deeds, their positions and their wealth which will quickly perish? Only the good righteous Word of God and those who live thereby, will last forever!

Psalm 52:1 Why boastest thou thyself in mischief, O mighty man? the goodness of God endureth continually.

The wicked deceive with their speech to gain followings and advantage over others

52:2 The tongue deviseth mischiefs; like a sharp razor, working deceitfully. **52:3** Thou [deceivers] lovest evil more than good; and lying rather than to speak righteousness. Selah.

The deceitful words of the wicked devour the people and their means, teaching the brethren to make idols of men and thereby stealing their lives as well as their goods

52:4 Thou lovest all devouring words, O thou deceitful tongue.

Those who deceive the brethren into idolizing men and corporate entities above any zeal to live by every Word of God will surely feel the wrath of God

52:5 God shall likewise destroy thee for ever, he shall take thee away, and pluck thee out of thy dwelling place, and root thee out of the land of the living. Selah.

Those who live by the righteous Word of God will see the destruction of the unrepentant wicked who do as they decide for themselves and refuse to live by every Word of God

52:6 The righteous also shall see, and fear, and shall laugh at him [scorn wickedness]:

Those who live by the righteousness of every Word of God shall see the end of the unrepentant and say:

52:7 Lo, this is the man that made not God his strength; but trusted in the abundance of his riches, and strengthened himself in his wickedness.

Those who live by the righteousness of every Word of God shall flourish with the oil of the Holy Spirit like a strong growing olive tree, full of oil.

52:8 But I am like a green olive tree in the house of God: I trust in the mercy of God for ever and ever.

The godly know that their righteousness is not their own, but is the gift of God; and they wait on and live by every Word of the Righteousness of God

52:9 I will praise thee for ever, because thou hast done it: and I will wait on thy name; for it is good before thy saints.

Psalm 53

A prophecy of conditions just before the tribulation

> **Luke 17:26** And as it was in the days of Noe, so shall it be also in the days of the Son of man.

In these latter days all mankind is corrupted and wickedness abounds

Psalm 53:1 The fool hath said in his heart, There is no God. Corrupt are they, and have done abominable iniquity: there is none that doeth good.

As in the days of Noah, today God looks for righteousness on the earth and finds almost none, for even the spiritual Ekklesia is corrupted

53:2 God looked down from heaven upon the children of men, to see if there were any that did understand, that did seek God.

There is none righteous on the earth today, yet a very small fraction of today's called out Ekklesia, a very few; are repentant and seeking that the worthiness and righteousness of Christ be applied to them

53:3 Every one of them is gone back: they are altogether become filthy; there is none that doeth good, no, not one. **53:4** Have the workers of iniquity [most of today's elders and church leaders Isaiah 56:10-12] no knowledge? who eat up my people as they eat bread: they have not called upon God.

Our fears and the tribulation will fall upon us in a time of peace (1 Thess 5:3)

53:5 There were they in great fear, where no fear was: for God hath scattered the bones of him that encampeth against thee [those who refuse to be subject to God will be corrected in great tribulation]: thou [God will correct today's wicked earth in great tribulation] hast put them [those who reject living by every Word of God] to shame, because God hath despised them.

Longing for deliverance

53:6 Oh that the salvation of Israel were come out of Zion! When God bringeth back the captivity of his people, Jacob shall rejoice, and Israel shall be glad.

Psalm 54

A prayer for the deliverance of the sincerely repentant

Psalm 54:1 Save me, O God, by thy name, and judge me by thy strength. **54:2** Hear my prayer, O God; give ear to the words of my mouth. **54:3** For strangers are risen up against me, and oppressors seek after my soul: they have not set God before them. Selah.

All flesh must die, both the godly and the wicked; the difference being that those who put their trust in God to live by every Word of God will be delivered from death into eternal life as incorruptible spirit; while the unrepentant wicked, after all hope for them is gone; will be destroyed forever. **54:4** Behold, God is mine helper: the Lord is with them that uphold my soul [life].

Satan and sin are the real enemies, and God will destroy Satan, sin and death itself

54:5 He shall reward evil [destroy] unto mine enemies [the real enemies are Satan and sin]: cut them off in thy truth.

After they are delivered from bondage to Satan and sin, all humanity will rejoice in God

54:6 I will freely sacrifice unto thee: I will praise thy name, O LORD; for it is good. **54:7** For he hath delivered me out of all trouble: and mine eye hath seen his desire upon mine enemies.

Psalm 55

Trust in God and run to him for deliverance, remembering that God allows trials for our good to teach us to be holy as he is holy.

> **Leviticus 19:2** Speak unto all the congregation of the children of Israel, and say unto them, Ye shall be holy: for I the Lord your God am holy.

David cries out to God over his sufferings and we should also run to our Mighty God in all our trials, instead of trying to bear them on our own or trying to relieve them by compromising with the Word of God.

Psalm 55:1 Give ear to my prayer, O God; and hide not thyself from my supplication. **55:2** Attend unto me, and hear me: I mourn [seek God when we are overwhelmed by afflictions] in my complaint, and make a noise [weeping in sorrow]; **55:3** Because of the voice [because of the false accusations and slanders] of the enemy, because of the oppression of the wicked: for they cast iniquity upon me, and in wrath they hate me.

Those who live by every Word of God we will be afflicted; and God will allow many trials to teach us lessons in his righteousness which will last in us for eternity

55:4 My heart is sore pained within me: and the terrors of death are fallen upon me. **55:5** Fearfulness and trembling are come upon me, and horror hath overwhelmed me.

We may seek to fly away from our bitter sorrows, but if we double down in seeking our LORD and living by every Word of God; his reward of eternal life in peace and joy is sure.

55:6 And I said, Oh that I had wings like a dove! for then would I fly away, and be at rest. **55:7** Lo, then would I wander far off, and remain in the wilderness. Selah. **55:8** I would hasten my escape from the windy storm and tempest [of many afflictions and trials].

God will deliver his faithful and will bring down those who persecute his faithful who live by the Righteous Word of God.

55:9 Destroy, O Lord, and divide their tongues: for I have seen violence and strife in the city.

The deceits and persecutions against those who seek God in sincerity and truth never seem to cease, but in due time God will correct the wicked

55:10 Day and night they go about it upon the walls thereof: mischief also and sorrow are in the midst of it. **55:11** Wickedness is in the midst thereof: deceit and guile depart not from her streets.

The greatest affliction is to be betrayed and hated by those who are closest to us, who we love so much. There is no greater pain than to be betrayed and rejected by a cherished spouse, a child or a beloved brother or close friend.

55:12 For it was not an enemy that reproached me; then I could have borne it: neither was it he that hated me that did magnify himself against me; then I would have hid myself from him: **55:13** But it was thou, a man mine equal, my guide, and mine acquaintance. **55:14** We took sweet counsel together, and walked unto the house of God in company.

God will destroy the unrepentant wicked one, Satan the Adversary; for separating many brethren from God the Father and their Beloved espoused Husband Jesus Christ, by deceiving them into following false traditions, corporate idols and idols of men.

55:15 Let death seize upon them, and let them go down quick into hell: for wickedness is in their dwellings, and among them.

Despite all the trials and afflictions that we may face, those who truly love God will remain absolutely faithful to him and will remain dedicated to live by every Word of God; they will continually put their trust in the Husband of their baptismal betrothal and will hear his voice and live by every Word of God the Father.

55:16 As for me, I will call upon God; and the LORD shall save me. **55:17** Evening, and morning, and at noon, will I pray, and cry aloud: and he shall hear my voice.

Our LORD will deliver all his faithful from the Adversary, Satan, and from all bondage to sin and death; and he will pour out his love on his faithful

55:18 He hath delivered my soul in peace from the battle that was against me: for there were many with me. **55:19** God shall hear, and afflict them, even he that abideth of old. Selah. Because they have no changes [many have no fear of God because things remain the same and no correction comes for a long time], therefore they fear not God.

Satan the Adversary is full of deceit, seeking to destroy the godly

55:20 He hath put forth his hands against such as be at peace with him: he hath broken his covenant. **55:21** The words of his mouth were smoother than butter [slick, smooth, to deceive], but war was in his heart: his words were softer than oil, yet were they drawn swords.

The faithful will put their trust in God and God's Word forever, and he will deliver them and will destroy the true enemy; Satan and bondage to sin and death

55:22 Cast thy burden upon the LORD, and he shall sustain thee: he shall never suffer the righteous to be moved. **55:23** But thou, O God, shalt bring them down into the pit of destruction: bloody and deceitful men shall not live out half their days; but I will trust in thee.

Psalm 56

A prayer for mercy and God's deliverance

Our Adversary Satan oppresses the godly with many trials and temptations daily, and we need to cleave to our God trusting in him for deliverance

Psalm 56:1 Be merciful unto me, O God: for man [the wicked] would swallow me up; he fighting daily oppresseth me.

Our real enemy is Satan who is behind the acts of wicked men

56:2 Mine enemies would daily swallow me up: for they be many that fight against me, O thou most High. **56:3** What time [whenever] I am afraid, I will trust in thee.

Trust in God, for if we live by every Word of God which is Wisdom and Righteousness we need not fear what men or Satan can do; because our Deliverer will raise us up from death itself, granting the gift of eternal life to all those who love God and keep his Word

56:4 In God I will praise his word, in God I have put my trust; I will not fear what flesh can do unto me.

The wicked twist the words of God and men, to deceive men to turn away from living by every Word of God

56:5 Every day they wrest my words: all their thoughts are against me for evil.

Many false teachers conceal themselves behind a facade of godliness, while like wolves in sheep's clothing they use clever words to deceive us.

> **2 Timothy 3:5** Having a form of godliness, but denying the power [the authority of God's Word by declaring that they are the deciders] thereof: from such turn away.

Psalm 56:6 They gather themselves together, they hide [conceal or disguise] themselves, they mark my steps, when they wait for my soul.

Can the wicked escape the judgment of God by deceits?

56:7 Shall they escape by iniquity? in thine anger cast down the [wicked] people, O God.

God knows our paths in this life and he knows our trials and sorrows

56:8 Thou tellest my wanderings: put thou my tears into thy bottle: are they not in thy book?

When we put our trust in God to live by his Word, God will deliver us

56:9 When I cry unto thee, then shall mine enemies turn back: this I know; for God is for me.

God is to be praised because his Word is Wisdom and Righteousness

56:10 In God will I praise his word: in the LORD will I praise his word. **56:11** In God have I put my trust: I will not be afraid what man can do unto me.

The faithful KEEP their baptismal commitment to live by every Word of God and they will follow no man [no matter who they claim to be] contrary to God's Word

56:12 Thy vows are upon me, O God: I will render praises unto thee.

Only Almighty God can deliver men from bondage to Satan, sin and eternal death.

56:13 For thou hast delivered my soul from death: wilt not thou deliver my feet from falling, that I may walk before God in the light of the living?

Psalm 57

A prayer of repentance for God's merciful deliverance, by those who put their trust in God

Psalm 57:1 Be merciful unto me, O God, be merciful unto me: for my soul trusteth in thee: yea, in the shadow of thy wings will I make my refuge, until these calamities be overpast. **57:2** I will cry unto God most high; unto God that performeth all things for me.

Satan would swallow up the godly in death and the grave, but if we are faithful to follow and to live by every Word of God; God will deliver us from Satan and death

57:3 He shall send from heaven, and save me from the reproach of him that would swallow me up. Selah. God shall send forth his mercy and his truth [God's Word is truth, John 17:17].

The wicked are like roaring lions surrounding those who are faithful to God (1 Peter 5:8)

57:4 My soul is among lions: and I lie even among them that are set on fire, even the sons of men, whose teeth are spears and arrows, and their tongue a sharp sword.

Even in great distress and death; let us exalt the Eternal and his Word above all else

57:5 Be thou exalted, O God, above the heavens; let thy glory be above all the earth.

The wicked attempt to deceive those who trust in God and live by every Word of God, but the wicked will fall into their own snares because they believe their own lies and deceits, not living by every Word of God

57:6 They have prepared a net for my steps; my soul is bowed down: they have digged a pit [a grave] before me, into the midst whereof they are fallen themselves. Selah.

The hearts and minds of the faithful are always dedicatedly fixed on God and on living by every Word of God

57:7 My heart is fixed, O God, my heart is fixed [on God and living by God's every Word]: I will sing and give praise.

In the resurrection the faithful will awaken in a resurrection to a glorious eternal spirit body

57:8 Awake up, my glory; awake, psaltery and harp: I myself will awake early.

The faithful to God praise him and rejoice in him always, but when they are resurrected to spirit their joy will be full and they will shout by his Mighty Power we live!" The faithful will praise and rejoice in God and his Word FOREVER!

57:9 I will praise thee, O Lord, among the people: I will sing unto thee among the nations. **57:10** For thy mercy is great unto the heavens, and thy truth unto the clouds. **57:11** Be thou exalted, O God, above the heavens: let thy glory be above all the earth.

Psalm 58

Is there righteousness in men, or do they need the righteousness of God?

Psalm 58:1 Do ye [men] indeed speak righteousness, O congregation? do ye judge uprightly, O ye sons of men? **58:2** Yea, in heart ye work wickedness; ye weigh [fill the earth with injustice and violence] the violence of your hands in the earth.

People are born without any knowledge of anything and people must be taught what is right and what is wrong by every Word of God.

Romans 8:7 Because the carnal mind is enmity against God: for it is not subject to the law of God, neither indeed can be.

Psalm 58:3 The wicked are estranged from the womb: they go astray as soon as they be born, speaking lies.

The unrepentant wicked are like those serpents which cannot be charmed [pacified and controlled], the wicked rejoice in their sins and will not be instructed in righteousness.

58:4 Their poison is like the poison of a serpent: they are like the deaf adder that stoppeth her ear; **58:5** Which will not hearken to the voice of charmers, charming never so wisely.

May God deliver his faithful from the poison tongues and pens of deceivers and from the mouth of the roaring lion [Satan]

58:6 Break their teeth, O God, in their mouth: break out the great teeth of the young lions, O LORD.

May God deliver his faithful from the devices of the wicked and bring the evil to nothing.

58:7 Let them melt away as waters which run continually: when he bendeth his bow to shoot his arrows, let them be as cut in pieces. **58:8** As a snail which melteth [in the hot sun], let every one of them [the unrepentant wicked] pass away: like the untimely birth [stillborn miscarriage] of a woman, that they may not see the sun.

Verse 9 is a reference to the burning of thorns for fire to cook with, meaning: before your pots can be warmed by the fire. This is a reference to the sudden and complete overthrow of the wicked at the coming of Christ

58:9 Before your pots can feel the [heat of the burning thorns] thorns, he shall take them away as with a whirlwind, both living, and in his wrath. **58:10** The righteous shall rejoice when he seeth the [the coming of Christ as King of kings to destroy wickedness from off the earth] vengeance: he shall wash his feet in the blood of the wicked.

When Christ comes to resurrect the chosen and destroy the unrepentant wicked, the whole earth will know the justice of God and everyone will see that there is a reward of eternal life for faithfulness, and a reward of destruction for wickedness

58:11 So that a man shall say, Verily there is a reward for the righteous: verily he is a God that judgeth in the earth.

Psalm 59

A prayer seeking deliverance

Our real enemies are spiritual, we need deliverance from Satan, bondage to sin and from death; which deliverance can only come through sincere repentance, a commitment to "go and sin no more" and the application of the redeeming sacrifice of the Lamb of God

Psalm 59:1 Deliver me from mine enemies [spiritually Satan and sin], O my God: defend me from them that rise up against me. **59:2** Deliver me from the workers of iniquity, and save me from bloody men.

The closer to God people are, the more the wicked will rise up against them

59:3 For, lo, they lie in wait for my soul: the mighty are gathered against me; not for my transgression, nor for my sin, O LORD. **59:4** They run and prepare themselves without my fault: awake to help me, and behold.

God will not be merciful but will sternly rebuke and correct unrepentant sinners

59:5 Thou therefore, O LORD God of hosts, the God of Israel, awake to visit all the heathen: be not merciful to any wicked transgressors. Selah.

With their deceits, the wicked prey on men

59:6 They return at evening: they make a noise [speak lies and deceit] like a dog, and go round about the city [seeking prey]. **59:7** Behold, they belch [pour] out [wickedness, lies and deceit] with their mouth: swords [wickedness, destruction and death] are in their lips: for who, say they, doth hear?

The wicked, including many leaders of today's spiritual Ekklesia, are like greedy dogs each doing his own thing to exalt themselves or their organizations and false traditions. They water down the Sabbath and the sound doctrine of Holy Scripture to try to attract more personal followers.

Godly understanding is withheld from them because of their lack of zeal for God's Sabbath and for living by every Word of God the Father.

Isaiah 56:11 Yea, they are greedy dogs which can never have enough, and they are shepherds that cannot understand: they all look to their own way, every one for his gain, from his quarter.

They fill themselves with the strong drink of their own imaginations, and become intoxicated with pride and their own ways.

All of the wicked together including Satan are nothing before God

Psalm 59:8 But thou, O LORD, shalt laugh at them; thou shalt have all the heathen [unrepentant wicked] in derision.

The Adversary is stronger than physical people, but God is vastly stronger than the Adversary; therefore the faithful put all their trust in God and wait on him

59:9 Because of his strength will I wait upon thee: for God is my defence.

God will give his faithful deliverance over our enemies; Satan, bondage to sin and death

59:10 The God of my mercy shall prevent me [from being destroyed]: God shall let me see my desire upon mine enemies.

God will correct the proud and self-willed wicked, so that all the people will see the justice and might of God

59:11 Slay them not, lest my people forget: scatter them by thy power; and bring them down, O Lord our shield. **59:12** For the sin of their mouth and the words of their lips let them even be taken in their pride: and for cursing and lying which they speak. **59:13** Consume them in wrath, consume them, that they may not be: and let them know that God ruleth in Jacob unto the ends of the earth. Selah.

Do not fret that the wicked continue in their wickedness and are grown prosperous, for their end is destruction

59:14 And at evening let them [the wicked] return; and let them make a noise [howl for hunger] like a dog, and go round about the city. **59:15** Let them wander up and down [searching for food] for meat, and grudge [fight one another] if they be not satisfied.

God will bring down the wicked, but God will be the strong defense and refuge of those who live by every Word of God

59:16 But I will sing of thy power; yea, I will sing aloud of thy mercy in the morning: for thou hast been my defence and refuge in the day of my trouble. **59:17** Unto thee, O my strength, will I sing: for God is my defence, and the God of my mercy.

Psalm 60

A prophecy of the captivities of Israel and Judah and the final tribulation on the whole earth; and a prayer for deliverance by the repentant

Psalm 60:1 O God, thou hast cast us off, thou hast scattered us, thou hast been displeased; O turn thyself to us again. **60:2** Thou hast made the earth to tremble; thou hast broken it: heal the breaches thereof; for it shaketh. **60:3** Thou hast shewed thy people hard things [many sorrows]: thou hast made us to drink the wine of astonishment.

The wicked will be corrected and those who live by every Word of God shall be a shining example of godliness for the whole earth

60:4 Thou hast given a banner [YHWH - Nissi; God our Banner] to them that fear thee, that it may be displayed because of the truth [God's Word is truth]. Selah.

60:5 That thy beloved [the faithful godly spiritual bride] may be delivered; save with thy right hand, and hear me.

When Christ comes he will again divide the land of Israel to her tribes

60:6 God hath spoken in his holiness; I will rejoice, I will divide Shechem [the land will be distributed by Messiah], and mete out the valley of Succoth [in the Jordan River Valley].

Jesus Christ will rule over all the earth and the resurrected David will be king over Judah and Israel including the Golan and beyond.

60:7 Gilead is mine, and Manasseh is mine; Ephraim also is the strength of mine head; Judah is my lawgiver;

David will also rule over Gaza, Jordan and Turkey

60:8 Moab [modern Jordan] is my washpot [under David's control]; over Edom [Turkey] will I [David will dominate Turkey] cast out my shoe: Philistia [Gaza], triumph thou because of me [Gaza will prosper because she will submit to Christ and to David].

God will cast Israel and Judah into great tribulation under Turkey and the New Europe (Psalm 83) to correct them for their sins; and God will also deliver all Israel and Judah and they shall dominate those who had afflicted them.

60:9 Who will bring me into the strong city? who will lead me into Edom? **60:10** Wilt not thou, O God, which hadst cast us off? and thou, O God, which didst not go out with our armies? **60:11** Give us help from trouble: for vain is the help of man.

60:12 Through God we shall do valiantly: for he it is that shall tread down our enemies.

Psalms 61 - 70

Psalm 61

The eternal unity between God and his faithful

God hears and delivers all those who love him enough to live by every Word of God. God's faithful put their trust in him.

Psalm 61:1 Hear my cry, O God; attend unto my prayer. **61:2** From the end of the earth will I cry unto thee, when my heart is overwhelmed: lead me to the rock [Messiah the Christ the Rock of Salvation] that is higher than I.

God will deliver all those who live by every Word of God from the enemies of Satan and bondage to sin and death, raising them up to eternal life

61:3 For thou hast been a shelter for me, and a strong tower from the enemy.

God's faithful will abide in the presence of God forever, through God's gift of eternal life

61:4 I will abide in thy tabernacle for ever [be faithful to God for eternity]: I will trust in the covert of thy wings. Selah.

God has heard our baptismal commitment to go and sin no more which the faithful have kept, and God will reward our faithfulness with a resurrection to spirit and eternal unity with God the Father and the Husband of our baptismal espousal.

61:5 For thou, O God, hast heard my vows [baptismal commitment]: thou hast given me the heritage of those that fear thy name.

The resurrection of David in the resurrection to eternal life of all those who live by every Word of God

61:6 Thou wilt prolong the king's life: and his years as many generations [eternal life]. **61:7** He [David and the faithful] shall abide before God for ever [for eternity]: O prepare mercy and truth [God's mercy for the repentant who live by the truth of God's Word will be eternal Salvation], which may preserve him.

God's faithful will keep their marriage covenant to follow the Husband of their baptismal espousal in all things, including living by every Word of God the Father (Mat 4:4, Rev 14:4).

61:8 So will I sing praise unto thy name for ever, that I may daily perform my vows.

Psalm 62

The absolute trust of the faithful in God the Father and Messiah the Christ, the Rock of Salvation

Psalm 62:1 Truly my soul waiteth upon God: from him cometh my salvation.

The faithful put their trust ONLY in God and in every Word of God

62:2 He only is my rock and my salvation; he is my defence; I shall not be greatly moved.

The source of wickedness and the inspiration of the wicked is Satan, he is the true enemy. Satan and all unrepentant sinners will perish forever.

62:3 How long will ye [the wicked] imagine mischief against a man? ye shall be slain all of you: as a bowing [collapsing] wall shall ye be, and as a tottering [falling] fence.

62:4 They [Satan and the wicked] only consult to cast him [the faithful to God] down from his excellency: they delight in lies: they bless with their mouth, but they curse inwardly [secretly]. Selah.

Those who live by every Word of God can expect God's deliverance; therefore they patiently live by his Word waiting on God's salvation.

62:5 My soul, wait thou only upon God; for my expectation is from him. **62:6** He only [God the Father and Jesus Christ the Husband of our baptismal espousal; and no one else, no matter what titles they may claim] is my rock and my salvation: he is my defence; I shall not be moved

The true godly faithful will never be moved from their dedicated commitment to live by every Word of God.

62:7 In God is my salvation and my glory: the rock of my strength, and my refuge, is in God.

Trust ONLY in God and set your hearts to live by every Word of God

62:8 Trust in him at all times; ye people, pour out your heart before him: God is a refuge for us. Selah.

Put not your trust in men because the wisdom of men great or lowly, is as nothing beside the Wisdom of every Word of God

62:9 Surely men of low degree are vanity, and men of high degree are a lie: to be laid in the balance, [men's words balanced against the Word of God are nothing in comparison] they are altogether lighter than vanity.

Do not trust in physical wealth and never compromise with the Word of God to attain physical wealth, and thereby lose eternity

62:10 Trust not in oppression, and become not vain in robbery: if riches increase, set not your heart upon them.

All people have sinned and Almighty God will judge every person by every Word of God; therefore all will perish unless they sincerely repent of all past sins and commit to sin no more, throwing ourselves at his feet and trusting in his mercy

62:11 God hath spoken once; twice have I heard this; that power belongeth unto God. **62:12** Also unto thee, O Lord, belongeth mercy: for thou renderest to every man according to his work.

Psalm 63

A declaration of loyalty to God

The godly faithful thirst and hunger like a starving man for every Word of God, while the wicked do whatever they please.

> **Matthew 5:6** Blessed are they which do hunger and thirst after righteousness [of God and God's Word]: for they shall be filled.

Psalm 63:1 O God, thou art my God; early will I seek thee: my soul thirsteth for thee, my flesh longeth for thee in a dry and thirsty land, where no water is; **63:2** To see thy power and thy glory, so as I have seen thee in the sanctuary. **63:3** Because thy lovingkindness is better than life, my lips shall praise thee. **63:4** Thus will I bless thee while I live: I will lift up my hands in thy name. **63:5** My soul shall be satisfied as with marrow and fatness; and my mouth shall praise thee with joyful lips:

In the night the wicked meditate on how to gain advantage over others, while the faithful considers how to apply the Word of God to every situation

63:6 When I remember thee upon my bed, and meditate on thee in the night watches.

The faithful are safe under the wings of the Mighty One of Moses; and are secure, putting all their trust in the Mighty Hand of God

63:7 Because thou hast been my help, therefore in the shadow of thy wings will I rejoice. **63:8** My soul followeth hard after thee: thy right hand upholdeth me.

God will deliver his faithful; and the unrepentant wicked will surely be destroyed

63:9 But those that seek my soul [the wicked who seek to destroy the life of the faithful to God], to destroy it, shall go into the lower parts of the earth [eternal death] . **63:10** They shall fall by the sword: they shall be a portion for foxes [scavengers].

The faithful first fruits that live by every Word of God will be resurrected to live forever as the kings and priests of the Most High

63:11 But the king shall rejoice in God; every one that sweareth [keeps his baptismal commitment] by him shall glory: but the mouth of them that speak lies shall be stopped.

Psalm 64

God will save his faithful from the ultimate enemy, Satan and bondage to sin and death

Psalm 64:1 Hear my voice, O God, in my prayer: preserve my life from fear of the enemy. **64:2** Hide [deliver] me from the secret counsel [schemes] of the wicked; from the insurrection of the workers of iniquity: **64:3** Who [have sharp vicious deceitful tongues] whet their tongue like a sword, and bend their bows to shoot their arrows, even bitter words:

The wicked will secretly start lying rumors, and falsely slander, libel and attack those who are faithful to God

64:4 That they may shoot in secret at the perfect: suddenly do they shoot at him, and fear not.

The wicked secretly conspire together to attack the faithful to God, or to deceive them. The wicked love darkness but the godly love light and God will bring all things into the light in his good time

64:5 They encourage themselves in an evil matter: they commune of laying snares privily; they say, Who shall see them?

The wicked lay awake at night imagining how to deceive the faithful for their own advantage and how to attack those who cannot be deceived

64:6 They search out iniquities [to do them]; they accomplish a diligent search: both the inward thought of every one of them, and the heart, is deep [deep in thought to do evil].

Almighty God will correct the wicked and their own words shall condemn them. When the people see the correction of God they shall fear God and they will be delivered from the deceits of the wicked

64:7 But God shall shoot at them with an arrow; suddenly shall they be wounded. **64:8** So they shall make their own tongue to fall upon themselves: all that see them shall flee away. **64:9** And all men shall fear, and shall declare the work of God; for they shall wisely consider of his doing.

When God corrects the wicked and delivers those who live by the righteous Word of God, the faithful will greatly rejoice that righteousness has triumphed over evil

64:10 The righteous shall be glad in the LORD, and shall trust in him; and all the upright in heart shall glory [in God].

Psalm 65

The faithful shall keep their baptismal commitment [vow] and will praise God the Almighty their Deliverer

Psalm 65:1 Praise waiteth for thee, O God, in Sion: and unto thee shall the vow be performed.

When Christ comes he will rule all the earth, and in the main harvest all flesh shall come to God

65:2 O thou that hearest prayer, **unto thee shall all flesh come**.

God calls the people out from their bondage to sin and when they sincerely repent he washes away all iniquity by the application of the sacrifice of Christ and the washing of water [the Holy Spirit] of the Word.

> **Ephesians 5:25** Husbands, love your wives, even as Christ also loved the church, and gave himself for it;

Christ lived and died for the good of his collective bride

> **5:26** That he might sanctify and cleanse it with the washing of water by the word, **5:27** That he might present it to himself a glorious church, not having spot, or wrinkle, or any such thing; but that it should be holy and without blemish.

The true spiritual Ekklesia consists of those who are called out by God the Father, who have sincerely repented and resolved not to sin anymore and who have been atoned for by the sacrifice of Christ, and who have been given God's Spirit.

The true spiritual Ekklesia is not a corporate organization. It is not a corporation. It is not one group or another group. It is the individuals, and collectively all the individuals who are filled with the Spirit of God and passionately live by every Word of God.

Christ lived a life of teaching and service and living by every Word of God, setting an example for the people; and we need to live by every Word of God the Father like Jesus did. It was his sinless passionate obedience to every Word of God as an example for us that we should do likewise, that made Jesus Christ the Lamb of God an effectual sacrifice for the sins of the world!

WE should be pure from all defilement [blemishes] of sin and all evil.

To be a chaste, pure virgin means being washed clean through the sacrifice of Christ and living by every Word of God by the power of the Holy Spirit, so that we are cleansed from the pollution of following after other lovers. Christ becomes one with the faithful and we become one with him; in total unity of Spirit through internalizing and living by every Word of God as Jesus did!

Psalm 65:3 Iniquities prevail against me: as for our transgressions, thou shalt purge them away

Once we sincerely repent the sacrifice of the Lamb of God will be applied to us and we will be completely cleansed.

Those who are faithful to live by every Word of God and are chosen as part of the bride will be blessed, for they shall be raised up to eternal life

65:4 Blessed is the man whom thou choosest, and causest to approach unto thee, that he may dwell in thy [temple] courts: we shall be satisfied with the [the Word of God] goodness of thy house, even of thy holy temple.

Ultimately virtually all people will put their trust in God

65:5 By terrible [powerful, mighty, awesome] things in righteousness wilt thou answer us, O God of our salvation; who art the confidence of all the ends of the earth, and of them that are afar off upon the sea:

Ultimately all the governments of the earth will be given by God to his chosen ones

65:6 Which by his strength setteth fast the mountains [a type of governments]; being girded with power:

The seas are types of many people

65:7 Which stilleth the **noise of the seas, the noise of their waves, and the tumult of the people**.

When Christ comes and later when God the Father comes, the whole earth and all people both near and people very far off, shall see the signs of God's majesty and they will rejoice and glorify him

65:8 They also that dwell in the uttermost parts are afraid at thy tokens [the power and glory of God]: thou makest the outgoings of the morning and evening to rejoice.

65:9 Thou visitest the earth, and waterest it: thou greatly enrichest it with the river [water representing the Holy Spirit] of God, which is full of water: thou preparest them corn [grain, representing the unleavened Bread of Life, the Word of God], when thou hast so provided for it.

The earth shall be greatly blessed both physically and spiritually

65:10 Thou waterest the ridges thereof abundantly: thou settlest the furrows thereof: thou makest it soft with showers: thou blessest the springing thereof.

65:11 Thou crownest the year [the main harvest at the end of the year, the Feast of the Ingathering of Nations, called Tabernacles] with thy goodness; and thy paths drop fatness. **65:12** They drop upon the pastures of the wilderness: and the little hills rejoice on every side. **65:13** The pastures are clothed with flocks; the valleys also are covered over with corn [grain]; they shout for joy, they also sing [the nations will rejoice at the Feast of Tabernacles for the great physical and spiritual blessings from God].

Psalm 66

A Psalm for the Feasts of the LORD

Rejoice and proclaim the goodness of the LORD throughout all the earth

Psalm 66:1 Make a joyful noise unto God, all ye lands: **66:2** Sing forth the honour of his name: make his praise glorious. **66:3** Say unto God, How terrible art thou in thy works! through the greatness of thy power shall thine enemies submit themselves unto thee.

In the millennium, all people will worship and live by every Word of God; and later once the plan is completed and God the Father comes to the earth with the New Jerusalem, all humanity will rejoice in God forever

66:4 All the earth shall worship thee, and shall sing unto thee; they shall sing to thy name. Selah.

The mighty deeds of God

66:5 Come and see the works of God: he is terrible [awesome] in his doing [in his mighty deed for men] toward the children of men.

God divided the Red Sea and the river Jordan

66:6 He turned the [Red] sea into dry land: they went through the flood on foot: there did we rejoice in him.

God justly judges the nations and all the deeds of men, none can rebel against his Word and live

66:7 He ruleth by his power for ever; his eyes behold the nations: let not the rebellious exalt themselves. Selah.

Let the faithful praise God for he delivers us from death

66:8 O bless our God, ye people, and make the voice of his praise to be heard: **66:9** Which holdeth [God gives eternal life to his faithful] our soul in life, and suffereth not our feet to be moved.

66:10 For thou, O God, hast proved [tested, purified and refined] us: thou hast tried us, as silver is tried [refined and purified].

Physical Israel endured much in the wilderness before entering the physical promised land and spiritual Israel must endure many afflictions before they may enter the spiritual Promised Land of eternal life.

God allows the faithful to be tested by many afflictions so that they might learn the righteousness of living by every Word of God and prove their loyalty to God

66:11 Thou broughtest us into the net; thou laidst affliction upon our loins. **66:12** Thou hast caused men to ride over our heads; we went through fire and through water [great affliction]: but thou broughtest us out into a wealthy place [the Promised Land of eternal life].

The faithful will keep their baptismal vow [commitment] of espousal to Jesus Christ to be his bride and to live by every Word of God.

Sin offerings cover sin and burnt offerings are symbolic of patient willing wholehearted service to live by every Word of God

66:13 I will go into thy house with burnt offerings [symbolic of patient willing wholehearted service to God]: I will pay thee my vows, **66:14** Which my lips have uttered, and my mouth hath spoken, when I was in trouble.

The faithful will give to God the offerings of faithful dedicated wholehearted service to live by every Word of God, and their prayers will rise up like sweet incense to God

66:15 I will offer unto thee burnt sacrifices of fatlings, with the incense of rams; I will offer bullocks with goats. Selah.

The faithful will extol the Eternal and praise him always for his marvelous Word and his mighty deeds

66:16 Come and hear, all ye that fear God, and I will declare what he hath done for my soul. **66:17** I cried unto him with my mouth, and he was extolled with my tongue.

God hears and answers the prayers of those who live by every Word of God, God refuses to even hear the prayers of those who compromise with his Word. If we even find sin desirable in our hearts God will not hear us.

66:18 If I regard iniquity in my heart, the Lord will not hear me: **66:19** But verily God hath heard me; he hath attended to the voice of my prayer. **66:20** Blessed be God, which hath not turned away my prayer, nor his mercy from me [because we sincerely seek to live by every Word of God].

Psalm 67

God's mercies and blessings on his faithful will be made known to all humanity when the dead are resurrected.

Psalm 67:1 God be merciful unto us, and bless us; and cause his face to shine upon us; Selah.

The ways of God will be revealed to all peoples and they will seek to live by every Word of God which shall be their saving health

67:2 That thy way may be known upon earth, thy saving health among all nations.

When the King of kings comes and rules all nations all humanity will praise him for his justice in ruling all nations by the righteous Word of God.

67:3 Let the people praise thee, O God; let all the people praise thee. **67:4** O let the nations be glad and sing for joy: for thou shalt judge the people righteously, and govern the nations upon earth. Selah.

67:5 Let the people praise thee, O God; let all the people praise thee. **67:6** Then shall the earth yield her increase; and God, even our own God, shall bless us. **67:7** God shall bless us; and all the ends of the earth shall fear him.

Psalm 68

A song of God's deliverance for his faithful who live by his Word

When Messiah the Christ comes the enemies of the righteous Word of God who will not repent will be destroyed.

Psalm 68:1 Let God arise, let his enemies be scattered: let them also that hate him flee before him. **68:2** As smoke [the wicked shall be cast away as smoke is dissipated by the wind] is driven away, so drive them away: as wax melteth before the fire, so let the wicked perish at the presence of God.

When Christ comes the unrepentant wicked who compromise with any part of the Word of God weill perish, but those who love and live by every Word of God shall be exceedingly glad

68:3 But let the righteous [those who live by every Word of God] be glad; let them rejoice before God: yea, let them exceedingly rejoice. **68:4** Sing unto God, sing praises to his name: extol him that rideth upon the heavens by his name JAH [the letter J was invented in the middle ages and this should properly be rendered YAH; YHWH], and rejoice before him.

68:5 [God is] A father of the fatherless, and a judge [a justice giver] of the widows, is God in [from] his holy habitation.

God brings the lonely into his family and delivers those in bondage to sin, but the unrepentant wicked will perish without the water of God's Holy Spirit

68:6 God setteth the solitary in families: he bringeth out those which are bound with chains: but the rebellious dwell in a dry land.

God called physical Israel out of Egypt and delivered them with mighty deeds; an d God calls spiritual Israel out from bondage to sin and delivers them with mighty deeds.

68:7 O God, when thou wentest forth before thy people, when thou didst march through the wilderness; Selah: **68:8** The earth shook, the heavens also dropped at the presence of God: even Sinai itself was moved at the presence of God, the God of Israel.

God blessed the faithful of physical Israel with rain in a dry land; which is a type of the rain of the Holy Spirit upon the spiritually faithful.

Physical Israel was given the physical promised land as an inheritance from God, and spiritual Israel will be given the Promised Land of eternal life as their heritage from God

68:9 Thou, O God, didst send a plentiful rain, whereby thou didst confirm thine inheritance, when it was weary. **68:10** Thy congregation hath dwelt therein [in the promised land]: thou, O God, hast prepared of thy goodness for the poor [those poor in the spirit of pride and stubborn self-will Mat 5:3].

Ultimately every Word of God will be published to all people in the whole earth, and all humanity will live by every Word of God.

68:11 The Lord gave the word: great was the company of those that published it.

When Christ comes the kings of the earth will submit to him, giving up their kingdoms to God's chosen ones

68:12 Kings of armies did flee apace: and she that tarried at home [physical and spiritual Israel] divided the spoil.

Those who live by every Word of God, even though they are common and humble in this physical life, will be exalted in the resurrection to eternal life and they will receive offices of kings and priests over the earth under the coming King of kings.

> **Revelation 5:10** And hast made us unto our God kings and priests: and we shall reign on the earth.

Psalm 68:13 Though ye have lien among the pots [though we may have been of humble station in this life] , yet shall ye be [exalted in the resurrection of the godly] as the wings of a dove covered with silver, and her feathers with yellow gold. **68:14** When the Almighty scattered kings in it, it was white as snow in Salmon.

The temple mount [and the government of God which it symbolizes] will be exalted above all the mountains [governments] of the earth

68:15 The hill [government] of God is as the hill of Bashan [fruitful prosperous Golan]; an high hill as the hill of Bashan.

God has chosen Jerusalem and his Holy Hill the Temple Mount, to be ultimately replaced by the New Jerusalem (Revelation 21); to dwell in that place forever

68:16 Why leap ye, ye high hills? this is the hill which God desireth to dwell in; yea, the LORD will dwell in it for ever. **68:17** The chariots of God are twenty thousand, even thousands of angels: the Lord is among them, as in Sinai, in the holy place.

The Lamb of God sacrificed for the repented sins of the world; was resurrected to eternal life and lifted up on high

68:18 Thou hast ascended on high, thou hast led captivity [Messiah conquered death and was exalted] captive: **thou hast received gifts** [Messiah has received the gifts of forgiveness and reconciliation with God and the gift of the Holy Spirit from God the Father; to give to men John 16:7.] **for men;** yea, for the rebellious [while we were still sinners God gave his son to be sacrificed for us, so that the rebellious could sincerely repent and be reconciled to God] also, that the LORD God might dwell among them.

Blessed be the LORD God who was made flesh and gave himself for his creation, so that mankind could be reconciled to God the Father and delivered from bondage to Satan and sin

68:19 Blessed be the Lord, who daily loadeth us with benefits, even the God of our salvation. Selah.

God alone will judge between the righteous to eternal life and the unrepentant wicked to eternal death

68:20 He that is our God is the God of salvation; and unto GOD the Lord belong the issues from death.

The sincerely repentant who go on to sin no more shall be saved, but the unrepentant wicked shall be grievously corrected to humble them in the hope that they might repent and be saved

68:21 But God shall wound the head of his enemies, and the hairy scalp of such an one as goeth on still in his trespasses.

God will deliver his physical people from all the places where they have been scattered, and he will deliver his faithful spiritual people to everlasting life

68:22 The Lord said, I will bring again from Bashan, I will bring my people again from the depths of the sea: **68:23** That thy foot may be dipped in the blood of thine enemies, and the tongue of thy dogs in the same.

The whole earth will see and know the mighty deeds of God to save humanity from bondage to Satan, sin and death, and the vast majority of mankind will sincerely repent, rejoicing in God

68:24 They have seen thy goings [deeds], O God; even the goings [deeds] of my God, my King, in the sanctuary.

The tribes [nations] of Israel shall all gather before God at the new Ezekiel Temple in Jerusalem to praise and worship God

68:25 The singers went before, the players on instruments followed after; among them were the damsels playing with timbrels. **68:26** Bless ye God in the congregations, even the Lord, from the fountain of Israel. **68:27** There is little Benjamin with their ruler, the princes of Judah and their council, the princes of Zebulun, and the princes of Naphtali.

The coming Messiah the Christ will save and strengthen the tribes of physical Israel, and will go on to deliver all humanity from bondage to Satan, sin and death

68:28 Thy God hath commanded thy strength: strengthen, O God, that which thou hast wrought for us.

All nations shall come up to worship God at the Ezekiel Temple in Jerusalem

68:29 Because of thy temple at Jerusalem shall kings bring presents unto thee.

The coming Christ will rebuke and scatter all those who delight in violence and rebellion against God, until the whole earth submits to God and lives by every Word of God

68:30 Rebuke the company of spearmen, the multitude of the bulls, with the calves of the people, till every one submit himself with pieces of silver: scatter thou the people that delight in war.

Egypt and Ethiopia [a type of all Africa] will turn to worship God and they will live by every Word of God

68:31 Princes shall come out of Egypt [to worship God at the Ezekiel Temple]; Ethiopia shall soon stretch out her hands unto God. **68:32** Sing unto God, ye kingdoms [nations and peoples] of the earth; O sing praises unto the Lord; Selah:

Messiah the Christ shall come with his resurrected chosen ones to rule all nations; in the righteousness of every Word of God

68:33 To him that rideth upon the heavens of heavens, which were of old; lo, he doth send out his voice, and that a mighty voice. **68:34** Ascribe ye strength unto God: his excellency is over Israel, and his strength is in the clouds. **68:35** O God, thou art terrible [Awesome] out of thy holy places: the God of Israel is he that giveth strength and power unto his people. Blessed be God.

Psalm 69

A prophecy of the sacrificial death of Messiah the Christ, the curse of the present spiritual blindness on Israel, and the final deliverance of Israel

Multitudes of enemies are likened to a flood of waters, and being helpless before the enemy is like trying to get free from deep mud and quicksand.

Psalm 69:1 Save me, O God; for the waters [many enemies] are come in unto my soul [to take my life]. **69:2** I sink in deep mire [a prophecy of mire as a type of the grave], where there is no standing: I am come into deep waters, where the floods [a flood of enemies] overflow me.

Messiah the Christ put his trust in God even when the situation seemed hopeless, and was rewarded with the resurrection to eternal life and exalted on high

69:3 I am weary of my crying: my throat is dried: mine eyes fail while I wait for my God. **69:4** They that hate me without a cause are more than the hairs of mine head: they that would destroy me, being mine enemies wrongfully, are mighty: then I restored that which I took not away.

The faithful know that God knows all things and that all those reproached and shamed by the enemy will receive a good reward. The reward of the faithful called out is sure; and the reward of Christ the first born is double.

> **Isaiah 61:7** For your shame ye shall have double; and for confusion they shall rejoice in their portion: therefore in their land they shall possess the double: everlasting joy shall be unto them.

Jesus knew that if he had sinned, God the Father would know it

Psalm 69:5 O God, thou knowest my foolishness; and my sins are not hid from thee.

The true servant's of God will never be ashamed of Christ their Deliverer, because he gave his life for us

69:6 Let not them that wait on thee, O Lord GOD of hosts, be ashamed for my sake: let not those that seek thee be confounded for my sake, O God of Israel. **69:7** Because for thy sake I have borne reproach; shame hath covered my face.

A prophecy of Messiah the Christ and his love for God and the Word of God, which love of godliness estranged him from Judah. Similarly the love of God to live by every Word of God will estrange godly brethren from today's apostate spiritual Ekklesia.

69:8 I am become a stranger unto my brethren, and an alien unto my mother's [Messiah the Christ was not accepted by the tribe of Judah, most of the Jews] children.

Messiah is zealous for God the Father's Temple [House] both physical and spiritual, and he will not permit any uncleanness of sin in the lives of God's faithful who are the spiritual Temple of God (1 Cor 3:16-17, 6:19).

69:9 For the zeal of thine house hath eaten me up; and the reproaches of them that reproached thee are fallen upon me.

Christ wept over the sins of the people and humbled himself before God in fasting

69:10 When I wept, and chastened my soul with fasting, that was to my reproach. **69:11** I made sackcloth [mourning and humility] also my garment; and I became a proverb to them.

Messiah was mocked by the people, but he was always absolutely faithful to God the Father

69:12 They that sit in the gate speak against me; and I was the song of the drunkards. **69:13** But as for me, my prayer is unto thee, O LORD, in an acceptable time: O God, in the multitude of thy mercy hear me, in the truth of thy salvation. **69:14** Deliver me out of the mire [the grave], and let me not sink: let me be delivered from them that hate me, and out of the deep waters [Christ was delivered from the grave and from the hands of many enemies].

69:15 Let not the waterflood [of enemies] overflow me, neither let the deep [a type of the grave See Jonah] swallow me up, and let not the pit [grave] shut her mouth upon me.

69:16 Hear me, O LORD; for thy lovingkindness is good: turn unto me according to the multitude of thy tender mercies. **69:17** And hide not thy face from thy servant; for I am in trouble: hear me speedily. **69:18** Draw nigh unto my soul, and redeem [save my life] it: deliver me because of mine enemies.

Jesus calls on God to remember his reproach and to raise him up from the grave

69:19 Thou hast known my reproach, and my shame, and my dishonour: mine adversaries are all before thee. **69:20** Reproach hath broken my heart; and I am full of heaviness: and I looked for some to take pity, but there was none; and for comforters, but I found none.

69:21 They gave me also gall for my meat; and in my thirst they gave me vinegar to drink.

Judah was corrected by the Roman Prince Titus, and Judah and Israel were largely darkened from understanding until Christ should return.

The stumbling block before Judah is their Unitarian belief concerning the nature of God.

The stumbling blocks before the ten tribes is the false belief that the sacrifice of Christ did away with any need to keep the whole Word of God and that now only the Ten Commandments are now binding, and that religious leaders have the authority to bind and loose the Word of God. See the **"Ecclesiastical Authority"** book.

69:22 Let their table become a snare before them: and that which should have been for their welfare, let it become a trap. **69:23** Let their eyes be darkened, that they see [do not understand for a time] not; and make their loins continually to shake [being oppressed]. **69:24** Pour out thine indignation upon them, and let thy wrathful anger take hold of them. **69:25** Let their habitation be desolate; and let none dwell in their tents.

> **Romans 11:25** For I would not, brethren, that ye should be ignorant of this mystery, lest ye should be wise in your own conceits; that **blindness in part is happened to Israel, until the fulness of the Gentiles be come in.**

This curse is upon those who rejected and persecuted Messiah, because God the Father had allowed Christ to be smitten for the sins of the people

Psalm 69:26 For they persecute him whom thou hast smitten; and they talk to the grief of those [they speak against Messiah, who God wounded for the sins of the people] whom thou hast wounded.

69:27 Add iniquity unto their iniquity: and let them not come into thy righteousness. **69:28** Let them be blotted out of the book of the living, and not be written with the righteous [until Christ returns to deliver them].

Christ was poor in the spirit of stubborn self-will and greatly grieved by sin, he lived enthusiastically by every Word of God and was resurrected and raised on high for doing so

69:29 But I am poor and sorrowful: let thy salvation, O God, set me up on high. **69:30** I will praise the name of God with a song, and will magnify him with thanksgiving.

Humility and obedience before God, is better than a sacrifice of animals.

69:31 This also shall please the LORD better than an ox or bullock that hath horns and hoofs.

Those who humbly seek to live by every Word of God will greatly rejoice in the application of the sacrifice of Christ to cleanse them from all repented past sins, and they shall live forever

69:32 The humble shall see this, and be glad: and your heart shall live that seek God.

God remembered his Son to raise him up and God will remember Israel and Judah after the coming tribulation and will end the curse and save them

69:33 For the LORD heareth the poor, and despiseth not his prisoners. **69:34** Let the heaven and earth praise him, the seas, and every thing that moveth therein. **69:35** For God will save Zion, and will build the cities of Judah: that they may dwell there, and have it in possession.

The hearts of Israel and Judah will yet be converted and their spiritual blindness will be healed, then they shall live in the Word of the LORD forever more

69:36 The seed also of his servants shall inherit it: and they that love his name shall dwell therein.

Psalm 70

An appeal for deliverance by Messiah the Christ, and from those faithful to live by every Word of God

Psalm 70:1 MAKE HASTE, O GOD, TO DELIVER ME; MAKE HASTE TO HELP ME, O LORD.

This is a prophecy about Christ and includes all those who are Christ's and have suffered for their faithfulness to God

70:2 Let them be ashamed and confounded that seek after my soul [life]: let them be turned backward, and put to confusion, that desire my hurt. **70:3** Let them be turned back for a reward of their shame that say, Aha, aha.

Let those who mock the righteousness of zeal to live by every Word of God; be put to shame by God's deliverance of the faithful and his correction of the wicked.

70:4 Let all those that seek thee rejoice and be glad in thee: and let such as love thy salvation say continually, Let God be magnified.

Those poor in the spirit of stubborn self-will, who are humble to acknowledge that they truly NEED and THIRST after godliness; will be saved to eternal life

70:5 But I am poor and needy: make haste unto me, O God: thou art my help and my deliverer; O LORD, make no tarrying.

Psalms 71 - 80

Psalm 71

Those who put their trust in God to live as God lives [by every Word of God] will be delivered and the faithful will praise him eternally for his love. David remembers his love for God in his youth and prays that God will keep him close, in his old age. This is very important as so very many get weary in their zeal for God as they age.

Psalm 71:1 In thee, O LORD, do I put my trust: let me never be put to confusion. **71:2** Deliver me in thy righteousness [God's Word is righteousness], and cause me to escape: incline thine ear unto me, and save me.

Those who live by God's Word are God's people and dwell with God, therefore God will deliver all those who trust in him

71:3 Be thou my strong habitation, whereunto I may continually resort: thou hast given commandment to save me; for thou art my rock and my fortress. **71:4** Deliver me, O my God, out of the hand of the wicked, out of the hand of the unrighteous and cruel man.

God the Father is the hope of his people, for he will deliver them from bondage to Satan, sin and death

71:5 For thou art my hope, O Lord GOD: thou art my trust from my youth. **71:6** By thee have I been holden up from the womb: thou art he that took me out of my mother's bowels: my praise shall be continually of thee.

Jesus Christ and those who follow God the Father seem very strange to many, but Messiah and God's people always place their trust in God the Father; who will deliver them, dumbfounding the naysayers

71:7 I am as a wonder [those who follow and trust in God seem strange to many] unto many; but thou art my strong refuge. **71:8** Let my mouth be filled with thy praise and with thy honour all the day.

God will love his faithful forever

71:9 Cast me not off in the time of old age; forsake me not when my strength faileth. **71:10** For mine enemies speak against me; and they that lay wait for my soul take counsel together, **71:11** Saying, God hath forsaken him: persecute and take him; for there is none to deliver him. **71:12** O God, be not far from me: O my God, make haste for my help.

When Christ comes to resurrect the godly dead to eternal life, and he puts down the wicked, the evil doers will be dumbfounded and humbled before God

71:13 Let them be confounded and consumed that are adversaries to my soul [life]; let them be covered with reproach and dishonour that seek my hurt.

Those who live by the righteousness of every Word of God shall be delivered from bondage to Satan, sin and death and they shall declare God's praises in great rejoicing forever

71:14 But I will hope continually, and will yet praise thee more and more. **71:15** My mouth shall shew forth [proclaim, teach] thy righteousness and thy salvation all the day; for I know not the numbers thereof. **71:16** I will go in the strength of the Lord GOD: I will make mention of thy righteousness, even of thine only.

David declares that he has been faithful to God from a child and prays the God will remain with him in his old age. Yes David sinned, but whenever he discovered his sin he immediately repented with a whole heart!

71:17 O God, thou hast taught me from my youth: and hitherto have I declared thy wondrous works. **71:18** Now also when I am old and greyheaded, O God, forsake me not; until I have shewed thy strength unto this generation, and thy power to every one that is to come.

The righteousness of God and God's Word is very great, and the Wisdom [Word] of God is greater than the wisdom of all men together

71:19 Thy righteousness also, O God, is very high, who hast done great things: O God, who is like unto thee! **71:20** Thou, which hast shewed me great and sore troubles, shalt quicken me again, and shalt bring me up again from the depths of the earth.

God will resurrect the godly dead to eternal life and he will grant the called out and chosen first fruits to be kings on the earth.

Messiah the Christ and all of the godly faithful say of God the Father:

71:21 Thou shalt increase my greatness, and comfort me on every side.

The faithful love truth, and the truth of the Word of God; they would never reject truth to cleave to any false tradition of men

71:22 I will also praise thee with the psaltery, even thy truth, O my God: unto thee will I sing with the harp, O thou Holy One of Israel. **71:23** My lips shall greatly rejoice when I sing unto thee; and my soul, which thou hast redeemed. **71:24** My tongue also shall talk of thy righteousness all the day long: for they are confounded, for they are brought unto shame, that seek my hurt.

Psalm 72

Psalm 72:1 Give [teach] the king thy judgments [God's Word], O God, and thy righteousness [God's Word] unto the king's son.

In the Kingdom of God Messiah will rule the whole earth and the resurrected David will rule all Israel while the resurrected saints will rule all nations in the righteousness of every Word of God

72:2 He shall judge thy people with righteousness, and thy poor with judgment.

72:3 The mountains [national governments will bring peace and not war] shall bring peace to the people, and the little hills [local governments will teach the righteous Word of God], by righteousness.

The King of kings and his Bride [the resurrected chosen] will rule the nations in the righteousness of every Word of God

72:4 He shall judge the poor of the people, he shall save the children of the needy, and shall break in pieces the oppressor.

God the Father and Messiah the Christ will be honored and greatly respected and obeyed forever

72:5 They shall fear thee as long as the sun and moon endure, throughout all generations.

When the nations turn to live by every Word of God, the whole earth will be blessed by the righteousness of God and the rule of Messiah the King of kings. God's Spirit will rain down upon the earth and the physical rains will fall in due season.

72:6 He shall come down like rain upon the mown grass: as showers that water the earth.

In the millennium peace will flourish and when God the Father comes down to the cleansed earth, peace and the righteousness of every Word of God shall flourish forever

72:7 In his days shall the righteous flourish; and abundance of peace so long as the moon endureth. **72:8** He shall have dominion also from sea to sea, and from the river unto the ends of the earth.

Every enemy of God who refuses to live by every Word of God, will either sincerely repent or they will be destroyed forever.

72:9 They that dwell in the wilderness shall bow before him; and his enemies shall lick the dust. **72:10** The kings of Tarshish and of the isles shall bring presents: the kings of Sheba and Seba shall offer gifts. **72:11** Yea, **all kings shall fall down before him: all nations shall serve him.**

72:12 For he shall deliver the needy when he crieth; the poor also, and him that hath no helper.

When Christ comes he will deliver all those who were poor in the spirit of pride and stubborn self-will and who hungered and thirsted to live by every Word of God. Christ will raise them up from death to life eternal

72:13 He [Messiah the Christ] shall spare the poor [in the spirit of self will] and needy [who hunger and thirst after godliness], and shall save the souls [lives] of the needy. **72:14** He shall redeem their soul from deceit and violence: and precious shall their blood [the death of the righteous is precious to God, because God will resurrect them from their rest] be in his sight.

Jesus Christ [Hebrew: Yeshua Mashiach] was resurrected to become the King of kings, and the chosen who loved and lived by every Word of God, will arise in the resurrection to eternal life as spirit.

72:15 And he shall live [to reign as King of kings], and to him shall be given of the gold of Sheba: prayer also shall be made for him continually; and daily shall he be praised.

When Christ comes after the devastation of the tribulation, the remnant of Israel will be a mere handful of her former self, but from that handful a great harvest [mighty nations] shall spring forth, like a tree barely able to stand, shaking for the abundance of its fruit.

72:16 There shall be an handful of corn [grain] in the earth upon the top of the mountains; the fruit thereof shall shake like Lebanon: and they of the city shall flourish like grass of the earth.

Jesus Christ the King of kings shall rule under God the Father; forever

72:17 His name shall endure for ever: his name shall be continued as long as the sun: and men shall be blessed in him: all nations shall call him blessed.

72:18 Blessed be the LORD God, the God of Israel, who only doeth wondrous things. **72:19** And blessed be his glorious name for ever: and let the whole earth be filled with his glory; Amen, and Amen.

72:20 The prayers of David the son of Jesse are ended.

Psalm 73

This Psalm is about why the godly suffer and the wicked often prosper in this physical life. Solomon the son of David, having learned about such questions from his father, discusses the subject further in Ecclesiastes. This question is also a main topic of Job.

God was good to the faithful of Mosaic Covenant, and God is good to the faithful of the New Covenant spiritual Israel

Psalm 73:1 Truly God is good to Israel, even to such as are of a clean heart.

How foolish it is to be envious of the prosperity of the wicked, because they and their prosperity will quickly perish

73:2 But as for me, my feet were almost gone [envy at the prosperity of the wicked can tempt us to slip into sin and depart from the path of godliness]; my steps [walk (life of godliness) with God] had well nigh slipped. **73:3** For **I was envious at the foolish, when I saw the prosperity of the wicked.**

The wicked will die but in life the prosperous wicked have nothing to restrain them and are set above all because of Satan's blessings on them

73:4 For there are no bands in their death: but their strength is firm. **73:5** They are not in trouble as other men; neither are they plagued like other men.

Wicked men who are exalted to any office [including elder] become full of pride, and being unrestrained by faithfulness to God they abuse others for their own advantage

73:6 Therefore pride compasseth them about as a chain; violence covereth them as a garment. **73:7** Their eyes stand out with fatness: they have more than heart could wish. **73:8** They are corrupt, and speak wickedly concerning oppression: they speak loftily. **73:9** They set their mouth against the heavens, and their tongue walketh through the earth.

73:10 Therefore his people return hither [those the wicked deceive, serve the wicked deceivers]: and waters of a full cup are wrung out to them.

The cunning deceiver is filled with material goods and has the respect of those he deceives.

The wicked deceivers convince themselves that they are righteous, pointing to their prosperity as a sign, and think that God will not punish them for their deeds

73:11 And they say, How doth God know? and is there knowledge in the most High? **73:12** Behold, these are the ungodly, who prosper in the world; they increase in riches.

If we see the prosperity of the wicked and begin to think that we are serving God in many trials for nothing, we are tempted to follow the wicked to receive physical prosperity and relieve our trials

73:13 Verily I have cleansed my heart in vain, and washed my hands in innocency.

When we envy the prosperity of the wicked, we tempt ourselves and begin to think that we have purified ourselves to godliness for nothing, because the godly face many trials

73:14 For all the day long have I been plagued [suffered trials], and chastened every morning [because we try to live by every Word of God].

The faithful who teach godliness are offensive to the wicked, who reject living by every Word of God preferring the pleasures of sin

73:15 If I say, I will speak thus; behold, I should offend against the generation of thy children.

The reason that the wicked prosper and those who love to live by every Word of God suffer, can be a very troubling question until we seek the answer from God

73:16 When I thought to know [understand] this, it was too painful for me;

Once we understand the Word of God, we realize that the prosperity of the wicked is as transitory as a wisp of smoke in a gale; but those who learn to live by Every Word of God, internalizing the very nature of God, will be resurrected and changed to spirit and will live in great prosperity FOREVER

73:17 Until I went into the sanctuary of God; then understood I their end.

The unrepentant wicked are appointed to eternal death

73:18 Surely thou didst set them in slippery places: thou castedst them down into destruction. **73:19** How are they brought into desolation, as in a moment! they are utterly consumed with terrors.

The unrepentant wicked will soon die and remain dead forever, fading from the memory of the faithful like a night dream fades in the light of the day

73:20 As a dream when one awaketh; so, O Lord, when thou awakest, thou shalt despise their image.

When we understand that the end of the wicked is eternal death and that their supposed apparent prosperity is just a shadow which will fade with them; then those who love God and live by every Word of God will know that the wicked are nothing to be envied

73:21 Thus my heart was grieved, and I was pricked in my reins.

Those who love God and live by every Word of God, will live in great prosperity FOREVER, while the unrepentant wicked will perish forever.

73:22 So foolish was I, and ignorant: I was as a beast before thee.

Once we realize that our trials come upon us because God is working with us now, teaching us lessons that will save us for eternity; we will remain steadfast in all trials and will never again envy the quickly perishing unrepentant wicked. We will remain steadfast to live by every Word of God FOREVER!

73:23 Nevertheless I am continually with thee: thou hast holden me by my right hand. **73:24** Thou shalt guide me with thy counsel [every Word of God], and afterward receive [God will resurrect the faithful to eternal life] me to glory.

The Eternal is the God of Salvation, there is NO other; though the flesh die, yet he will raise up his faithful to eternal life as spirit

73:25 Whom have I in heaven but thee? and there is none upon earth that I desire beside thee. **73:26** My flesh and my heart faileth: but God is the strength of my heart, and my portion for ever.

The unrepentant and their supposed physical prosperity shall ultimately perish, but those who put their trust in God and internalize God's nature through living by every Word of God will live forever with God

73:27 For, lo, they that are far from thee shall perish: thou hast destroyed all them that go a whoring from thee. **73:28** But it is good for me to draw near to God: I have put my trust in the Lord GOD, that I may declare all thy works.

Psalm 74

A prophecy of the future falls of Jerusalem by Babylon and Rome, which are types of the final fall of Jerusalem by the climax of the Babylonian system, the now rising New Federal Europe

The captive people call on God to remember them and their sufferings

Psalm 74:1 O God, why hast thou cast us off for ever? why doth thine anger smoke against the sheep of thy pasture? **74:2** Remember thy congregation, which thou hast purchased of old; the rod of thine inheritance [physical and spiritual Israel], which thou hast redeemed; this mount Zion, wherein thou hast dwelt.

God's people call upon God to see the desolation's wrought by the Adversary

74:3 Lift up thy feet unto the perpetual desolations; even all that the enemy hath done wickedly in the sanctuary. **74:4** Thine enemies roar in the midst of thy congregations; they set up their ensigns for signs.

The fame of the wicked is great because they have defeated the nations of Israel

74:5 A man was famous according as he had lifted up axes upon the thick trees.

A prophecy of the destruction of Jerusalem; the first time by Babylon and later by Rome when the city and Temple were burned; these being types of the final fall of Jerusalem to Babylon the Great [the rising New Europe and her allies] in our time

74:6 But now they break down the carved work thereof [of Jerusalem and the Temple] at once with axes and hammers. **74:7** [a prophecy of the destruction of the Temple] They have cast fire into thy sanctuary, they have defiled by casting down the dwelling place of thy name to the ground.

Here David says that all the synagogues will be destroyed in the land, proving that the synagogue system was known to David. The synagogue system originated with Moses and the setting up of Levitical schools to teach the people a basic education and the Word of God.

74:8 They said in their hearts, Let us destroy them together: they have burned up all the synagogues of God in the land.

74:9 We see not our signs [today's spiritual Ekklesia does not understand the Word of God, nor do they see their approaching correction]: there is no more any prophet: neither is there among us any that knoweth how long. **74:10** O God, how long shall the adversary reproach? shall the enemy blaspheme thy name for ever?

God is asked to lift up his hand and deliver the faithful and the repentant

74:11 Why withdrawest thou thy hand, even thy right hand? pluck it out of thy bosom. **74:12** For God is my King of old, working salvation in the midst of the earth.

David recounts the mighty deeds of God and calls for God's deliverance

74:13 Thou didst divide the sea by thy strength: thou brakest the heads of the dragons in the waters. **74:14** Thou brakest the heads of leviathan in pieces, and gavest him to be meat to the people inhabiting the wilderness. **74:15** Thou didst cleave the fountain and the flood: thou driedst up mighty rivers. **74:16** The day is thine, the night also is thine: thou hast prepared the light and the sun. **74:17** Thou hast set all the borders of the earth: thou hast made summer and winter.

God is asked to remember that the wicked who are destroying HIS people have reproached God, and asks for God's intervention

74:18 Remember this, that the enemy hath reproached [Thee], O LORD, and that the foolish people have blasphemed thy name.

God is asked to remember HIS Covenant with his beloved and deliver the faithful who are being persecuted; and to also deliver the apostates when they sincerely repent: this includes the apostate New Covenant spiritual Ekklesia who will quickly repent in their imminent correction

74:19 O deliver not the soul [life] of thy turtledove [beloved people, bride] unto the multitude of the wicked: forget not the congregation of thy poor for ever. **74:20** Have respect unto the covenant: for the dark places of the earth are full of the habitations of cruelty.

The persecuted for godliness will be delivered, and the apostates will sincerely repent and turn to God in wholehearted zeal

74:21 O let not the oppressed return ashamed [the faithful will not be ashamed for putting their trust in God]: let the poor [in self-will and rebellion against God] and needy praise thy name [because God will deliver them].

God will indeed arise and Messiah the Christ will come; first to resurrect his beloved faithful chosen, and then to come WITH them to save all Israel and destroy wickedness from off the earth.

74:22 Arise, O God, plead thine own cause: remember how the foolish man reproacheth thee daily. **74:23** Forget not the voice of thine enemies: the tumult of those that rise up against thee increaseth continually.

Psalm 75

David thanks God because he is near to delivering his people

Psalm 75:1 Unto thee, O God, do we give thanks, unto thee do we give thanks: for that thy name is near thy wondrous works declare.

When Jesus Christ comes he will rule all nations in the justice of every Word of God as King of kings

75:2 When I shall receive the congregation I will judge uprightly.

The earth itself will ultimately be made molten by fire after the millennium and after the Feast of Tabernacles ingathering of nations; but God will preserve it, making the earth anew; and God will judge and rule the resurrected nations by the righteousness of every Word of God.

75:3 The earth and all the inhabitants thereof are dissolved: I bear up the pillars of it. Selah.

> **2 Peter 3:10** But the day of the Lord will come as a thief in the night; in the which the heavens shall pass away with a great noise, and the elements shall melt with fervent heat, the earth also and the works that are therein shall be burned up.
>
> **3:11** Seeing then that all these things shall be dissolved, what manner of persons ought ye to be in all holy conversation and godliness,
>
> **3:12** Looking for and hasting unto the coming of the day of God, wherein the heavens being on fire shall be dissolved, and the elements shall melt with fervent heat? **3:13** Nevertheless we, according to his promise, look for new heavens and a new earth, wherein dwelleth righteousness.

All humanity will be called to sincere repentance, to turn to and live by every Word of God

75:4 I said unto the fools, Deal not foolishly: and to the wicked, Lift not up the horn [do not be lifted up with pride]: **75:5** Lift not up your horn [power, self-exaltation] on high: speak not with a stiff neck [stubborn self-will].

God will judge all people justly: It is God who will exalt his faithful, and it is God who will correct the wicked

75:6 For promotion cometh neither from the east, nor from the west, nor from the south. **75:7** But God is the judge: he putteth down one, and setteth up another.

The wine of the wrath of God will be poured out on all those who refuse to live by every Word of God

75:8 For in the hand of the LORD there is a cup, and the wine is red; it is full of mixture; and he poureth out of the same: but the dregs thereof, all the wicked of the earth shall wring them out, and drink them.

The righteous will be glad when the LORD comes to deliver God's faithful from the grave and correct the wicked

75:9 But I will declare for ever; I will sing praises to the God of Jacob.

The strength of those who live by every Word of God shall be greatly increased, while the power of the wicked will vanish forevermore

75:10 All the horns [power, strength] of the wicked also will I cut off [totally destroy]; but the horns [power, strength] of the righteous shall be exalted.

Psalm 76

A prophecy of the coming of Messiah the Christ as King of kings

When Messiah the Christ comes, all Israel and Judah will sincerely repent and all Israel shall turn to and know God

Psalm 76:1 In Judah is God known: his name is great in Israel. **76:2** In Salem [Jerusalem, which shall be known as the city of peace] also is his tabernacle, and his dwelling place in Zion.

When Christ comes he will come to Jerusalem and he will break the power of the wicked

76:3 There brake he the arrows of the bow, the shield, and the sword, and the battle. Selah.

Messiah's victory over the wicked at Jerusalem will be complete

76:4 Thou [Messiah the Christ] art more glorious and excellent [much wiser and more powerful] than the mountains of prey [governments that make war].

When Christ comes with his resurrected chosen, the wicked will either sincerely repent or perish

76:5 The stouthearted [the wicked are overcome] are spoiled, they have slept their sleep [perished in death]: and none of the men of might have [none of the wicked have any strength against Messiah] found their hands.

At the rebuke of the coming Christ, the mightiest of the wicked shall fall

76:6 At thy rebuke, O God of Jacob, both the chariot and horse are cast into a dead sleep [destruction, death].

No one will be able to stand against God or resist the coming Christ

76:7 Thou, even thou, art to be feared: and who may stand in thy sight when once thou art angry?

When the King of kings comes he will rule all nations in the justice and righteousness of every Word of God

76:8 Thou didst cause judgment to be heard from heaven; the earth feared, and was still, **76:9** When God arose to judgment, to save all the meek of the earth. Selah.

Those who survive will have their eyes opened and will sincerely repent to praise God, and people will no longer resist God

76:10 Surely the wrath [mankind's enmity against God will vanish and men will serve God when God's Spirit is poured out (Joel 2:28)] of man shall praise thee: the remainder of wrath shalt thou restrain [Satan will be removed and man's resistance to God will vanish].

The people will then repent and make a baptismal commitment to live by every Word of God, and they will serve God the Father and Messiah the Christ

76:11 Vow, and pay unto the LORD your God: let all that be round about him bring presents unto him that ought to be feared.

When Christ comes he will destroy the power and pride of the nations, and HE will rule over all nations as King of kings, with his faithful servants ruling the individual nations

76:12 He shall cut off the spirit of princes: he is terrible [kings and princes will be awed and cowed to submission by the King of kings] to the kings of the earth.

Psalm 77

A prophecy of the repentance of Israel during the tribulation

The nations and peoples of physical and spiritual Israel will cry out to God for deliverance in the hour of her correction

Psalm 77:1 I cried unto God with my voice, even unto God with my voice; and he gave ear unto me.

The sufferings of the nations will be grave during the hour of correction, bringing great lamentation and sorrow and people will cry out to God for deliverance

77:2 In the day of my trouble I sought the Lord: my sore ran in the night, and ceased not: my soul refused to be comforted.

Then the people will remember God and cry out to HIM; then they will be ready to enter a New Covenant with God (Jer 31:31).

77:3 I remembered God, and was troubled: I complained, and my spirit was overwhelmed. Selah.

The people shall suffer so greatly that the time will come when they are sleepless with sorrows so overwhelming that they will be unable to properly express them

77:4 Thou holdest mine eyes waking: I am so troubled that I cannot speak.

Then the people will consider and remember the good times and realize that they were blessed from the God, whom they refused to follow

77:5 I have considered the days of old, the years of ancient times. **77:6** I call to remembrance my song [past joys] in the night: I commune with mine own heart: and my spirit made diligent search.

The people will remember God and acknowledge that they sinned against him in return for his blessings; and they will cry out in sincere repentance begging God not to forsake them any longer

77:7 Will the Lord cast off for ever? and will he be favourable no more? **77:8** Is his mercy clean gone for ever? doth his promise fail for evermore? **77:9** Hath God forgotten to be gracious? hath he in anger shut up his tender mercies? Selah.

The people will remember God and will turn unto him

77:10 And I said, This is my infirmity [my fault because of my sin]: but I will remember the years of the right hand [the blessings] of the most High. **77:11** I will remember the works [the mighty deeds] of the LORD: surely I will remember thy wonders of old.

Then the people will think on the mighty deeds and marvelous wisdom of God

77:12 I will meditate also of all thy work, and talk of thy doings.

Going to God's sanctuary is an allegory for seeking God

Then the people will seek God with all their hearts and they will acknowledge the greatness, glory, power and wisdom of God.

77:13 Thy way, O God, is in the sanctuary: who is so great a God as our God?

At his coming the wisdom and power of Messiah the Christ will be manifest to all peoples

77:14 Thou art the God that doest wonders: thou hast declared thy strength among the people. **77:15** Thou hast with thine arm redeemed thy people, the sons of Jacob and Joseph. Selah.

God is so mighty in his power that the waters of the Red Sea parted before God and Mount Sinai shook and trembled at his presence.

When Christ comes all people will learn that God is able to go where he wills, and to do as he wills; and they will rejoice that God is just and full of mercy and will deliver humanity from bondage to Satan and sin and mankind will turn to him with a whole heart.

77:16 The waters saw thee, O God, the waters saw thee; they were afraid: the depths also were troubled. **77:17** The clouds poured out water: the skies sent out a sound: thine arrows also went abroad. **77:18** The voice of thy thunder was in the heaven: the lightnings lightened the world: the earth trembled and shook. **77:19** Thy way is in the sea, and thy path in the great waters, and thy footsteps are not known.

77:20 Thou leddest thy people like a flock by the hand of Moses and Aaron.

Psalm 78

A recounting of the history of physical Israel from Egypt to David as a lesson in loyalty and rebellion for us today

In this Psalm David rehearses the failures of Israel to keep the Mosaic Covenant with God and explains the need for a New Covenant; beginning by calling the people to listen to the law.

Psalm 78:1 Give ear, O my people, to my law: incline your ears to the words of my mouth.

78:2 I will open my mouth in a parable: I will utter [explain secrets] dark sayings of old: **78:3** Which we have heard and known, and our fathers have told us.

The Word of God will be taught to all generations

78:4 We will not hide them from their children, shewing to the generation to come the praises of the LORD, and his strength, and his wonderful works that he hath done.

The New Covenant is the addition of a more efficacious sacrifice and the gift of the Holy Spirit to write God's law and every Word of God on the hearts and in the minds of the people; so that the people would be enabled to live by every Word of God (Jer 31:31)

78:5 For he established a testimony in Jacob [Israel], and appointed a law in Israel, which he commanded our fathers, that they should make them known to their children:

The New Covenant will begin in its fullness on the Feast of Pentecost when Christ comes, and a spiritual New Covenant Israel would then live by every Word of God forever

78:6 That the generation to come might know them, even the children which should be born; who should arise and declare them to their children:

The New Covenant spiritual Israel [into which all nations will be grafted], through the indwelling of God's Spirit, will internalize and live by EVERY Word of God, and their hope will be in God throughout all generations

78:7 That they might set their hope in God, and not forget the works of God, but keep his commandments:

Physical Mosaic Covenant Israel was a rebellious people who continually departed from God, but New Covenant Israel (Jer 31:31) will be different and they will never again depart from living by every Word of God

78:8 And might not be as their fathers, a stubborn and rebellious generation; a generation that set not their heart aright, and whose spirit was not stedfast with God.

Recounting the departure of Ephraim [a type of all Israel] from God

78:9 The children of Ephraim, being armed, and carrying bows, turned back in the day of battle. **78:10 They kept not the covenant of God, and refused to walk in his law; 78:11 And forgat his works, and his wonders** that he had shewed them.

The mighty deeds of God are forgotten by most of Israel and are considered ancient cultural myths today.

Recounting the mighty deeds of God in delivering physical Israel out from bondage in Egypt; which are an allegory of the mighty deeds of God in delivering the people out from bondage to sin and Satan the god-king of this world.

78:12 Marvellous things did he in the sight of their fathers, in the land of Egypt, in the field of Zoan. **78:13** He divided the sea, and caused them to pass through [being drowned at the bottom of the sea was death, and dividing the sea was a picture of God opening the graves and resurrecting the people in the future]; and he made the waters to stand as an heap. **78:14** In the daytime also he led them with a cloud, and all the night with a light of fire [the cloud and fire signifying God's presence in his people].

78:15 He clave the rocks in the wilderness [picturing **the application of the sacrifice** of the Lamb of God for repented sin so that the waters of the Holy Spirit could be poured out on the sincerely repentant], and gave them drink as out of the great depths [of water pouring out of the rock] . **78:16** He brought streams also out of the rock, and caused waters to run down like rivers [as an allegory of the pouring out of the Word of God and the Holy Spirit when Messiah comes].

78:17 And they sinned [Israel rebelled in the wilderness in spite of the miracles from God] yet more against him by provoking the most High in the wilderness. **78:18** And they tempted God in their heart by asking meat for their lust.

78:19 Yea, they spake against God; they said, Can God furnish a table [feed us with flesh] in the wilderness? **78:20** Behold, he smote the rock, that the waters gushed out, and the streams overflowed; can he give bread also? can he provide flesh for his people?

God was angry because the people had no faith or trust in him after all his miracles

78:21 Therefore the LORD heard this, and was wroth: so a fire was kindled against Jacob, and anger also came up against Israel; **78:22** Because they believed not in God, and trusted not in his salvation: **78:23** Though he had commanded the clouds from above, and opened the doors of heaven, **78:24** And had rained down manna upon them to eat, and had given them of the corn of heaven. **78:25** Man did eat angels' food [manna]: he sent them meat [the flesh of quails] to the full.

Then God gave them the flesh of quails in the wilderness and the people gorged themselves in their lust, still rejecting to trust and live by every Word of God

78:26 He caused an east wind to blow in the heaven: and by his power he brought in the south wind. **78:27** He rained flesh also upon them as dust, and feathered fowls like as the sand of the sea: **78:28** And he let it fall in the midst of their camp, round about their habitations. **78:29** So they did eat, and were well filled: for he gave them their own desire;

The people did not give glory to God or trust in him and continued in their sins, so God, the Being who later gave up his God-hood to become flesh as Jesus Christ; poured out his fury on them.

78:30 They were not estranged from their lust. But while their meat was yet in their mouths, **78:31** The wrath of God came upon them, and slew the fattest of them, and smote down the chosen men of Israel. **78:32** For all this they sinned still, and believed not for his wondrous works.

Because Israel would not put their trust in God to live by his Word, they suffered through their generations

78:33 Therefore their days did he consume in vanity, and their years in trouble. **78:34** When he slew them, then they sought him: and they returned and enquired early after God.

They would remember God in the extremity of their distress and then quickly forgot God in better times.

78:35 And they remembered that God was their rock, and the high God their redeemer.

To this very day physical and spiritual Israel pay lip-service to God while refusing to live by every Word of God.

78:36 Nevertheless they did flatter him with their mouth, and they lied unto him with their tongues. **78:37** For their heart was not right with him, neither were they stedfast in his covenant [which Covenant; BOTH the Mosaic and the New is to live by every Word of God].

Israel provoked God very often, yet he forgave them.

78:38 But he, being full of compassion, forgave their iniquity, and destroyed them not: yea, many a time turned he his anger away, and did not stir up all his wrath. **78:39** For he remembered that they were but flesh; a wind that passeth away, and cometh not again. **78:40** How oft did they provoke him in the wilderness, and grieve him in the desert! **78:41** Yea, they turned back and tempted God, and limited the Holy One of Israel.

The miraculous plagues on ancient Egypt by which God delivered Israel listed.

78:42 They remembered not his hand, nor the day when he delivered them from the enemy. **78:43** How he had wrought his signs in Egypt, and his wonders in the field of Zoan. **78:44** And had turned their rivers into blood; and their floods, that they could not drink. **78:45** He sent divers sorts of [biting] flies among them, which devoured them; and frogs, which destroyed them. **78:46** He gave also their increase unto the caterpiller, and their labour unto the locust.

78:47 He destroyed their vines with hail, and their sycomore trees with frost. **78:48** He gave up their cattle also to the hail, and their flocks to hot thunderbolts. **78:49** He cast upon them the fierceness of his anger, wrath, and indignation, and trouble, by sending evil angels [spirits] among them. **78:50** He made a way to his anger; he spared not their soul from death, but gave their life over to the pestilence; **78:51** And smote all the firstborn in Egypt; the chief of their strength in the tabernacles of Ham:

God afflicted the Egyptians and delivered his called out, as an allegory that God will ultimately afflict the wicked and will deliver the sincerely repentant out of bondage to sin

78:52 But made his own people to go forth like sheep, and guided them in the wilderness like a flock. **78:53** And he led them on safely, so that they feared not: but the sea overwhelmed their enemies. **78:54** And he brought them to the border of his sanctuary [to the land of promise and the temple mount, as a type that God will deliver the sincerely repentant out of bondage to sin and bring them into the household of God], even to this mountain, which his right hand had purchased.

Once they repent in the time of correction God will deliver and restore Israel and divide the land among them

78:55 He cast out the heathen [a general term for unbelievers and wicked] also before them, and divided them an inheritance by line, and made the tribes of Israel to dwell in their tents.

Yet even in the promised land Israel was repeatedly unfaithful to God.

78:56 Yet they tempted and provoked the most high God, and kept not his testimonies: **78:57** But turned back, and dealt unfaithfully like their fathers: they were turned aside like a deceitful bow.

They were commanded to worship God at his temple in God's presence, and most simply would not go up to the temple of God and claimed that they were worshiping God when they went to the pagan high places. Thus they paid lip-service to God while refusing to do what God commanded; just as today's spiritual called out Ekklesia of the New Covenant does.

78:58 For they provoked him to anger with their high places, and moved him to jealousy with their graven images.

God then removed his Ark from among the people because they had forsaken him.

78:59 When God heard this, he was wroth, and greatly abhorred Israel:

78:60 So that he forsook the tabernacle of Shiloh, the tent which he placed among men;

God strengthened the Philistines to correct Israel.

78:61 And delivered his strength [the Ark of God's presence] into captivity [to the Philistines], and his glory into the enemy's hand (1 Sam 4-5).

78:62 He gave his people over also unto the sword; and was wroth with his inheritance. **78:63** The fire consumed their young men; and their maidens were not given to marriage. **78:64** Their priests fell by the sword; and their widows made no lamentation.

Then the people called on God to deliver them, and God arose and plagued the Philistines.

78:65 Then the LORD awaked as one out of sleep, and like a mighty man that shouteth by reason of wine. **78:66** And he smote his enemies in the hinder parts [with hemorrhoids]: he put them to a perpetual reproach.

Then God chose David of Judah as king of Israel

78:67 Moreover he refused the tabernacle of Joseph, and chose not the tribe of Ephraim: **78:68** But chose the tribe of Judah, the mount Zion which he loved.

God then chose Jerusalem and chose the temple mount as his sanctuary instead of Shiloh

78:69 And he built his sanctuary like high palaces, like the earth which he hath established for ever.

David is made the shepherd king over all Israel, and a resurrected spirit David will be king over a once again united Israel when Messiah comes; and they will feed the flock of Israel with every Word of God!

78:70 He chose David also his servant, and took him from the sheepfolds: **78:71** From following the ewes great with young he brought him to feed Jacob his people, and Israel his inheritance. **78:72** So he fed them according to the integrity of his heart; and guided them by the skilfulness of his hands.

Psalm 79

A prophecy of the future captivities and the destruction of the temple

Psalm 79:1 O God, the heathen are come into thine inheritance; thy holy temple have they defiled; they have laid Jerusalem on heaps.

The past destructions of the city Jerusalem and the temple were fore runners of a final treading down of the city and the captivity of physical Israel for 42 months; and the captivity of spiritual Israel, the spiritual temple of God.

79:2 The dead bodies of thy servants have they given to be meat unto the fowls of the heaven, the flesh of thy saints unto the beasts of the earth. **79:3** Their blood have they shed like water round about Jerusalem; and there was none to bury them. **79:4** We are become a reproach to our neighbours, a scorn and derision to them that are round about us.

Speaking of the tribulation in our time David asks how long will these things be? Later God will answer through Daniel, for 1,260 days (Dan 12:7)

79:5 How long, LORD? wilt thou be angry for ever? shall thy jealousy burn like fire?

David then asks that the oppressors also be humbled.

79:6 Pour out thy wrath upon the heathen that have not known thee, and upon the kingdoms that have not called upon thy name. **79:7** For they have devoured Jacob, and laid waste his dwelling place.

David pleads sincere repentance and asks deliverance for Israel; which prayer will be granted with the coming of Messiah the Christ.

79:8 O remember not against us former iniquities: let thy tender mercies speedily prevent us: for we are brought very low.

David pleads for deliverance so that God will be made known and glorified as the Great Deliverer.

79:9 Help us, O God of our salvation, for the glory of thy name: and deliver us, and purge away our sins, for thy name's sake. **79:10** Wherefore should the heathen say, Where is their God? let him be known among the heathen in our sight by the revenging of the blood of thy servants which is shed.

God will deliver his sincerely repentant of both physical and spiritual Israel who have been corrected, and they shall never more depart from living by every Word of God

79:11 Let the sighing [repentance] of the prisoner come before thee; according to the greatness of thy power preserve thou those that are appointed to die;

The nations will also repent after their own correction, and they will turn to embrace the Eternal with a whole heart (Isaiah 60).

79:12 And render unto our neighbours sevenfold into their bosom their reproach, wherewith they have reproached thee, O Lord.

79:13 So we thy people [all sincerely repentant people] and sheep of thy pasture will give thee thanks for ever: we will shew forth thy praise to all generations.

Psalm 80

A call to God for deliverance from the correction of great tribulation

Psalm 80:1 Give ear, O Shepherd [God, YHVH] of Israel, thou that leadest Joseph like a flock; thou that dwellest between the cherubims, shine forth.

God will reveal his strength and deliver the repentant

80:2 Before Ephraim [today's British peoples] and Benjamin [Benjamin is part of the two tribe kingdom of Judah] and Manasseh [the founding peoples of America] stir up thy strength, and come and save us [from the correction of the now imminent great tribulation].

80:3 Turn us again, O God, and cause thy face to shine [shine on us with the blessing of deliverance]; and we shall be saved.

David calls on God to save us after we sincerely repent

80:4 O LORD God of hosts, how long wilt thou be angry against the prayer of thy people? **80:5** Thou feedest them with the bread of tears; and givest them tears to drink in great measure. **80:6** Thou makest us a strife unto our neighbours: and our enemies laugh among themselves.

80:7 Turn us again [in sincere repentance to God], O God of hosts, and cause thy face to shine [the light of deliverance]; and we shall be saved.

80:8 Thou hast brought a vine [Israel] out of Egypt: thou hast cast out the heathen [ejected the wicked from the promised land], and planted [Israel in the land] it.

Israel was given the land of promise and she grew and overspread the land.

80:9 Thou preparedst room before it, and didst cause it to take deep root, and it filled the land. **80:10** The hills were covered with the shadow of it, and the boughs thereof were like the goodly cedars. **80:11** She sent out her boughs unto the sea, and her branches unto the river.

Why has God corrected his vine Israel? We are corrected because we have turned away from God into many sins.

80:12 Why hast thou then broken down her hedges, so that all they which pass by the way do pluck her? **80:13** The boar [spiritually unclean sinners] out of the wood [world] doth waste it, and the wild beast [unconverted aliens] of the field doth devour it.

Oh God, remember us in our distress and save your vine, Israel [both physical and spiritual]; when they sincerely repent and turn to embrace godliness.

80:14 Return, we beseech thee, O God of hosts: look down from heaven, and behold, and visit [save] this vine [Israel]; **80:15** And the vineyard which thy right hand hath planted, and the branch that thou madest strong for thyself.

Physical and spiritual Israel will sincerely repent at the rebuke and correction of the LORD.

80:16 It is burned with fire, it is cut down: **they perish at the rebuke of thy countenance.** **80:17** Let thy hand be upon [strengthen the repentant to zealously live by every Word of God] the man of thy right hand, upon the son of man whom thou madest strong for thyself.

Preserve us from ever again turning away from God

80:18 So will not we go back from thee: quicken us, and we will call upon thy name. **80:19** Turn us again [back to God, to live by every Word of God], O LORD God of hosts, cause thy face to shine; and we shall be saved.

Psalms 81 - 90

Psalm 81

All God's faithful will ejoice in the New Moons and the Feasts of the LORD

81:1 Sing aloud unto God our strength: make a joyful noise unto the God of Jacob. **81:2** Take a psalm, and bring hither the timbrel, the pleasant harp with the psaltery.

81:3 Blow up the trumpet in the new moon, [all the New Moons of each year including the Feast of Trumpets] in the time appointed, on our solemn feast day [the Feast of Trumpets]. **81:4** For this was [made] a statute for Israel, and a law of the God of Jacob.

81:5 This he [God] ordained in Joseph for a testimony, when he [God commanded and ordained the New Moon celebrations with the first New Moon of the first month and commanded the Feasts of the LORD at Sinai.] went out through the land of Egypt [at the time that Jacob went out of Egypt; including the giving of the Word of God at Sinai]: where I heard a language that I understood not.

God delivered them from the burden of bondage in Egypt, and God has delivered us from the burden of bondage to sin: and God will yet call all humanity to himself in the main fall harvest of mankind!

81:6 I removed his shoulder from the burden [of bondage] his [the hands of the called out] hands were delivered from the pots [pots of slime for making bricks in Egypt].

As physical Israel called out for deliverance, let us also call out for deliverance from spiritual bondage. When Israel called, God answered; and when we call in sincere repentance, God will answer us with his deliverance.

81:7 Thou calledst in trouble, and I delivered thee; I answered thee in the secret place of thunder: I proved thee at the waters of Meribah. Selah.

What does God require of us? We are to obey and exalt God alone above any and all others: We must NEVER allow anyone or anything to come between us and God or to separate us from zealously living by every Word of God.

81:8 Hear, O my people, and I will testify unto thee: O Israel, if thou wilt hearken unto me; **81:9** There shall no strange god be in thee; neither shalt thou worship [obey] any strange god.

Seek out the Eternal God, hungering and thirsting after his righteousness; and love to live by every Word of God in exuberant enthusiasm; and we shall be filled.

81:10 I am the Lord thy God, which brought thee out of the land of Egypt: open thy mouth wide [to physically eat, figurative of internalizing the Word of God], and I will fill it [If we hunger and thirst after godliness, God will fill us with the righteousness of his Word].

At their appointed time all humanity will be delivered from bondage to sin; and called to come to God!

The following is true of physical Israel and it is also true of today's spiritually called out Ekklesia

81:11 But my people would not hearken to my voice; and Israel would [have nothing in God] **none of me. 81:12 So I gave them up unto their own hearts' lust: and they walked in their own counsels.**

We know the history of Physical Israel; even so the conditions in today's spiritual Ekklesia [where every one trusts in their own counsels] are at the point where we will be rejected by God the Father and Jesus Christ (Rev 3:15-22) and given over to the affliction of the flesh, so that God may perchance save the spirit and bring us to sincere repentance.

God calls on physical Israel to sincerely repent and the remnant will do so when Messiah comes; God is also calling today's spiritual Ekklesia to sincerely repent, so that God can save us in the resurrection to eternal life.

81:13 Oh that my people had hearkened unto me, and Israel had walked in my ways! **81:14** I should soon have subdued their enemies, and turned my hand against their adversaries.

The remnant will repent when Christ comes and the ancients will be resurrected back to physical life (Ezek 37) and they will eventually repent in the fall main harvest typified by the Feast of Tabernacles, and then they will run to the Mighty One of Abraham!

81:15 The haters of the LORD should have submitted themselves unto him: but their time should have endured for ever. **81:16** He should [If we will only sincerely repent and turn to live by every Word of God with a whole heart, God will feed the sincerely repentant with the sweet honey and unleavened bread of every Word of God] have fed them also with the finest of the wheat: and with honey out of the rock should I have satisfied thee.

God wants to save all humanity; and God will do so at their appointed times.

Psalm 82

May the people be like God the Just Judge in all their judgments and doings

Psalm 82:1 God standeth in the congregation of the mighty; he judgeth among the gods [mighty ones].

How long will the leaders of today's physical and spiritual Israel judge unjustly and permit living contrary to the Word of God?

82:2 How long will ye judge unjustly, and accept the persons of the wicked? Selah.

Godly judges defend the oppressed from the wicked and execute righteous judgments according to every Word of God.

82:3 Defend the poor and fatherless [godly leaders give justice to the oppressed]: do justice to the afflicted and needy. **82:4** Deliver the poor and needy: rid them out of the hand of the wicked.

Today's judges in both physical and spiritual Israel are ignorant of true godly justice

82:5 They know not, neither will they understand; they walk on in darkness: all the foundations of [justice on the earth] the earth are out of course.

God has called out some to become the spiritual children of God (Romans 8:15), yet the errant in the spiritual Ekklesia shall die without hope like all flesh; unless we turn to live by every Word of God in sincere repentance.

82:6 I have said, Ye are gods; and all of you are children of the most High. **82:7** But ye shall die like men, and fall like one of the princes.

When he comes, Messiah and those with him will judge the earth in the righteousness of every Word of God.

82:8 Arise, O God, judge the earth: for thou shalt inherit all nations.

Psalm 83

A prophecy of the latter days when the nations of Europe, Turkey, Jordan, Syria, Lebanon and the Arab States will confederate against the nations of Judah and Israel

Psalm 83:1 Keep not thou silence, O God: hold not thy peace, and be not still, O God.

David speaks about the nations seeking to destroy the nations of Israel, which is a type of the proud lifting themselves up against God to reject the Word of God and live according to their own false ways and persecute God's faithful.

83:2 For, lo, thine enemies make a tumult: and they that hate thee have lifted up the head. **83:3** They have taken crafty counsel against thy people, and consulted against thy hidden [protected faithful] ones.

83:4 They have said, Come, and let us cut them off from being a nation; that the name of Israel may be no more in remembrance [this as an allegory that the wicked also seek to destroy God's faithful].

83:5 For they have consulted together with one consent: they are confederate against thee:

83:6 The tabernacles of Edom [Turkey], and the Ishmaelites [true Arabs, sons of Ishmael; sons of Abraham and Agar]; of Moab [northern Jordan today], and the Hagarenes [Arabs who are sons of Agar by another than Abraham, and also not the sons of Ishmael];

83:7 Geba [Lebanon], and Ammon [southern Jordan today], and Amalek [a tribe of the Turks]; the Philistines [Gaza] with the inhabitants of Tyre [Lebanon];

83:8 Assur [Germany, Austria, Hungary] also is joined with them: they have holpen the children of Lot [the New Europe will help modern Jordan; Ammon and Moab].

Selah.

David prophesies that the nations who attack the Judah and Israel in these latter days will be corrected in their turn [by the men of the east]

83:9 Do unto them as unto the Midianites; as to Sisera, as to Jabin, [whose armies were slaughtered (Judges 4)] at the brook of Kison: **83:10** Which perished at Endor: they became as dung for the earth. **83:11** Make their nobles like Oreb, and like Zeeb: yea, all their princes as Zebah (Judges 8), and as Zalmunna:

God will drive away the attackers who delight in destroying; like the wind drives stubble before it and wheels roll away

83:12 Who said, Let us take to ourselves the houses of God in possession. **83:13** O my God, make them like a wheel; as the stubble before the wind.

God will destroy the armies of the New Europe and her Turkish, Jordanian, Lebanese, Syrian and Arab allies with armies from the east and consume them like a raging fire consumes its fuel.

83:14 As the fire burneth a wood, and as the flame setteth the mountains on fire;

David calls on God to correct the nations of the New Europe Babylon the Great and her Turkish, Jordanian and Arab allies, to humble them and turn them to God

83:15 So persecute them with thy tempest, and make them afraid with thy storm. **83:16** Fill their faces with shame [humble them]; that they may seek thy name, O LORD.

83:17 Let them [the wicked] be confounded and troubled for ever; yea, let them be put to shame, and perish:

83:18 That [all] men may know that thou, whose name alone is JEHOVAH [YHVH], art the most high over all the earth.

Psalm 84

The heart, mind and spirit of the righteous man longs for the things of God, he longs to be in the presence of God and to learn about the precious holy Word of God

Psalm 84:1 How amiable are thy tabernacles, O LORD of hosts! **84:2** My soul longeth, yea, even fainteth for the courts [to be in the presence] of the LORD: my heart and my flesh crieth out for the living God.

Like wondering birds, man cannot find his way to life and peace; man needs God to show him the path to peace and life.

84:3 Yea, the sparrow hath found an house, and the swallow a nest for herself, where she may lay her young, even thine altars, O LORD of hosts, my King, and my God.

Those who dwell in the presence of God will sing his praises forever; because of the awesome wonder and glorious wisdom of his ways.

84:4 Blessed are they that dwell in thy house: they will be still praising thee. Selah.

Those who are faithful to put their trust in God to live by his Word will be greatly blessed for they shall live forever through the wisdom and Word of God.

84:5 Blessed is the man whose strength is in thee; in whose heart are the ways of them.

84:6 Who passing through the valley of Baca [the valley of Bracha on the border of the promised land at the Jordan River near Jericho, a type of going down into death and then rising up to a Promised Land of eternal life on the other side of the grave] make it a well; the rain also filleth the pools.

Those who put their trust in God may have trials in this life, but they shall be resurrected to strength and eternal life if they keep on living by every Word of God.

84:7 They go from strength to strength, every one of them in Zion appeareth before God.

God will look upon the sincerely repentant to bless them, and God will hear the prayers of all those who are faithful to live by every Word of God

84:8 O LORD God of hosts, hear my prayer: give ear, O God of Jacob. Selah. **84:9** Behold, O God our shield, and look upon the face of thine anointed.

A day in the presence of God is better than a thousand days far from God. It is far better to be a humble person in the presence of God, then to have enormous riches and be beloved of men but estranged from God.

84:10 For a day in thy courts [tabernacle - temple courtyards] is better than a thousand. I had rather be a doorkeeper in the house of my God, than to dwell in the tents of wickedness.

84:11 For the LORD God is a sun [light of wisdom] and shield [a defense and protector]: the LORD will give grace and glory: no good thing will he withhold from them that walk uprightly.

84:12 O LORD of hosts, blessed is the man that trusteth in thee.

Psalm 85

Repentance and rejoicing over God's deliverance

Physical Israel will be delivered from her captivity and Spiritual Israel will be delivered from her correction; and when God's correction has brought forth the fruits of sincere repentance our sins will be forgiven.

Psalm 85:1 Lord, thou hast been favourable unto thy land: thou hast brought back the captivity of Jacob. **85:2 Thou hast forgiven the iniquity of thy people, thou hast covered all their sin.** Selah. **85:3** Thou hast taken away all thy wrath: thou hast turned thyself from the fierceness of thine anger.

Yes, LORD, turn us to you and bring us to sincere repentance even if we need correction.

85:4 Turn us, O God of our salvation, and cause thine anger toward us to cease.

God will not be angry forever neither will our correction last over long, for when God has brought us to sincere repentance he will deliver us and raise us up in his Love.

85:5 Wilt thou be angry with us for ever? wilt thou draw out thine anger to all generations? **85:6** Wilt thou not revive us again: that thy people may rejoice in thee?

When we have been corrected and humbled God will show mercy and save us; and we will hear the Word of God and we will live by every Word of God from thenceforth and forever more.

85:7 Shew us thy mercy, O LORD, and grant us thy salvation.

Then we shall be reconciled to God the Father and we will dwell in peace with God forever, never again departing into the folly of sin against our Mighty God.

85:8 I will hear what God the LORD will speak: for he will speak peace unto his people, and to his saints: but let them not turn again to folly.

Those that respect God and fear to sin against the Word of God will be blessed with eternal salvation.

85:9 Surely his salvation is nigh them that fear him; that glory may dwell in our land.

Messiah the Christ will bring truth, righteousness and peace to the earth; God's Word is Truth and God's Word is Righteousness.

The righteousness of living by every Word of God brings peace and unity between people and God and brings peace and true unity between all godly people.

85:10 Mercy and truth are met together; righteousness and peace have kissed each other. **85:11** Truth shall spring out of the earth; and righteousness shall look down from heaven. **85:12** Yea, the LORD shall give that which is good; and our land shall yield her increase. **85:13** Righteousness shall go before him; and shall set us in the way of his steps.

Psalm 86

An entreaty for God to hear our prayers

The entreaty begins with a declaration of our NEED for God and our humility before God, acknowledging that we are spiritually poor and needy of God's Righteousness; the exact opposite of today's called out spiritual Ekklesia and their pride (Rev 3:14-22).

Psalm 86:1 Bow down thine ear, O LORD, hear me: for I am poor and needy.

God will hear the plea for salvation of all those who put their trust in God to live by his Word

86:2 Preserve my soul; for I am holy: O thou my God, save thy servant that trusteth in thee. **86:3** Be merciful unto me, O Lord: for I cry unto thee daily.

God will accept and rejoice in all those who live by every Word of God and dedicate their lives to him.

86:4 Rejoice the soul of thy servant: for unto thee, O Lord, do I lift up my soul [dedicate my life].

All who live by every Word of God and put their trust in him to call on him will be delivered

86:5 For thou, Lord, art good, and ready to forgive; and plenteous in mercy unto all them that call upon thee. **86:6** Give ear, O LORD, unto my prayer; and attend to the voice of my supplications. **86:7** In the day of my trouble I will call upon thee: for thou wilt answer me. **86:8** Among the gods there is none like unto thee, O Lord; neither are there any works like unto thy works. **86:9** All nations whom thou hast made shall come and worship before thee, O Lord; and shall glorify thy name (Joel 2:32).

There is NO other God but the Family of YHVH and all nations will sincerely repent and call upon the LORD to worship [live by every Word of] God.

86:10 For thou art great, and doest wondrous things: thou art God alone.

All people must and most people will sincerely repent of going contrary to the Word of God and they will hunger and thirst to internalize and live by every Word of God (Mat 5:6).

86:11 Teach me thy way, O LORD; I will walk [we will live by God's Word] in thy truth: unite my heart to fear thy name.

If we shout praises and do not live by every Word of God we do not glorify God, we are merely paying lip-service as we rebel against Him.

We truly glorify and praise God through living by every Word of God.

86:12 I will praise thee, O Lord my God, with all my heart: and I will glorify thy name for evermore.

God's mercy is great towards the sincerely repentant, who STOP living contrary to the Word of God.

86:13 For great is thy mercy toward me: and thou hast delivered my soul from the lowest hell.

The proud reject the Word of God and they reject those who live by the Word of God, preferring their own imaginations.

86:14 O God, the proud are risen against me, and the assemblies of violent men have sought after my soul; and have not set thee before them.

The proud reject those who seek to live by every Word of God, and God rejects the proud.

God is merciful and accepts the repentant.

86:15 But thou, O Lord, art a God full of compassion, and gracious, long suffering, and plenteous in mercy and truth.

The godly welcome and even pray for God's correction to keep them in God's ways; but the proud wicked will not hear correction.

86:16 O turn unto me, and have mercy upon me; give thy strength unto thy servant, and save the son of thine handmaid.

God will do good for his faithful, resurrecting them to eternal life; the wicked will see this and be humbled.

86:17 Shew me a token for good; that they which hate me may see it, and be ashamed: because thou, LORD, hast holpen me, and comforted me.

Psalm 87

The situation of Jerusalem is in the mountains and the Temple of God is on the Holy Mount. Those who seek to be in the presence of God have a sure foundation for life eternal and peace everlasting.

Psalm 87:1 His foundation is in the holy mountains.

God loves Jerusalem, the place he has chosen; above all other places.

This is an allegory that God loves the spiritual New Covenant faithful within whom he dwells.

87:2 The LORD loveth the gates of Zion more than all the dwellings of Jacob.

Those who live in the presence of God's dwelling place in the physical millennial Jerusalem Temple are greatly blessed; and those who are the faithful spiritual house in whom God dwells trough God's Holy Spirit are even more blessed.

87:3 Glorious things are spoken of thee, O city of God. Selah.

The city of God, Jerusalem, is an allegory of the faithful to God in whom God dwells through his Holy Spirit.

87:4 I will make mention of Rahab [a term meaning prideful boaster; used for the Egypt of the exodus as a type of sin] and Babylon to them that know me: behold Philistia, and Tyre, with Ethiopia; this man was born there.

Jerusalem will be considered the great city because God's Temple and presence is there and anyone born there will be greatly blessed.

This is a type that those faithful to God in whom God's Spirit dwells will be greatly blessed, because God will resurrect and exalt them and they shall be born of God

87:5 And of Zion it shall be said, This and that man was born in her: and the highest himself shall establish her. **87:6** The LORD shall count, when he writeth up the people, that this man was born there. Selah.

87:7 As well the singers as the players on instruments shall be there: all my springs [The physical Temple is an instructional allegory that the salvational water of the Word and Spirit of God comes from God in the heavenly Jerusalem (Gal 4:26).] are in thee.

Psalm 88

A prayer of repentance

Psalm 88:1 O lord God of my salvation, I have cried day and night before thee: **88:2** Let my prayer come before thee: incline thine ear unto my cry; **88:3** For my soul is full of troubles: and my life draweth nigh unto the grave. **88:4** I am counted with them that go down into the pit [grave]: I am as a man that hath no strength [we cannot save ourselves]: **88:5** Free [in death we are free from the afflictions of life, having neither sorrows nor hope] among the dead, like the slain that lie in the grave, whom thou rememberest no more: and they are cut off from thy hand.

God corrects the pride of the sinner out of love, to bring him to sincere repentance in order to save him.

88:6 Thou hast laid [the proud must be humbled before God] me in the lowest pit, in darkness, in the deeps [to the depths of contrition].

88:7 Thy wrath lieth hard upon me, and thou hast afflicted me with all thy waves [repeated corrections]. Selah.

88:8 Thou hast put away mine acquaintance [friends and associates] far from me; thou hast made me an abomination unto them: I am shut up [isolated], and I cannot come forth.

Let us call on God in sincere repentance before we are totally destroyed

88:9 Mine eye mourneth [pours out tears] by reason of affliction: LORD, I have called daily upon thee, I have stretched out my hands unto thee.

The dead are inanimate and know nothing; therefore save us in our repentance while we still live and cry out to Thee.

> **Ecclesiastes 9:5** For the living know that they shall die: but the dead know not any thing

Psalm 88:10 Wilt thou shew wonders to the dead? shall the dead arise and praise thee? Selah. **88:11** Shall thy lovingkindness be declared in the grave? or thy faithfulness in destruction? **88:12** Shall thy wonders be known in the dark? and thy righteousness in the land of forgetfulness?

88:13 But unto thee have I cried, O LORD; and in the morning shall my prayer prevent [hasten to God; Lexicon H6923] thee.

We must ASK God to reveal and teach us why he corrects us

88:14 LORD, why castest thou off my soul? why hidest thou thy face from me?

88:15 I am afflicted and ready to die from my youth up: while I suffer thy terrors I am distracted. **88:16** Thy fierce wrath goeth over me; thy terrors have cut me off. **88:17** They came round about me daily like water; they compassed me about together.

88:18 Lover and friend hast thou put far from me, and mine acquaintance into darkness.

Psalm 89

A song of praise for the wondrous mercy of God

This Psalm is a lesson for us that the spiritually called out also have the promise of eternal life and an eternal kingdom; **if we persevere and faint not in all our distresses,** which are allowed for our own good to make of us the people that God wants us to be.

Psalm 89:1 I will sing of the mercies of the LORD for ever: with my mouth will I make known thy faithfulness to all generations.

89:2 For I have said [God promises], Mercy shall be built up [mercy for the faithful who repent of their mistakes will continue and increase] for ever: thy faithfulness shalt thou establish in the very heavens.

YHVH's covenant with David is that David would be in the resurrection of the faithful and would be king over a united Israel forever; just as the spiritually called out will also inherit eternal life and an eternal kingdom if we persevere and learn from God's corrections.

89:3 I have made a covenant with my chosen, I have sworn unto David my servant, **89:4** Thy seed will I establish for ever, and build up thy throne to all generations. Selah.

The LORD [the YHVH family is greater than anything else in the earth and in heaven

89:5 And the heavens [the holy angels and all that is in heaven] shall praise thy wonders, O LORD: thy faithfulness also in the congregation of the saints. **89:6** For who in the heaven can be compared unto the LORD? who among the sons of the mighty can be likened unto the LORD?

Those who respect God enough to live by every Word of God shall be covered by God's mercy and saved by His strength.

89:7 God is greatly to be feared in the assembly of the saints, and to be had in reverence of all them that are about him. **89:8** O LORD God of hosts, who is a strong LORD like unto thee? or to thy faithfulness round about thee? **89:9** Thou rulest the raging of the sea: when the waves thereof arise, thou stillest them.

89:10 Thou hast broken Rahab [a term meaning prideful boaster; used for the Egypt of the exodus as a type of sin; Strong's 7294] in pieces, as one that is slain; thou hast scattered thine enemies with thy strong arm.

The YHVH family created all things on earth and in the heavens; they belong to God!

89:11 The heavens are thine, the earth also is thine: as for the world and the fulness thereof, thou hast founded them. **89:12** The north and the south thou hast created them: Tabor and Hermon shall rejoice in thy name.

89:13 Thou hast a mighty arm: strong is thy hand, and high is thy right hand. **89:14** Justice and judgment are the habitation of thy throne: mercy and truth shall go before thy face.

Every Word of God is wise and just and all those who live by every Word of God will ultimately be greatly blessed.

In this world Satan hates the Word of God and burdens and persecutes all those zealous to live by every Word of God, but in the end Satan will be destroyed and the persevering godly shall be greatly blessed.

It is not God's Word that is difficult, it is Satan's attacks that make it seem difficult!

89:15 Blessed is the people that know the joyful sound [of deliverance and the teaching of the Word of God]: they shall walk [live], O LORD, in the light of thy countenance [a poetic way of saying that the righteous will live in the presence of God and they will live by the light of every Word of God].

89:16 In thy name shall they [the godly] rejoice all the day: and in thy righteousness [which is every Word of God] shall they be exalted. **89:17** For thou art the glory of their strength: and in thy favour our horn shall be exalted. **89:18** For the LORD is our defence; and the Holy One of Israel is our king.

Now David reminds God of God's promises to David; and the spiritually called out have similar promises.

89:19 Then thou spakest in vision to thy holy one, [prophet Samuel] and saidst, I have laid help upon one that is mighty [to serve God]; I have exalted one chosen out of the people. **89:20 I have found David my servant; with my holy oil have I anointed him: 89:21** With whom my hand shall be established: mine arm also shall strengthen him.

God promises David and similarly every person who is faithful to live by every Word of God: a place in the coming resurrection to eternal life.

89:22 The enemy shall not exact upon him; nor the son of wickedness afflict him. **89:23** And I will beat down his foes before his face, and plague them that hate him.

David shall have mercy and he will be resurrected to eternal life as king over a united and repentant Israel forever; just as other faithful called out persons who overcome and remain faithful, will also be resurrected to eternal life and receive a good reward.

89:24 But my faithfulness and my mercy shall be with him [and with all those who are similarly repentant and faithful to live by every Word of God]: and in my name shall his horn be exalted.

David's future kingdom will stretch from the Mediterranean Sea to the rivers [the river of Egypt in Sinai the El Arish, and the Euphrates].

89:25 I will set his hand also in the sea, and his right hand in the rivers.

David will be utterly faithful to God forever and he shall rule a united repentant Israel forever; and the other resurrected faithful will also live forever and they will have a good reward.

89:26 He shall cry unto me, Thou art my father, my God, and the rock of my salvation. **89:27** Also I will make him my firstborn, higher than the kings of the earth. **89:28** My mercy will I keep for him for evermore, and my covenant shall stand fast with him. **89:29** His seed also will I make to endure for ever, and his throne as the days of heaven.

Because David made his mistakes but was quick to repent with a whole heart, God will not withhold correction but will correct and save David and his descendants.

Likewise God will not withhold correction from his spiritually called out so that we also may be corrected to sincere repentance and saved.

9:30 If his children forsake my law, and walk not in my judgments; **89:31** If they break my statutes, and keep not my commandments; **89:32** Then will I visit their transgression with the rod, and their iniquity with stripes.

89:33 Nevertheless my lovingkindness will I not utterly take from him, nor suffer my faithfulness to fail. **89:34** My covenant will I not break, nor alter the thing that is gone out of my lips. **89:35** Once have I sworn by my holiness that I will not lie unto David.

David's throne will last forever; this is referring to the resurrection of David and his eternal kingship over Israel.

89:36 His seed shall endure for ever, and his throne as the sun before me. **89:37** It shall be established for ever as the moon, and as a faithful witness in heaven. Selah.

After remembering God's promises, David begins to rehearse his distress

89:38 But thou hast cast off and abhorred, thou hast been wroth with thine anointed. **89:39** Thou hast made void the covenant of thy servant: thou hast profaned his crown by casting it to the ground. **89:40** Thou hast broken down all his hedges; thou hast brought his strong holds to ruin. **89:41** All that pass by the way spoil him: he is a reproach to his neighbours. **89:42** Thou hast set up the right hand of his adversaries; thou hast made all his enemies to rejoice.

89:43 Thou hast also turned the edge of his sword, and hast not made him to stand in the battle. **89:44** Thou hast made his glory to cease, and cast his throne down to the ground. **89:45** The days of his youth hast thou shortened: thou hast covered him with shame. Selah.

David asks God for deliverance

89:46 How long, LORD? wilt thou hide thyself for ever? shall thy wrath burn like fire? **89:47** Remember how short my time is: wherefore hast thou made all men in vain? **89:48** What man is he that liveth, and shall not see death? shall he deliver his soul from the hand of the grave? Selah. **89:49** Lord, where are thy former lovingkindnesses, which thou swarest unto David in thy truth?

David asks God to remember and to deliver him.

This is a lesson for us that the spiritually called out also have the promise of eternal life and an eternal kingdom; if we persevere and faint not in all our distresses, which distresses are allowed for our own good to make of us the people that God wants us to be.

89:50 Remember, Lord, the reproach of thy servants; how I do bear in my bosom the reproach of all the mighty people; **89:51** Wherewith thine enemies have reproached, O LORD; wherewith they have reproached the footsteps of thine anointed.

89:52 Blessed be the LORD for evermore. Amen, and Amen.

Psalm 90

The LORD has lived through all the generations of man, indeed the LORD was before man existed and God created all that is.

Psalm 90:1 Lord, thou hast been our dwelling place in all generations. **90:2** Before the mountains were brought forth, or ever thou hadst formed the earth and the world, even from everlasting to everlasting, thou art God.

All flesh is born and all flesh dies and returns to the earth but God lives forever.

90:3 Thou turnest man to destruction; and sayest, Return [to dust], ye children of men.

The Eternal God lives forever.

90:4 For a thousand years in thy sight are but as yesterday when it is past, and as a watch in the night.

> **2 Peter 3:8** But, beloved, be not ignorant of this one thing, that one day is with the Lord as a thousand years, and a thousand years as one day.

Men grow like the grass and flowers, lasting for a short time and then passing away.

Psalm 90:5 Thou carriest them away as with a flood; they are as a sleep: in the morning they are like grass which groweth up. **90:6** In the morning it flourisheth, and groweth up; in the evening it is cut down, and withereth.

Carnal man is hostile to the Word of God; unconverted physical humanity cannot understand the things of God and is doomed to death and the grave.

Romans 8:7 Because the carnal mind is enmity against God: for it is not subject to the law of God, neither indeed can be.

The human mind rebels against the Word of God which brings life; and man dies as a result of rejecting the way to life.

Psalm 90:7 For we are consumed by thine anger, and by thy wrath are we troubled.

God knows our every sin and he knows all our rebellions against the way to life.

90:8 Thou hast set our iniquities before thee, our secret sins in the light of thy countenance. **90:9** For all our days are passed away in [we live in bondage to sin and we are doomed to everlasting death, unless God saves us] thy wrath: we spend our years as a tale that is told.

90:10 The days of our years are threescore years and ten [70 years]; and if by reason of strength they be fourscore [80] years, yet is their strength [our years are full of sorrows] labour and sorrow; for it is soon cut off, and we fly away.

God's power and his anger at sin has been recorded in a true record throughout the scriptures, and the wrath of God the Father and Jesus Christ at our refusal to live by every Word of God is very real.

God corrected Israel and Judah many times for not living by the Word of God and he will do so again.

90:11 Who knoweth the power of thine anger? even according to thy fear [awesome reputation], so is thy wrath.

Instead of relying on our own ways and the traditions of men which bring death; we ought to seek life and righteousness from God and we should live by every Word of God in Christ-like zeal.

90:12 So teach us to number our days, that we may apply our hearts unto wisdom [God's Word is Wisdom].

A prayer of repentance and plea for God's mercy

90:13 Return, O LORD, how long? and let it repent thee concerning thy servants. **90:14** O satisfy us early with thy mercy; that we may rejoice and be glad all our days.

When God's correction has brought us to repentance, we will be glad that we were corrected and been turned back to God and saved from eternal death.

90:15 Make us glad according to the days wherein thou hast afflicted us, and the years wherein we have seen evil.

May God's correction of our wickedness bear the bountiful fruit of sincere repentance.

90:16 Let thy work appear unto thy servants, and thy glory unto their children.

The correction and affliction of the flesh is intended to save us spiritually to eternal life.

90:17 And let the beauty of the LORD our God be upon us: and establish thou the work of our hands upon us; yea, the work of our hands establish thou it.

Psalms 91 – 100

Psalm 91

This is a prophecy of Jesus Christ in the flesh, and also for us if we follow Christ's example of passionate zeal to live every Word of God the Father.

If we - like Jesus did - put our trust in the Almighty to live by every Word of God; God the Father himself will be our refuge and deliverer from the grave and death, and we shall live forever with him.

Psalm 91:1 He that dwelleth in the secret [Most Holy Place] place of the most High shall abide under the shadow of the Almighty. **91:2** I will say of **the LORD, He is my refuge and my fortress: my God; in him will I trust. 91:3** Surely he shall deliver thee from the snare [which snare is sin] of the fowler [Satan], and from the noisome pestilence [death].

91:4 He shall cover thee with his feathers [poetic for God's protection], and under his wings shalt thou trust: his truth [God's Word is Truth] shall be thy shield and buckler.

If we put our trust in God to live by every Word of God we need not fear death or the grave because our Mighty God will deliver his faithful from death to eternal life.

91:5 Thou shalt not be afraid for the terror by night; nor for the arrow that flieth by day; **91:6** Nor for the pestilence that walketh in darkness; nor for the destruction that wasteth at noonday.

Poetically speaking of the second death, even if we see thousands of wicked people fall around us, the faithful to live by every Word of God will live forever.

91:7 A thousand shall fall at thy side, and ten thousand at thy right hand; but it [death] shall not come nigh thee. **91:8** Only with thine eyes shalt thou behold and see the reward of the wicked.

The faithful to live by every Word of God shall be delivered from death to eternal life, while the unrepentant wicked will perish.

A prophecy of Jesus Christ

91:9 Because thou hast made the LORD, which is my refuge, even the most High, thy habitation; **91:10** There shall no evil befall thee, neither shall any plague come nigh thy dwelling.

91:11 For he shall give his angels charge over thee, to keep thee in all thy ways. **91:12** They shall bear thee up in their hands, lest thou dash thy foot against a stone. **91:13** Thou shalt tread upon the lion and adder: the young lion and the dragon shalt thou trample under feet.

91:14 Because he hath set his love upon me, therefore will I [God the Father] deliver him: I will set him on high, because he hath known my name.

91:15 He shall call upon me, and I will answer him: I will be with him in trouble; I will deliver him, and honour him.

Jesus Christ was resurrected to eternal life as the first born of many more, who will also be resurrected to eternal life for their zeal faithful to live by every Word of God the Father.

91:16 With long life will I satisfy him, and shew him my salvation.

Psalm 92

A prophecy of the resurrection of Jesus Christ as the first of many

It is good to rejoice in the mighty deeds of deliverance of our God for his beloved faithful.

Psalm 92:1 It is a good thing to give thanks unto the LORD, and to sing praises unto thy name O MOST HIGH: **92:2** To shew forth thy lovingkindness in the morning, and thy faithfulness every night, **92:3** Upon an instrument of ten strings, and upon the psaltery; upon the harp with a solemn sound.

92:4 For thou, LORD, hast made me glad through thy work [of salvation and resurrection]: I will triumph [over sin and death] in the works of thy hands [by the power of God]. **92:5** O LORD, how great are thy works! and thy thoughts are very deep.

Carnal minds cannot even begin to understand the wisdom and works of God, the unrepentant wicked flourish only for a moment and will then perish forever

92:6 A brutish man knoweth not; neither doth a fool understand this. **92:7** When the wicked spring as the grass, and when all the workers of iniquity do flourish; it is that they shall be destroyed for ever:

God is from everlasting and those who delight in the righteousness of every Word of God shall live forever.

92:8 But thou, LORD, art most high for evermore.

The unrepentant wicked will perish in their sins, but those who delight to live by every Word of God will live forever.

92:9 For, lo, thine enemies, O LORD, for, lo, thine enemies shall perish; all the workers of iniquity shall be scattered.

92:10 But my horn [strength, life] shalt thou exalt like the horn of an unicorn: I shall be anointed with fresh oil [a type of the Holy Spirit].

92:11 Mine eye also shall see my desire on mine enemies [Satan and sin], and mine ears shall hear my desire [that all wickedness is at an end] of the wicked that rise up against me.

The LORD the Righteous, will bless his faithful with eternal life, peace and all good things in the resurrection.

92:12 The righteous shall flourish like the palm tree: he shall grow like a cedar in Lebanon. **92:13** Those that be planted in the house of the LORD shall flourish in the courts [presence] of our God. **92:14** They shall still bring forth fruit in old age; they shall be fat [blessed] and flourishing;

92:15 To shew that the LORD is upright: he is my rock, and there is no unrighteousness in him.

Psalm 93

God the Father rules from heaven and on a soon coming Feast of Pentecost Messiah the Christ will establish the Kingdom of God over all the earth.

God the Father and the one who gave up his God-hood to become flesh and was resurrected back to his former glory, are the present two members of the YHVH family of Elohim.

Psalm 93:1 The LORD [YHVH] reigneth [God the Father rules from heaven and the Son will be King of kings ruling all nations from Jerusalem], he is clothed with majesty; the LORD is clothed with strength, wherewith he hath girded himself: the world also is stablished, that it cannot be moved.

93:2 Thy throne is established of old: thou art from everlasting.

Many waters are an allegory of all nations who will lift up their voice in rejoicing and praise of God when they are delivered from bondage to Satan and sin.

> **Revelation 17:15** And he saith unto me, The waters which thou sawest, where the whore sitteth, are peoples, and multitudes, and nations, and tongues.

Psalm 93:3 The floods have lifted up, O LORD, the floods have lifted up their voice; the floods lift up their waves.

93:4 The LORD on high is mightier than [all peoples] the noise of many waters, yea, than the mighty waves of the sea.

Every Word of God is pure and holy and true

> **Romans 7:12** Wherefore the law is holy, and the commandment holy, and just, and good.

God's people are to be set apart from worldliness to live by every Word of God.

> **John 17:17** Sanctify them [living by every Word of God will set us apart from sin] through thy truth: thy word is truth.

Psalm 93:5 Thy testimonies are very sure [God's Word is everlasting]: holiness becometh thine house, O LORD, for ever.

Psalm 94

Psalm 94 speaks of the actions of the wicked and God's ultimate deliverance of the sincerely repentant.

When it speaks of wicked people, we must realize that such people are inspired by that ultimate source of evil, Satan the Adversary of God.

Most wicked people are deceived and being used by that ultimate wicked being, who is the one which will ultimately be totally destroyed; while the vast majority of evil people will ultimately sincerely repent and be saved.

We are not to seek our own revenge; it is up to God to make a final judgment.

Psalm 94:1 O Lord God, to whom vengeance belongeth; O God, to whom vengeance belongeth, shew thyself.

Let us call upon our God in sincere repentance; calling on Him for our deliverance, this is also a specific prophecy of the people calling for Messiah to come and deliver them from their affliction during the tribulation.

94:2 Lift up thyself, thou judge [the King of kings will come to the earth and will rule in justice] of the earth: render a reward to [to correct the proud who live in their own wicked ways] the proud.

94:3 LORD, how long shall the wicked, how long shall the wicked triumph? **94:4** How long shall they utter and speak hard things? and all the workers of iniquity boast themselves? **94:5** They break in pieces thy people, O LORD, and afflict thine heritage. **94:6** They slay the widow and the stranger, and murder the fatherless.

This is about the wicked afflicting the truly faithful of God in all ages, but is specifically a prophecy of the tribulation just before the coming of Messiah the Christ to judge [rule] the earth.

94:7 Yet they [the wicked will] say, The LORD shall not see, neither shall the God of Jacob regard it [what we do].

God knows the minds of all men and he will chastise the evil doers and will deliver the sincerely repentant who become zealous to live by every Word of God.

94:8 Understand, ye brutish [those who will not live by God's Word] among the people: and ye fools, when will ye be wise? **94:9** He that planted [created] the ear, shall he not hear? he that formed the eye, shall he not see [the wicked things we do]? **94:10** He that chastiseth the heathen [the unconverted], shall not he correct [those God has called out to live by His Word]? he that teacheth man knowledge, shall not he know [the ultimate source of truth and knowledge knows what men do]? **94:11** The LORD knoweth the thoughts of man, that they are vanity [wickedness bringing death].

Speaking of the people that God chastens by afflicting the flesh to save the spirit, such people are indeed blessed if they accept their chastisement (Heb 12:6-8) and turn to live by every Word of God their Father. Those who sincerely repent and turn to the Eternal will be greatly blessed.

94:12 Blessed is the man whom thou chastenest, O LORD, and teachest him out of thy law; **94:13** That thou mayest give him rest from the days of adversity, until the pit be digged for the wicked.

> **Hebrews 12:6** For whom the Lord loveth he chasteneth, and scourgeth every son whom he receiveth. **12:7** If ye endure chastening, God dealeth with you as with sons; for what son is he whom the father chasteneth not? **12:8** But if ye be without chastisement, whereof all are partakers, then are ye bastards, and not sons.

When we sincerely repent and turn to the Eternal he will remember us and deliver us. This is a prophecy about the coming of Messiah to deliver humanity after the trial of affliction that is to come upon all the earth.

Psalm 94:14 For the LORD will not cast off his people [those who love God enough to live by every Word of God], neither will he forsake his inheritance. **94:15** But judgment [correction] shall [shall bring repentance and godly righteousness] return unto righteousness: and all the upright in heart shall follow it.

It is God the Eternal who will deliver the sincerely repentant who turn to the righteousness of living by every Word of God

94:16 Who will rise up for me against the evildoers? or who will stand up for me against the workers of iniquity? **94:17** Unless the LORD had been my help, my soul had almost dwelt in silence.

When we unintentionally slip, our Maker will deliver us if we acknowledge our sin and call out to God.

94:18 When I said, My foot slippeth; thy mercy, O LORD, held me up.

The zealous people of God find comfort in thinking on and living by every Word of God.

94:19 In the multitude of my thoughts within me thy comforts delight my soul.

God will have nothing to do with iniquity and the unrepentant wicked, and neither should the godly except by necessity of living on this earth.

> **1 Corinthians 5:9** I wrote unto you in an epistle not to company with fornicators: **5:10** Yet not altogether with the fornicators of this world, or with the covetous, or extortioners, or with idolaters; for then must ye needs go out of the world. **5:11** But now I have written unto you not to keep company, if any man that is called a brother be a fornicator, or covetous, or an idolator, or a railer, or a drunkard, or an extortioner; with such an one no not to eat.

Psalm 94:20 Shall the throne of iniquity have fellowship with thee, which frameth mischief by a law?

The wicked despise and persecute the godly righteous, but the Eternal delivers the faithful. This is a prophecy about Messiah delivering the sincerely repentant in the resurrection to spirit at His coming.

94:21 They [the wicked who will not live by every Word of God] gather themselves together against the soul [life] of the righteous [those who do live by every Word of God], and condemn the innocent blood.

Messiah the Christ will defend God's people and will raise them up when he comes.

94:22 But the LORD is my defence; and my God is the rock of my refuge.

The unrepentant wicked will be cut off

94:23 And he shall bring upon them their own iniquity, and shall cut them off in their own wickedness; yea, the LORD our God shall cut them off.

Psalm 95

Psalm 95 is a song of praise and joy over the deliverance of those who have turned in sincere repentance to live by every Word of God.

This song is about standing in the presence of the Eternal, but is also a prophecy about the literal coming of Christ to deliver the people and to rule all nations as King of kings and Lord of all lords. At that time the ultimate source of evil will be removed for one thousand years and all remaining people will repent, then God's Spirit will be poured out on all flesh (Joel 2:28).

After Christ comes and builds the Ezekiel Temple, all nations will come into his presence with great rejoicing because he has bound Satan and saved humanity and he will teach all humanity the Righteousness of the Word of God to eternal salvation (Is 11:10, 42:1-6, 49:6. 60:3-5).

Psalm 95:1 O come, let us sing unto the LORD: let us make a joyful noise to the rock of our salvation. **95:2** Let us come before his presence with thanksgiving, and make a joyful noise unto him with psalms.

Messiah the Christ together with God the Father is above all gods including that would be god, Satan himself.

The greatness of God

95:3 For the LORD is a great God, and a great King above all gods. **95:4** In his hand [control] are the deep places of the earth: the strength of the hills is his also. **95:5** The sea is his, and he made it: and his hands formed the dry land.

If we will only hear and live by every Word of God, we shall receive God's deliverance and inherit all good things.

95:6 O come, let us worship and bow down: let us kneel before the LORD our maker. **95:7** For he is our God; and we are the people of his pasture, and the sheep of his hand. To day if ye will hear his voice,

Those who resist the Word of God, refusing to obey and live by every Word of God, and insisting on doing whatever seems right in their own eyes; will not enter into the Promised Land of eternal life.

95:8 Harden not your heart, as in the provocation, and as in the day of temptation in the wilderness: **95:9** When your fathers tempted me, proved me, and saw my work. **95:10** Forty years long was I grieved with this generation, and said, It is a people that do err in their heart, and they have not known my ways: **95:11** Unto whom I sware in my wrath that **they should not enter into my rest**.

Psalm 96

A true New World Order will begin with the coming of Christ.

Both physical and spiritual Israel will be delivered and the Word of God will be opened up to all nations and peoples. God's Spirit will be poured out on all flesh on the Feast of Pentecost (Joel 2:28), and all who call on the LORD will be saved

> **Joel 2:32** And it shall come to pass, that **whosoever shall call on the name of the Lord shall be delivered: for in mount Zion and in Jerusalem shall be deliverance**, as the Lord hath said, and in the remnant [all those who survive the tribulation will be called to God] whom the Lord shall call.

Psalm 96:1 O sing unto the LORD a new song: sing unto the LORD, all the earth. **96:2** Sing unto the LORD, bless his name; shew forth his salvation [we receive salvation from bondage to sin through sincere repentance, the application of the sacrifice of Christ and then going forward to live by every Word of God] from day to day.

96:3 Declare his glory among the heathen [the unconverted], **his wonders among all people.**

96:4 For the LORD is great, and greatly to be praised: he is to be feared above all gods. **96:5** For all the gods of the nations are idols: but the LORD made the heavens. **96:6** Honour and majesty are before him: strength and beauty are in his sanctuary.

All nations and peoples will be called to God the Father when Messiah the Christ comes

96:7 Give unto the LORD, O ye kindreds of the people, give unto the LORD glory and strength. **96:8** Give unto the LORD the glory due unto his name: bring an offering, and come into his courts. **96:9** O worship the LORD in the beauty of holiness: fear before him, all the earth.

96:10 Say among the heathen that the LORD reigneth [over all the earth]: the world [the worldwide Kingdom of God] also shall be established that it shall not be moved: he shall judge the people righteously.

96:11 Let the heavens rejoice, and let the earth be glad; let the sea roar, and the fulness thereof. **96:12** Let the field be joyful, and all that is therein: then shall all the trees of the wood rejoice

96:13 Before the LORD: for he cometh, for he cometh to judge [rule, govern] the earth: he shall judge the world with righteousness, and the people with his truth [God's Word is truth].

John 17:17 Sanctify them through thy truth: thy word is truth

Psalm 97

The Kingdom of God will be established and on a future Feast of Shavuot or Pentecost the New Covenant will be extended to all humanity; and Messiah the Christ shall rule all nations as King of kings and Lord of all lords.

Psalm 97:1 The LORD reigneth; let the earth rejoice; let the multitude of isles be glad thereof.

At his coming the earth will tremble, and when his throne and Kingdom are established; on the Feast of Pentecost, God's Spirit will be poured out on all flesh (Joel 2:28) and all people shall rejoice.

97:2 Clouds and darkness are round about him: righteousness and judgment are the habitation of his throne. **97:3** A fire goeth before him, and burneth up his enemies round about. **97:4** His lightnings enlightened the world: the earth saw, and trembled. **97:5** The hills melted like wax at the presence of the LORD, at the presence of the Lord of the whole earth.

The glory of the Lord

97:6 The heavens declare his righteousness, and all the people see his glory.

Those who trust in their own ways and idols of wood and stone or idols of men, and will be confounded and brought to humble contrition; and all people will worship the Eternal.

97:7 Confounded be all they that serve graven images, that boast themselves of idols: worship him, all ye gods.

All physical and spiritual Israel will rejoice in Messiah the King, and all nations will be humbled before God.

97:8 Zion heard, and was glad; and the daughters of Judah rejoiced because of thy judgments, O LORD. **97:9** For thou, LORD [YHVH both Messiah the Christ and God the Father], art high above all the earth: thou [YHVH both Messiah the Christ and God the Father] art exalted far above all gods.

A good understanding and God's ultimate deliverance is given to all those who hate and loathe all evil; and love, follow and live by every Word of God.

97:10 Ye that love the LORD, hate evil: he preserveth the souls of his saints; he delivereth them out of the hand of the wicked. **97:11** Light is sown for the righteous, and gladness for the upright in heart.

True godly righteousness is living by every Word of God

97:12 Rejoice in the LORD, ye righteous; and give thanks at the remembrance of his holiness.

Psalm 98

A song for joy that Messiah has come and established the Kingdom of God as King of kings over all nations

First Christ saved men by being made flesh and giving his life for the sincerely repented sins of humanity; then he saves Israel and all humanity from destruction by coming with his resurrected chosen and destroying the destroyers of the earth.

When Christ comes in his power all nations will see and quickly turn to the righteousness of living by every Word of God and a New World Order of righteousness will be born.

Psalm 98:1 O sing unto the LORD a new song; for he hath done marvellous things: his right hand, and his holy arm, hath gotten him the victory.

Messiah the Christ will teach the only way to salvation which is sincere repentance, the application of Christ's sacrifice and embracing the righteousness of living by every Word of God.

98:2 The LORD hath made known his salvation: his righteousness hath he openly shewed in the sight of the heathen.

After their correction all Israel [both physical and spiritual] will sincerely repent and God will pour out his mercy on them and then on all humanity to the ends of the earth

98:3 He hath remembered his mercy and his truth toward the house of Israel: all the ends of the earth have seen the salvation of our God.

Let every mouth rejoice and every person sing, because repentance and eternal salvation is opened to all then living humanity! and will be opened up to all who have ever lived in due time!

98:4 Make a joyful noise unto the LORD, all the earth: make a loud noise, and rejoice, and sing praise. **98:5** Sing unto the LORD with the harp; with the harp, and the voice of a psalm. **98:6** With trumpets and sound of cornet make a joyful noise before the LORD, the King.

Let every breath be employed in rejoicing over the salvation of the LORD, let the earth herself rejoice for the time of her decay is past and her desolate places will flourish!

98:7 Let the sea roar, and the fulness thereof; the world, and they that dwell therein. **98:8** Let the floods clap their hands: let the hills be joyful together

May God speed the day!

98:9 Before **the LORD; for he cometh to judge the earth: with righteousness shall he judge the world, and the people with equity.**

Psalm 99

Let every mouth rejoice for the God of Moses and Aaron is coming to reign over the earth from Jerusalem!

Let all flesh rejoice and praise God that Messiah comes and he shall reign over all the earth in godly justice as King of kings. His mighty power will be employed to do justice, to teach all people to live by every Word of God and to extend eternal salvation to a repentant humanity.

Psalm 99:1 The LORD reigneth; let the people tremble: he sitteth between the cherubims; let the earth be moved. **99:2** The LORD is great in Zion;

and he is high above all the people. **99:3** Let them praise thy great and terrible name; for it is holy.

99:4 The king's [Messiah the King of kings] strength [will be employed to do justice] also loveth judgment; thou dost establish equity, thou executest judgment and righteousness in Jacob.

99:5 Exalt ye the LORD our God, and worship at his footstool [the earth is God's footstool (Isaiah 66:1) and all the earth shall obey the Father and the Son]; for he is holy.

The Messiah the Christ [and God the Father] is YHVH on whom Moses, Aaron and Samuel called, and they will serve God the Father and Christ again in the resurrection

99:6 Moses and Aaron among his priests, and Samuel among them that call upon his name; they called upon the LORD, and he answered them.

The YHVH who led Israel in the cloud and in the fire is the very Messiah the Christ who gave up his God-hood to become flesh as Jesus Christ and die in effectual sacrifice for the repented sins of humanity; he has been resurrected back to spirit and he will come to the earth to rule all nations as King of kings.

He is well deserving of being King over humanity because he gave up his God-hood to become flesh, sacrificing himself for the sins of humanity, and he was then resurrected and returned to his past glory.

99:7 He spake unto them in the cloudy pillar: they kept his testimonies, and the ordinance that he gave them.

The Being who became Jesus Christ corrects those who follow ways contrary to the Word of God, but he forgives the sincerely repentant.

99:8 Thou answeredst them, O LORD our God: thou wast a God that forgavest them, though thou tookest vengeance of their inventions.

99:9 Exalt the LORD our God, and worship [exalt and obey] at his holy hill [the Temple; the place of God's presence]; for the LORD our God is holy.

Psalm 100

Almost all nations and people will sincerely repent and greatly rejoice, entering into eternal life in the family of God; serving God through living by every Word of God.

Psalm 100:1 Make a joyful noise unto the LORD, all ye lands. **100:2** Serve the LORD with gladness: come before his presence with singing.

The eternal YHVH family has made us and is God alone, and is to be exalted and obeyed forever. We are to follow NO other; we are to live by every Word of God the Father!

100:3 Know ye that the LORD he is God: it is he that hath made us, and not we ourselves; we are his people, and the sheep of his pasture.

100:4 Enter into his gates [His household, His family] with thanksgiving, and into his courts [presence] with praise: be thankful unto him [for creating us and for saving us to eternal life], and bless his name.

God is merciful to all those who turn to God in sincere repentance; to STOP all sin and to live by every Word of God.

100:5 For the LORD is good; his mercy is everlasting; and his truth endureth to all generations.

Psalms 101 - 110

Psalm 101

The people will sing for joy because Messiah the Christ will teach the truth and judgment of every Word of God the Father and will teach us of his mercy for the sincerely repentant.

Psalm 101:1 I will sing of mercy and judgment: unto thee, O LORD, will I sing.

We are to commit ourselves to live by every Word of God just as Christ did and does.

101:2 I will behave myself wisely in a perfect way [the ways of the Word of God]. O when wilt thou come unto me? I will walk [live] within my house with a perfect [perfect in living by every Word of God the Father] heart.

Neither David nor Christ coveted to do evil contrary to the Word of God. Yes David slipped occasionally but he also quickly repented; it is Jesus Christ who never slipped who is our example in godliness.

101:3 I will set no wicked thing before mine eyes: I hate the work [deeds] of them that turn aside [turn away from God's Word]; it [the godly will have no part in sin against the Word of God] shall not cleave to me.

101:4 A froward [stubborn, self-willed] heart shall depart from me: I will not know [be a friend of wickedness] a wicked person.

Telling the truth openly is not slander; telling lies is slander.

101:5 Whoso privily [secretly speaks lies] slandereth his neighbour, him will I cut off: [Jesus Christ will not tolerate those full of pridr in their own ways] him that hath an high look and a proud heart will not I suffer.

101:6 Mine eyes shall be upon the faithful [to live by every Word of God] of the land, that they may dwell with me: he that walketh in a perfect way [lives by every Word of God], he shall serve me [God the Father and Jesus Christ].

It is very common in today's spiritual Ekklesia to take a small bit of truth out of its context and then spin it to mean the opposite of what it really meant in its complete context. That is LYING and it is deception which Jesus Christ and God the Father HATE!

101:7 He that worketh deceit shall not dwell within my house: he that telleth lies shall not tarry in my sight.

When Christ comes he will destroy all unrepentant transgressors of the Word of God.

101:8 I will early destroy all the wicked of the land; that I may cut off all wicked doers from the city of the LORD.

Psalm 102

A prayer of repentance in great tribulation

Correction of the flesh brings sorrow over sin unto sincere repentance, which brings deliverance to the spirit.

Psalm 102:1 Hear my prayer, O LORD, and let my cry come unto thee. **102:2** Hide not thy face from me in the day when I am in trouble; incline thine ear unto me: in the day when I call answer me speedily. **102:3** For my days are consumed [dissipate] like smoke, and my bones are burned as [in the fire] an hearth.

102:4 My heart is smitten [our pride must be broken to contrition], and withered like grass; so that I forget to eat my bread [we are to fast for sorrow and heaviness of spirit in sincere repentance over our sins]. **102:5** By reason of the voice of my groaning my bones cleave to my skin.

Those separated from God by their sins, are alone and wondering like a bird in the wilderness.

102:6 I am like a pelican of the wilderness: I am like an owl of the desert. **102:7** I watch, and am as a sparrow alone upon the house top.

Our enemies mock us because we are afflicted for our sins.

102:8 Mine enemies reproach me all the day; and they that are mad against me are sworn against me. **102:9** For I have eaten ashes [the sinful partake of affliction like daily eating until they sincerely repent] like bread, and mingled my drink with weeping.

God called us and lifted us up from bondage to sin, and God casts us back down and afflicts us when we turn away from him to sin against His Word.

102:10 Because of thine indignation and thy wrath: for thou hast lifted me up, and cast me down.

102:11 My days are like a shadow that declineth [my life is fading and withering away because of my sins]; and I am withered like grass.

David learns that man is but flesh which is temporary and passing; while God and the Word of God are forever and forever.

102:12 But thou, O LORD, shall endure for ever; and thy remembrance unto all generations.

God will have mercy on the sincerely repentant who turn to live by every Word of God

102:13 Thou shalt arise, and have mercy upon Zion [the Temple is a type of the people of God who seek to sincerely repent and live by every Word of God]: for the time [for the coming of Christ's coming is at hand] to favour her [Jerusalem and the people of God], yea, the set time, is come.

The true servants of God love his presence among them; they will love Jerusalem because the Temple of God the Father will be there and Messiah the Christ will rule all nations from Jerusalem.

102:14 For thy servants take pleasure in her stones, and favour the dust thereof.

When Christ comes all nations will sincerely repent, to serve and live by every Word of God.

102:15 So the heathen shall fear the name of the LORD, and all the kings of the earth thy glory.

When Christ comes as King of kings with his chosen, he will be glorified in all the earth.

102:16 When the LORD shall build up Zion, he shall appear in his glory.

Then God will regard the prayers of the sincerely repentant who acknowledge that they are spiritually destitute and in need of God.

102:17 He will regard the prayer of the destitute [poor in the spirit of pride and self-will], and not despise their prayer.

When Christ comes in his glory the story will be told from generation to generation.

102:18 This shall be written for the generation to come: and the people which shall be created shall praise the LORD.

Our Mighty One will hear the groaning of his afflicted and he will see their sincere repentance; and he will deliver them.

102:19 For he hath looked down from the height of his sanctuary; from heaven did the LORD behold the earth; **102:20** To hear the groaning of the prisoner; to loose those that are appointed to death;

Messiah will teach the Word of God the Father to all people when he comes, and they will worship God and live by every Word of God.

102:21 To declare the name of the LORD in Zion, and his praise in Jerusalem; **102:22** When the people are gathered together, and the kingdoms, to serve the LORD.

For a short time we will be afflicted because of our sins, so that by afflicting the flesh the spirit might repent and be saved.

102:23 He weakened my strength in the way; he shortened my days.

In our affliction we will acknowledge the transitory and meaningless nature of the flesh and our own ways, then we will sincerely repent turning to the things that last forever.

102:24 I said, O my God, take me not away in the midst of my days: thy years are throughout all generations. **102:25** Of old hast thou laid the foundation of the earth: and the heavens are the work of thy hands.

102:26 They shall perish, but thou shalt endure: yea, all of them shall wax old like a garment; as a vesture shalt thou change them, and they shall be changed:

102:27 But thou art the same, and thy years shall have no end.

Even if the earth itself should perish, God and every Word of God will last forever: What is man when God has power to change the very planets.

Men can also live forever if they are founded and established on the Word of God.

102:28 The children of thy servants shall continue, and their seed shall be established before thee.

Psalm 103

Praise to God for his deliverance

Psalm 103:1 Bless the LORD, O my soul: and all that is within me, bless his holy name. **103:2** Bless the LORD, O my soul, and forget not all his benefits:

God can heal physical diseases and does so to teach us that God heals our spiritual infirmities.

103:3 Who forgiveth all thine iniquities; who healeth all thy diseases;

Our LORD has redeemed our lives from death by the sacrifice of his own life.

103:4 Who redeemeth thy life from destruction; who crowneth thee with lovingkindness and tender mercies;

God makes the plants grow providing physical food, as an instruction that God is the source of the spiritual food of eternal life, the Word of God.

103:5 Who satisfieth thy mouth with good things; so that thy youth is renewed like the eagle's.

Every Word of God is Righteous and Just, bringing just judgment to humanity; saving the righteous and destroying the wicked.

103:6 The LORD executeth righteousness and judgment for all that are oppressed.

God gave HIS Word to Moses; the laws of Moses are really the Law and Word of Almighty God our LORD.

103:7 He made known his ways unto Moses, his acts unto the children of Israel.

God has patiently warned us to repent of our rebellion and sins, but he will not always warn and his patience will come to its end, bringing much deserved correction on the unrepentant. Yet God's correction is in love so that by afflicting the flesh he might bring us to sincere repentance and save the spirit.

103:8 The LORD is merciful and gracious, slow to anger, and plenteous in mercy. **103:9** He will not always chide: neither will he keep his anger for ever.

God has not utterly destroyed us immediately for our sins, but has, in his love and great mercy patiently warned us.

103:10 He hath not dealt with us after our sins; nor rewarded us according to our iniquities.

Once the people sincerely repent and turn to love and live by every Word of God; God will extend mercy and abundantly forgive those who have respect for Him and are willing to live by every Word of God.

103:11 For as the heaven is high above the earth, so great is his mercy toward them that fear him. **103:12** As far as the east is from the west, so far hath he removed our transgressions from us. **103:13** Like as a father pitieth his children, so the LORD pitieth them that fear [God forgives those who deeply respect God to live by God's Word] him.

God knows that the flesh is transitory and that our lives are as nothing compared to Him, therefore he is very patient and merciful to those that love and respect him, sincerely repenting and turning to live by every Word of God.

103:14 For he knoweth our frame; he remembereth that we are dust. **103:15** As for man, his days are as grass: as a flower of the field, so he flourisheth. **103:16** For the wind passeth over it, and it is gone; and the place thereof shall know it no more.

103:17 But the mercy of the LORD is from everlasting to everlasting upon them that fear [deeply respect] him, and his righteousness [the righteousness of God is revealed in EVERY WORD of God] unto children's children;

The Mosaic Covenant was to live by every Word of God; and the New Covenant of Jeremiah 31:31 is to live by every Word of God with the addition of a efficacious sacrifice and the enabling power of the Holy Spirit.

Those who keep the New Covenant to live by every Word of God; will be resurrected to eternal life, and will rule over all nations under Messiah the Christ in the millennium and beyond.

103:18 To **such as keep his covenant, and to those that remember his commandments to do them.** **103:19** The LORD hath prepared his [God's thrones are prepared in heaven but they shall rule over the earth Rev 5:10] throne in the heavens; and his kingdom ruleth over all.

From the heavenly angels to the hosts of humanity, all living shall praise God forever.

103:20 Bless the LORD, ye his angels, that excel in strength, that do his commandments, hearkening unto the voice of his word.

103:21 Bless ye the LORD, all ye his hosts; ye ministers [servants; all people will serve God] of his, that do his pleasure.

103:22 Bless the LORD, all his works in all places of his dominion: bless the LORD, O my soul.

Psalm 104

The greatness of God

Psalm 104:1 Bless the LORD, O my soul. O LORD my God, thou art very great; thou art clothed with honour and majesty.

In appearance, God is a brilliant light and his Word is the darkness and ignorance destroying Light of Truth. In his wisdom God created the physical universe.

104:2 Who coverest thyself with light as with a garment: who stretchest out the heavens like a curtain:

God created the earth and divided the waters from the land; God is spirit and is not limited by the physical laws which he has made.

104:3 Who layeth the beams of his chambers in the waters: who maketh the clouds his chariot: who walketh upon the wings of the wind: **104:4** Who maketh his angels spirits; his ministers a flaming fire: **104:5** Who laid the foundations of the earth, that it should not be removed for ever. **104:6** Thou coveredst it with the deep as with a garment: the waters stood above the mountains.

When God commanded:

> **Genesis 1:9 And God said, Let the waters under the heaven be gathered together unto one place, and let the dry land appear: and it was so.**

Psalm 104:7 At thy rebuke they fled; at the voice of thy thunder they [the waters removed and the dry land appeared] hasted away.

104:8 They go up by [it rains and the waters come down from the mountains] the mountains; they go down by the valleys unto the place which thou hast founded for them. **104:9** Thou hast set a bound that they [the seas and the waters] may not pass over; that they turn not again to cover the earth.

By his design God has provided fresh water for all to drink and live; which is an allegory of the water of the Word and Spirit of God which gives life eternal.

104:10 He sendeth the springs into the valleys, which run among the hills. **104:11** They give drink to every beast of the field: the wild asses quench their thirst. **104:12** By them shall the fowls of the heaven have their habitation, which sing among the branches. **104:13** He watereth the hills from his chambers: the earth is satisfied with the fruit of thy works.

God has designed and given every plant for the earth so that all creatures may eat and live; which is an allegorical lesson that those who hunger and thirst after the righteousness of every Word of God shall live forever (Mat 5).

104:14 He causeth the grass to grow for the cattle, and herb for the service of man: that he may bring forth food out of the earth;

Red wine is a symbol of the sacrifice of the Lamb of God which saves and sets apart the repentant unto godliness; the oil is a type of God's Spirit which enables us to live by every Word of God, the Word of life everlasting; unleavened bread is representative of every Word of God the Bread of Life Eternal!

104:15 And wine that maketh glad the heart of man, and oil to make his face to shine, and bread which strengtheneth man's heart.

Jesus tells us in John 15 that he is the tree and God's faithful are the branches grafted into him, and if we remain in him we will be nourished by God and we will bring forth much spiritual fruit to life everlasting

104:16 The trees of the LORD are full of sap; the cedars of Lebanon, which he hath planted; **104:17** Where the birds make their nests: as for the stork, the fir trees are her house.

God made the mountains and the hills for his purposes, and God designed different animals to reside in every place.

104:18 The high hills are a refuge for the wild goats; and the rocks for the conies.

The light of the moon was set in motion to set the beginning of the months, as the sun measures out the days.

104:19 He appointed the moon for seasons: the sun knoweth his going down.

In the darkness the wild beast's prowl, and in the daylight men work

104:20 Thou makest [the sun to go down] darkness, and it is night: wherein all the beasts of the forest do creep forth. **104:21** The young lions roar after their prey, and seek their meat from God. **104:22** The sun ariseth, they [the wild beasts] gather themselves together, and lay them down in their dens. **104:23** Man goeth forth unto his work and to his labour until the evening.

The great wisdom of God who made all the amazing things on the earth and in the universe.

104:24 O LORD, how manifold are thy works! in wisdom hast thou made them all: the earth is full of thy riches.

All the creatures of the sea were designed and given their roles in life by God.

104:25 So is this great and wide sea, wherein are things creeping innumerable, both small and great beasts. **104:26** There [over the sea] go the ships: there is that leviathan, whom thou hast made to play therein.

God made them all and God sustains all his creatures directing them to their intended purpose.

104:27 These wait all upon thee; that thou mayest give them their meat in due season. **104:28** That thou givest them they gather: thou openest thine hand, they are filled with good.

All physical creatures are transitory and exist by the bounty of God

104:29 Thou hidest thy face, they are troubled: thou takest away their breath, they die, and return to their dust. **104:30** Thou sendest forth thy spirit [power], they are created: and thou renewest the face of the earth.

God is spirit and exists from everlasting to everlasting; God will bring man to repentance and God's plan and will, will be fulfilled; and God shall rejoice to give eternal life to mankind.

104:31 The glory of the LORD shall endure for ever: the LORD shall rejoice in his works [to give eternal life to humanity].

God is Almighty and his purpose will be fulfilled

104:32 He looketh on the earth, and it trembleth: he toucheth the hills, and they smoke.

Let all that hath breath rejoice in the glory of God and in his merciful gifts.

104:33 I will sing unto the LORD as long as I live: I will sing praise to my God while I have my being.

104:34 My meditation [thoughts] of him shall be sweet: I will be glad in the LORD.

All those who refuse to live by every Word of God will be eternally destroyed, but God's faithful shall live forever with many good blessings.

104:35 Let the sinners be consumed out of the earth, and let the wicked be no more. Bless thou the LORD, O my soul. Praise ye the LORD.

Psalm 105

Remember the great deeds of God and rejoice in gratitude, exalting him forever

Psalm 105:1 O give thanks unto the LORD; call upon his name: make known his deeds among the people. **105:2** Sing unto him, sing psalms unto him: talk ye of all his wondrous works. **105:3** Glory ye in his holy name: let the heart of them rejoice that seek the LORD.

Seek God to live in the presence of God, living by his Word; because he is mighty to save his faithful.

105:4 Seek the LORD, and his strength: seek his face evermore. **105:5** Remember his marvellous works that he hath done; his wonders, and the judgments of his mouth;

All those who faithfully trust in God and live by every Word of God are the true spiritual children of Abraham and Jacob, being their spiritual children.

>**Galatians 3:7** Know ye therefore that they which are of faith, the same are the children of Abraham.

Psalm 105:6 O ye seed of Abraham his servant, ye children of Jacob his chosen.

God our Deliverer out of bondage to sin, will rule all the earth; and every nation and people will ultimately live by every Word of God or perish.

105:7 He is the LORD our God: his judgments are in all the earth.

All Israel and all humanity will be called into the eternal spiritual New Covenant of Jeremiah 31:31.

105:8 He hath remembered his covenant for ever, the word which he commanded to a thousand generations. **105:9** Which covenant he made with Abraham, and his oath unto Isaac; **105:10** And confirmed the same unto Jacob for a law, and to Israel for an everlasting covenant:

The physical promised land of Canaan will belong to a united Israel forever, and is an allegory that the sincerely repentant who live by every Word of God will enter the spiritual Promised Land of eternal life.

105:11 Saying, Unto thee will I give the land of Canaan, the lot of your inheritance:

The promise of the land was made when Abraham, Isaac and Jacob were wonderers in the land.

105:12 When they were but a few men in number; yea, very few, and strangers in it.

God protected them as strangers in the land.

105:13 When they went from one nation to another, from one kingdom to another people; **105:14** He suffered no man to do them wrong: yea, he reproved kings for their sakes; **105:15** Saying, Touch not mine anointed, and do my prophets no harm.

Joseph was tested by God until God called him out of prison. The spiritually called out are being tested by God until they are resurrected from the prison of death and the grave.

105:16 Moreover he called for a famine upon the land: he brake the whole staff of bread. **105:17** He sent a man before them, even Joseph, who was sold for a servant: **105:18** Whose feet they hurt with fetters: he was laid in iron: **105:19** Until the time that his word came: the word of the LORD tried him.

Joseph was made the ruler of Egypt by God after his testing; and God's faithful through the years are also being tested and will be made rulers by God when their resurrection comes.

105:20 The king sent and loosed him; even the ruler of the people, and let him go free. **105:21** He made him lord of his house, and ruler of all his substance: **105:22** To bind [command] his princes at his pleasure; and teach his senators wisdom.

Then Jacob came to Joseph in Egypt, and there Israel grew into a nation.

105:23 Israel also came into Egypt; and Jacob sojourned in the land of Ham. **105:24** And he [God] increased his people [Israel] greatly; and made them stronger than their enemies.

Then God hardened Pharaoh's heart to use him as an example of Satan and bondage to sin.

105:25 He turned their heart to hate his people, to deal subtilly with his servants.

Then God sent Moses to lead Israel out of bondage in Egypt, as an example that God will ultimate deliver all humanity from bondage to Satan and sin.

105:26 He sent Moses his servant; and Aaron whom he had chosen. **105:27** They shewed his [God's] signs among them, and wonders in the land of Ham. **105:28** He [God] sent darkness, and made it dark [in an allegory the at that time Egypt was representative of the darkness of idolatry, ignorance and sin]; and they [the light faded away and the darkness obeyed God] rebelled not against his word.

God made their waters to become like blood to teach us that worshiping [obeying] idols [including false teachers and false teachings] and refusing to live by every Word of God brings death, and living by the Word of God brings life.

105:29 He turned their waters into blood, and slew their fish.

The Eternal made the earthly things that the Egyptians held holy - from the Nile itself to the smallest insects - to become great plagues; to demonstrate that the Eternal is greater than and has power over all other gods.

105:30 Their land brought forth frogs in abundance, in the chambers of their kings. **105:31** He spake, and there came divers sorts of [biting, blood sucking insects] flies, and lice in all their coasts. **105:32** He gave them hail for rain, and flaming fire in their land.

105:33 He smote their vines also and their fig trees; and brake the trees of their coasts. **105:34** He spake, and the locusts came, and caterpillars, and that without number, **105:35** And did eat up all the herbs in their land, and devoured the fruit of their ground.

All of the gods of Egypt were but physical things, and God demonstrated his power over them all so that we would know that all our own idols are but vain and meaningless fantasies, and that our only deliverance is to live by every Word of God.

105:36 He smote also all the firstborn in their land, the chief of all their strength.

Israel was delivered out of Egypt by the power of God and greatly blessed. Even so, those who are faithful to live by every Word of God will be resurrected to spirit and they will receive great blessings and eternal life; if they persevere to live by every Word of God.

105:37 He brought them forth also with silver and gold: and there was not one feeble person among their tribes.

Just like ancient Egypt and the surrounding nations feared God and Israel, today's nations will regard and fear God when they see God's chosen rising from their graves to life eternal.

105:38 Egypt was glad when they departed: for the fear of them fell upon them.

In the wilderness God provided for his people; and God will watch over his spiritual faithful, giving them the Word of God which is the spiritual Bread of Life from heaven.

105:39 He spread a cloud for a covering; and fire to give light in the night. **105:40** The people asked, and he brought quails, and satisfied them with the bread of heaven.

When Christ comes with his chosen, the waters of the Holy Spirit will be poured out on all flesh (Joel 2:28)

105:41 He opened the rock, and the waters gushed out; they ran in the dry places like a river.

God remembered his promise to Abraham that his descendants would inherit that land; and God will remember the spiritual aspect of that promise, that all those who are faithful to God like Abraham was faithful to God - which people are the children of Abraham in spirit - will inherit the spiritual Promised Land of eternal life..

105:42 For he remembered his holy promise, and Abraham his servant.

God brought the physical descendants of Abraham out of bondage in Egypt; and God will bring forth the spiritual children of Abraham out from bondage to Satan and sin.

> **Galatians 3:7** Know ye therefore that they which are of faith, the same are the children of Abraham.

105:43 And he brought forth his people with joy, and his chosen with gladness:

God gave physical Israel a physical promised land; and God will give the spiritual children of Abraham the Promised Land of eternal life and dominion over all the earth and tthe universe under Messiah the King of kings.

105:44 And gave them the lands of the heathen: and they inherited the labour of the people;

The faithful to God will live by every Word of God forever and forever!

105:45 That they might observe his statutes, and keep his laws. Praise ye the LORD.

Psalm 106

The Greatness of God

Psalm 106:1 Praise ye the LORD. O give thanks unto the LORD; for he is good: for his mercy endureth for ever.

Who can declare all the wonders of God which are too many to number? Who can praise God as much as he deserves?

106:2 Who can utter the mighty acts of the LORD? who can shew forth all his praise?

Every Word of God is Truth, Wisdom and Righteousness; blessed are those who live by every Word of God!

106:3 Blessed are they that keep judgment, and he that doeth righteousness at all times.

106:4 Remember me, O LORD, with the favour that thou bearest [give me also of the blessings that are given to your faithful people] unto thy people: O visit me with thy salvation;

Physical Israel was chosen to be called out of Egypt, and God has chosen to call a spiritual people out of bondage to sin.

106:5 That I may see the good of thy chosen, that I may rejoice in the gladness of thy nation, that I may glory with thine inheritance.

A History of Israel

We of today's spiritual Ekklesia have sinned just like the ancients; yet God forgave the ancients and delivered them, and God will also deliver us if we sincerely repent and trust in him!

106:6 We have sinned with our fathers, we have committed iniquity, we have done wickedly. **106:7** Our fathers understood not thy wonders in Egypt; they remembered not the multitude of thy mercies; but provoked him at the sea, even at the Red sea. **106:8** Nevertheless he saved them for his name's sake, that he might make his mighty power to be known.

God opened up the Red Sea and Israel passed through dry shod as an allegorical example that God will deliver those faithful to live by every Word of God from the sea of death and the grave to eternal life.

106:9 He rebuked the Red sea also, and it was dried up: so he led them through the depths, as through the wilderness.

God saved Israel from Pharaoh the god king of Egypt as an example that God will deliver humanity from Satan the god king of this world.

106:10 And he saved them from the hand of him that hated them, and redeemed them from the hand of the enemy.

The Red Sea covered the wicked and the wicked who reject living by every Word of God will remain in the grave forever and ever.

106:11 And the waters covered their enemies: there was not one of them left.

When the people saw that they were saved from the Egyptians and the Sea, they greatly rejoiced on the seventh and High Holy last day of the Feast of Unleavened Bread: which seventh day of that Feast represents a future millennial rest.

106:12 Then believed they his words; they sang his praise.

Then with the boredom and pressures of everyday life, Physical Israel quickly forgot the miracles of God's deliverance

106:13 They soon forgat his works; they waited not for his counsel: **106:14** But lusted exceedingly in the wilderness, and tempted God in the desert.

When Israel forgot their zeal for God, God rebuked and corrected them; which is a lesson for us that God will rebuke and correct the spiritually called when they depart from zeal to live by God's Word.

106:15 And he gave them their request; but sent leanness into their soul.

Moses was the mediator of the Mosaic Covenant and was envied by some. Jesus Christ is the Mediator of the New Covenant and today in the Ekklesia many envy him, USING his name to lead the brethren to follow themselves

106:16 They envied Moses also in the camp, and Aaron the saint of the LORD.

God opened up the earth to swallow up those desirous of taking the people from Moses as an example for us; that the graves are open wide to receive those who desire the brethren to follow themselves in place of being passionately zealous to live by every Word of God.

106:17 The earth opened and swallowed up Dathan and covered the company of Abiram. **106:18** And a fire was kindled in their company; the flame burned up the wicked.

The people then dedicated an idol to represent God and God would have destroyed the people but Moses intervened.

Today we make idols of men and corporate churches to follow the traditions of men contrary to the Word of God; and God is about to severely correct us for this grave wickedness.

106:19 They made a calf in Horeb, and worshipped the molten image. **106:20** Thus they changed their glory [God their LORD] into the similitude of an ox that eateth grass.

Today's called out Ekklesia have forgotten the greatness of God and are content to follow the false traditions of man, making idols of men to follow them contrary to the Word of God.

We have allowed ourselves to be deceived by clever men who say "We are God's servants and you must follow us;" when of course they prove by their deeds that they are not God's servants, since if they were God's servants they would be obeying God as their Master and living by every Word of God! Which they refuse to do!

> **John 8:34** Jesus answered them, Verily, verily, I say unto you, Whosoever committeth sin is the servant of sin.

Psalm 106:21 They forgat God their saviour, which had done great things in Egypt; **106:22** Wondrous works in the land of Ham, and terrible things by the Red sea.

The people had made a gold calf, today our golden calves are our idols of men and corporate churches, which we love and follow more than we love and follow the Word of God.

Just as God wanted to destroy these people who had made an idol, God will correct us in his righteous fury for doing the same thing on a spiritual level.

106:23 Therefore he said that he would destroy them, had not Moses his chosen stood before him in the breach, to turn away his wrath, lest he should destroy them.

Then the people refused to enter the physical promised land out of faithlessness, just as today's spiritually spirtual Ekklesia refuse to live by every Word of God because of our lack of faith and trust in our Mighty One.

106:24 Yea, they despised the pleasant land, they believed not his word: **106:25** But murmured in their tents, and hearkened not unto the voice of the LORD.

God would not let those who had refused to enter the land, go into the land; but saved that promise to a new generation: as a lesson for us that the unrepentant faithless of today will not inherit the promises made to the first fruits early harvest of humanity to be raised in the first general resurrection and rule the nations (Rev 5:10).

106:26 Therefore he lifted up his hand against them, to overthrow them in the wilderness: **106:27** To overthrow their seed also among the nations, and to scatter them in the lands.

During the forty years in the wilderness the people were enticed into much sin because they had no faith or zeal to live by every Word of God. This is also a lesson for us because the spiritually called out Ekklesia have also gone astray following our idols of men into much sin.

106:28 They joined themselves also unto Baalpeor, and ate the sacrifices of the dead. **106:29** Thus they provoked him to anger with their inventions: and the plague brake in upon them.

Then one man from among the people stood up to make a stand in zeal for God and the people were saved.

106:30 Then stood up Phinehas, and executed judgment: and so the plague was stayed. 106:31 And that was counted unto him for righteousness unto all generations for evermore.

Then the people who had continually provoked God; provoked Moses beyond his endurance.

106:32 They angered him also at the waters of strife, so that it went ill with Moses for their sakes: **106:33** Because they provoked his spirit, so that he spake unadvisedly with his lips.

Then when Israel entered the land they did not obey God after the days of Joshua but rejected the Word of God and intermarried with the wicked and accepted their gods which are not gods.

Today's spiritual Israel has done this very same thing; rejecting zeal to live by every Word of God and following men who are not God. We have not destroyed wickedness and sin out from among us, we do not even rebuke habitual sin today! We pride ourselves in tolerate sin in our assemblies.

1 Corinthians 5:6 Your glorying [in tolerating sin] is not good. Know ye not that a little leaven [a little sin tolerated in the assemblies] leaveneth the whole lump [pollutes the whole body]? **5:7** Purge out therefore the old leaven [purge out sin and the habitually sinful], that ye may be a new lump [a new being in godliness], as ye are unleavened. For even Christ our passover is sacrificed for us:

5:8 Therefore let us keep the feast, not with old leaven [of sin], neither with the leaven of malice and wickedness; but with the unleavened bread of sincerity and truth.

5:9 I wrote unto you in an epistle not to company with fornicators: **5:10** Yet not altogether with the fornicators of this world, or with the covetous, or extortioners, or with idolaters; for then must ye needs go out of the world.

5:11 But now I have written unto you **not to keep company, if any man that is called a brother be a fornicator, or covetous, or an idolator, or a railer, or a drunkard, or an extortioner; with such an one no not to eat.**

Psalm 106:34 They did not destroy the nations [today we do not remove the wicked out from among the assemblies], concerning whom the LORD commanded them:

Today's called out Ekklesia have allowed those who lack any desire to live by every Word of God to intermingle with the zealous until today's church organizations have become so spiritually polluted that they are beyond saving and the righteous must leave them before they too fail.

106:35 But were mingled among the heathen, and learned their works.

Our idols of men have become a snare to take us astray from the Word of God.

106:36 And they served their idols: which were a snare unto them.

We follow such deceivers without question, and we teach our children to do likewise.

106:37 Yea, they sacrificed their sons and their daughters unto devils, **106:38** And shed innocent blood, even the blood of their sons and of their daughters, whom they sacrificed unto the idols of Canaan: and the land was polluted with blood.

We have gone far astray from living by every Word of God into much idolatry of men, rushing to our own destruction.

106:39 Thus were they defiled with their own works, and went a whoring with their own inventions.

David now speaks of the Judges; which are an example for us, to teach us that we must consistently and continually live by every Word of God.

106:40 Therefore was the wrath of the LORD kindled against his people, insomuch that he abhorred his own inheritance. **106:41** And he gave them into the hand of the heathen; and they that hated them ruled over them. **106:42** Their enemies also oppressed them, and they were brought into subjection under their hand.

106:43 Many times did he deliver them; but they provoked him with their counsel, and were brought low for their iniquity. **106:44** Nevertheless he regarded their affliction, when he heard their cry: **106:45** And he remembered for them his covenant, and repented according to the multitude of his mercies. **106:46** He made them also to be pitied [by their captor's] of all those that carried them captives.

When we are corrected in much tribulation, then we shall turn to our LORD in sincere repentance and God will save us!

106:47 Save us, O LORD our God, and gather us from among the heathen, to give thanks unto thy holy name, and to triumph in thy praise.

106:48 Blessed be the LORD God of Israel from everlasting to everlasting: and let all the people say, Amen. Praise ye the LORD.

Psalm 107

A prophecy of deliverance from Babylon for Judah and the latter day deliverance at the end of the tribulation by the coming of Messiah; and in its spiritual context a prophecy and song of rejoicing over deliverance from bondage to sin.

Psalm 107:1 O give thanks unto the LORD, for he is good: for his mercy endureth for ever.

Physically God will save his people from wherever they have been scattered, and spiritually the sincerely repentant will greatly rejoice over their redemption when they are resurrected to spirit.

107:2 Let the redeemed of the LORD say so, whom he hath redeemed from the hand of the enemy; **107:3** And gathered them out of the lands, from the east, and from the west, from the north, and from the south.

In the tribulation the people will be afflicted.

107:4 They wandered in the wilderness in a solitary way; they found no city to dwell in. **107:5** Hungry and thirsty, their soul fainted in them.

God will deliver us if we cry out to him in sincere repentance.

107:6 Then they cried unto the LORD in their trouble, and he delivered them out of their distresses. **107:7** And he led them forth by the right way, that they might go to a city of habitation.

Men ought to praise God for feeding the hungry, and God will fill the spiritually hungry with the meat of every Word of God.

107:8 Oh that men would praise the LORD for his goodness, and for his wonderful works to the children of men! **107:9** For he satisfieth the longing soul, and filleth the hungry soul with goodness.

God will correct and humble his rebellious children and when they repent and run to him; God will deliver them.

107:10 Such as sit in darkness and in the shadow of death, being bound in affliction and iron; **107:11** Because they rebelled against the words of God, and contemned the counsel of the most High: **107:12** Therefore he brought down their heart with labour; they fell down, and there was none to help.

God is worthy of much praise for he delivers the sincerely repentant who are bound in the darkness of ignorance and sin into the light of the truth, and he delivers the sincerely repentant from bondage to Satan, sin and the grave.

107:13 Then they cried unto the LORD in their trouble, and he saved them out of their distresses. **107:14** He brought them out of darkness and the shadow of death, and brake their bands in sunder.

God is worthy to be praised for he delivers humanity from bondage to Satan, sin and death.

107:15 Oh that men would praise the LORD for his goodness, and for his wonderful works to the children of men! **107:16** For he hath broken the gates of brass, and cut the bars of iron in sunder.

Sinful men will be delivered when they sincerely repent and cry out to God for deliverance.

107:17 Fools because of their transgression, and because of their iniquities, are afflicted.

The fool rejects the meat of God's Word until he is afflicted and approaches eternal death.

107:18 Their soul abhorreth all manner of meat; and they draw near unto the gates of death.

When the wicked finally sincerely repent, the Eternal will save them.

107:19 Then they cry unto the LORD in their trouble, and he saveth them out of their distresses.

If we turn to live by every Word of God he will heal the sincerely repentant sinner of his terminal disease of wickedness.

This is also a prophecy about the Logos the Word of God [Jesus Christ; Hebrew Yeshua Mashiach], who would give his life in sacrifice for sinners.

> **John 1:1 In the beginning was the Word, and the Word was with God, and the Word was God.**

Psalm 107:20 He sent his word, and healed them, and delivered them from their destructions.

Let all that has breath rejoice with thanksgiving before the LORD; God has power over all things and he will save humanity from Satan, sin and death.

107:21 Oh that men would praise the LORD for his goodness, and for his wonderful works to the children of men! **107:22** And let them sacrifice the sacrifices of thanksgiving, and declare his works with rejoicing.

God has power over the very seas and weather, and he has made the endless variety of creatures in the sea and on the earth.

107:23 They that go down to the sea in ships, that do business in great waters; **107:24** These see the works of the LORD, and his wonders in the deep. **107:25** For he commandeth, and raiseth the stormy wind, which lifteth up the waves thereof.

When the great storm rages the sailors fear and cry out to God for deliverance.

In the terrible storm of our great hour of trial we will also be afraid and call out to God for deliverance.

107:26 They [the waves] mount up to the heaven, they go down again to the depths: their [the sailors heart melts for fear in the storm] soul is melted because of trouble. **107:27** They [the seamen] reel to and fro, and stagger [in the heavy seas and raging waves] like a drunken man, and are at their wit's end. **107:28 Then they cry unto the LORD in their trouble, and he bringeth them out of their distresses.**

In our hour of great trial, once we sincerely repent and call out to God for deliverance; Messiah will come to deliver us and will calm the raging nations and bring his people to their land in peace.

107:29 He maketh the storm a calm, so that the waves thereof are still.

When Christ comes, spiritual Israel will greatly rejoice at their resurrection, and physical Israel will be saved and will greatly rejoice; all humanity will also be saved and rejoice in the Word of God to live by it.

107:30 Then are they glad because they be quiet [at peace]; so he bringeth them unto their desired haven [their land].

All the children of men will see and know the greatness of God, and they will praise him for his deliverance from bondage to Satan, sin and the grave.

107:31 Oh that men would praise the LORD [YHVH] for his goodness, and for his wonderful works to the children of men! **107:32** Let them exalt him also in the congregation of the people, and praise him in the assembly of the elders.

God has all power; he can turn the rich land into desert and he can correct the wicked to repentance.

107:33 He turneth rivers into a wilderness, and the watersprings into dry ground; **107:34** A fruitful land into barrenness, for the wickedness of them that dwell therein.

God's rich blessings on the sincerely repentant, who faithfully live by every Word of God.

107:35 He turneth the wilderness into a standing water, and dry ground into watersprings. **107:36** And there he maketh the hungry to dwell, that they may prepare a city for habitation; **107:37** And sow the fields, and plant vineyards, which may yield fruits of increase. **107:38** He blesseth them also, so that they are multiplied greatly; and suffereth not their cattle to decrease.

God corrects and humbles the proud who exalt their own imaginations above the Word of God.

107:39 Again, they [the proud will be diminished and humbled] are minished and brought low through oppression, affliction, and sorrow.

God is contemptuous of the leaders - including church elders - who lead the brethren astray from their zeal for God.

107:40 He poureth contempt upon princes [leaders], and causeth them to wander in the wilderness, where there is no way [road or highway].

The physically poor are a type of the spiritually poor in the spirit of self-will who are humble before God. The humble will be exalted and the proud will be abased.

> **Matthew 23:12** And whosoever shall exalt himself shall be abased; and he that shall humble himself shall be exalted.

Psalm 107:41 Yet setteth he the poor on high from affliction, and maketh him families like a flock. **107:42** The righteous [the godly] shall see it, and rejoice: and all iniquity shall [be ended] stop her mouth.

The wise will live by every Word of God.

107:43 Whoso is wise, and will observe these things, even they shall understand the lovingkindness of the LORD.

Psalm 108

A song of praise to God for deliverance when Messiah comes.

This Psalm is about the deliverance of Israel and their resurgence during the millennium, but it is an appropriate expression of gratitude for God's deliverance from any and all distress especially from bondage to Satan, sin and the grave.

Psalm 108:1 O God, my heart is fixed; I will sing and give praise, even with my glory.

Let the faithful rise early to think on God's Word, and rejoice with music and with song through the day.

108:2 Awake, psaltery and harp: I myself will awake early.

From the millennial Jerusalem and forever after, the Word of God and the way to his salvation will flow forth to all nations.

108:3 I will praise thee, O LORD, among the people: and I will sing praises unto thee among the nations. **108:4** For thy mercy is great above the heavens: and thy truth reacheth unto the clouds.

May all that lives and breathes, turn to God in sincere repentance and be saved; may all who live exalt the Eternal above all else.

108:5 Be thou exalted, O God, above the heavens: and thy glory above all the earth;

David speaks of Israel as God's beloved, but all nations shall sincerely repent and be grafted into the spiritual New Covenant Israel and every person will be beloved of the LORD.

May every person who lives be turned to live by every Word of God

108:6 That thy beloved may be delivered: save with thy right hand, and answer me.

David speaks of God's promise to him, that in the resurrection he will rule a united Israel under Messiah the Christ forever.

108:7 God hath spoken in his holiness; I will rejoice, I will divide Shechem, and mete out the valley of Succoth. **108:8** Gilead is mine; Manasseh is mine; Ephraim also is the strength of mine head; Judah is my lawgiver;

God has also promised that in the millennium after Christ comes; the resurrected David will be given rule over Moab [Jordan], Edom [Turkey], the Samaritans [Palestinians] and the Philistines [Gaza].

108:9 Moab [Jordan will be subject to David] is my washpot; over Edom [Turkey will be subject to David] will I cast out my shoe; over Philistia [Gaza] will I triumph.

These nations will be devastated by the armies from the East [Asia] when they gather at Jerusalem, and when Messiah the Christ comes he will give

Jordan, Turkey and Gaza to be subject to the resurrected David as autonomous states in the commonwealth of Israel.

108:10 Who will bring me into the strong city? who will lead me into Edom? **108:11** Wilt not thou, O God, who hast cast us off? and wilt not thou, O God, go forth with our hosts?

When Christ comes he will destroy the armies arrayed against Jerusalem.

108:12 Give us help from trouble: for vain is the help of man. **108:13** Through God we shall do valiantly: for he it is that shall tread down our enemies.

Psalm 109

This is primarily a prophecy about Caiaphas the high priest and his plot to murder Jesus Christ. The Psalm curses Caiaphas and his descendants in the flesh until they rise from the grave and are ashamed of what he had done in plotting the murder of the Christ.

Psalm 109:1 Hold not thy peace [against this wicked high priest], O God of my praise;

Caiaphas spoke deceit and lies against Christ to convince the Sanhedrin to kill him.

109:2 For the mouth of the wicked and the mouth of the deceitful are opened [speak against God the Father's faithful Son] against me [against Jesus Christ]: they have spoken against me with a lying tongue. **109:3** They compassed me about also with words of hatred; and **fought against me without a cause.**

109:4 For my love [because of Christ's love for God the Father and his rebuking of sin] they are [make themselves] my adversaries: but I give myself unto prayer.

Jesus gave his life for those who hated him.

109:5 And they have rewarded me evil for good, and hatred for my love.

A prophecy of the Aaronic high priest who conspired to kill Jesus Christ

> Joseph Caiaphas, known simply as Caiaphas **(Hebrew: בר יהוסף קיפא; Greek: Καϊάφας)** in the New Testament, was the high priest who organized the plot to kill Jesus. Caiaphas is also said to have

been involved in the Sanhedrin trial of Jesus. Caiaphas and his posterity are here prophesied to be accursed because he was the man behind the plot to kill Messiah the Christ.

The Curse on Caiaphas

109:6 Set thou a wicked man over him: and let Satan stand at his right hand. **109:7** When he shall be judged, let him be condemned: and let his prayer become sin. **109:8** Let his days be few; and let another take his office. **109:9** Let his children be fatherless, and his wife a widow. **109:10** Let his children be continually vagabonds, and beg: let them seek their bread also out of their desolate places.

109:11 Let the extortioner catch [take away] all that he hath; and let the strangers spoil his labour [the Roman prince Titus destroyed Jerusalem and the temple, stopping the Daily Sacrifice; which Daniel was told would not resume nor a new temple be built; **until after Christ returns**]. **109:12** Let there be none to extend mercy unto him: neither let there be any to favour his fatherless children. **109:13** Let his posterity be cut off; and in the generation following let their name be blotted out.

109:14 Let the iniquity of his fathers be remembered with the LORD; and let not the sin of his mother be blotted out. **109:15** Let them be before the LORD continually, that he may cut off the memory of them from the earth. **109:16** Because that he remembered not to shew mercy, but persecuted the poor and needy [poor in spirit and humble before God] man [Jesus Christ], that he might even slay the broken in heart [spiritually humble before God].

The murderous heart of Caiaphas sealed his doom.

109:17 As he loved cursing, so let it come unto him: as he delighted not in blessing, so let it be far from him. **109:18** As he clothed himself with cursing like as with his garment, so let it come into his bowels like water, and like oil into his bones. **109:19** Let it be unto him as the garment which covereth him, and for a girdle wherewith he is girded continually.

109:20 Let this be the reward of mine adversaries [the plotters to murder Jesus Christ] from the LORD, and of them that speak evil against my soul.

God the Father delivered Messiah his son from death and the grave, and exalted him to be a spiritual High Priest forever; thereby restoring the High Priesthood of Melchisedec which existed BEFORE Aaron, and replacing the transitory physical Aaronic priesthood with the permanent spiritual priesthood of Melchisedec [Messiah the Christ].

109:21 But do thou for me, O GOD the Lord, for thy name's sake: because thy mercy is good, deliver thou me.

Jesus Christ was poor in the spirit of self-will and pride, and very humble towards God the Father.

109:22 For I am poor and needy, and my heart is wounded within me.

Jesus allowed himself to be abused out of respect for God the Father's will that he submit to such indignities and be sacrificed for the sins of humanity.

109:23 I am gone like the shadow when it declineth: I am tossed up and down as the locust.

Jesus fasted especially as his time approached.

109:24 My knees are weak through fasting; and my flesh faileth of fatness. **109:25** I became also a reproach unto them: when they looked upon me they shaked their heads.

Jesus prayed for deliverance from death and the grave so that all might know that he loved God and was loved by God.

109:26 Help me, O LORD my God: O save me according to thy mercy: **109:27** That they may know that this is thy hand; that thou, LORD, hast done it.

Let those wicked men who curse Christ be greatly ashamed when they arise from the grave; but Messiah rejoices because he has overcome Satan and worldliness.

109:28 Let them curse, but bless thou: when they arise, let them be ashamed; but let thy servant rejoice. **109:29** Let mine adversaries be clothed with shame, and let them cover themselves with their own confusion, as with a mantle.

109:30 I will greatly praise the LORD [who will deliver all God's faithful] with my mouth; yea, I will praise him among the multitude.

109:31 For he shall stand at the right hand of the poor [the poor in the spirit of pride and self-will], to save him [all God's faithful] from those that condemn his soul.

Psalm 110

Jesus Christ, after giving his life in sacrifice for the sins of humanity was resurrected to spirit and ascended back to the glory which he had given up to be made flesh; and he remains with the Father waiting for the appointed time to return to the earth and rule all nations.

Psalm 110:1 The LORD [God the Father] said unto my Lord [Messiah the Christ], Sit thou at my right hand, until I make thine enemies thy footstool.

Jesus Christ will gather up God's faithful in a resurrection to spirit, and he will then come with God's chosen to rule all nations. Jesus Christ will rule the earth from Jerusalem and God's chosen will rule over the nations around the world.

110:2 The LORD shall send the rod of thy strength out of Zion: rule thou in the midst of thine enemies.

All peoples will be thoroughly humbled in great tribulation and when Messiah comes and destroys the wicked gathered at Jerusalem, the people of Jerusalem will be ready to welcome him with even greater rejoicing than when he entered the city before his crucifixion.

110:3 Thy people shall be willing in the day of thy power, in the beauties of holiness from the womb of the morning: thou hast the dew of thy youth.

This Jesus Christ was the High Priest of God the Father, Melchizedek; before he gave up his God-hood to be made flesh and die for the repented sins of mankind. He was then resurrected to spirit and returned to his office of spirit High Priest, Melchizedek; replacing the temporary Mosaic Covenant physical priesthood of Aaron which Covenant and priesthood ended with the death of the Husband of Israel.

110:4 The LORD hath sworn, and will not repent, Thou art a priest for ever after the order of Melchizedek.

When Christ comes he will destroy all wickedness and bring in a reign of godly righteousness.

110:5 The Lord at thy right hand shall strike through kings in the day of his wrath. **110:6** He shall judge among the heathen [the unrepentant wicked], he shall fill the places with the dead bodies; he shall wound the heads over many countries.

The water of the brook is an analogy of the Holy Spirit, and Christ was full of God's Spirit and an enthusiastic zeal to live by every Word of God; therefore he was lifted up in a resurrection to eternal life and exalted as King over all rulers.

110:7 He shall drink of the brook [Jesus Christ was filled with the water of the Holy Spirit and zeal for the Word of God] in the way: therefore shall he [God] lift up the head [resurrect and exalt him].

Psalms 111 - 118

Psalm 111

Praise to God for his many might deeds and marvelous blessings

When David is resurrected with God's chosen and the nations are delivered from bondage to Satan and sin, not only the chosen but the whole earth will be ecstatic with praise for God the Father and Messiah the Christ the Mighty One of our Salvation!

Psalm 111:1 Praise ye the LORD. I will praise the LORD with my whole heart, in the assembly of the upright, and in the congregation.

God has done many wonderful works for the sons of men, beginning with the creation itself and then God's mighty deeds in calling Israel out of Egypt as an instructional allegory of God calling and delivering humanity out of bondage to Satan and sin. From creating mankind to divesting himself of his God-hood to be made flesh and die for humanity, the

Awesome Deliverance of our LORD is so much greater than tongue can tell!

111:2 The works of the LORD are great, sought out of all them that have pleasure therein. **111:3** His work is honourable and glorious: and his righteousness endureth for ever.

The whole purpose of the Creator being made flesh and dying for our sins; is so that we will remember forever, and we will NEVER again be tempted to rebel or sin once given eternal life!

111:4 He hath made his wonderful works to be remembered: the LORD is gracious and full of compassion.

God gives the spiritual food of every Word of God to those who sincerely repent of sin and enter his New Covenant of living by every Word of God.

111:5 He hath given meat [food, the Word of God] unto them that fear [love and respect God to live by his Word] him: he will ever be mindful of his covenant [God's New Covenant of marriage to his collective spiritual bride, spiritual Israel].

Ultimately the unrepentant wicked will be destroyed and the faithful will inherit all things under our LORD and God the Father.

111:6 He hath shewed his people the power of his works, that he may give them the heritage of the heathen. **111:7** The works of his hands are verity [truth] and [just, fair, godly judgment] judgment; all his commandments are sure. **111:8** They stand fast for ever and ever, and are done in truth and uprightness [righteousness is defined by every Word of God].

111:9 He sent redemption unto his people: he hath commanded his [New Covenant of Jeremiah 31:31] covenant for ever: holy and reverend [highly esteemed] is his [God's reputation is great according to all his mighty deeds on behalf of the faithful] name.

Those who compromise with the Word of God and tolerate sin are most foolish, they are promoting their own destruction and death; because the Word of God is the path to salvation and life eternal.

The Word of God is the wisdom of God, and respect to live by every Word of God is the first step in attaining to the wisdom of God.

111:10 The fear of the LORD is the beginning of wisdom: a good understanding have all they that do his commandments: his praise endureth for ever.

Psalm 112

God is great and greatly to be praised for all he does for his faithful. Every person who lives by every Word of God; although they may suffer in this world, will be resurrected to spirit and eternal life with many blessings.

Psalm 112:1 Praise ye the LORD. Blessed is the man that feareth the LORD, that delighteth greatly in his commandments.

Those who live by every Word of God will be resurrected to eternal life and as they diligently teach their children to also live by every Word of God their children will also be greatly blessed if they remain in the way.

112:2 His seed shall be mighty upon earth: the generation of the upright [the faithful to God] shall be blessed.

Great spiritual wealth will accrue in the house of those who wholeheartedly seek to live by every Word of God, and that spiritual wealth will follow them in the resurrection to spirit and they shall be blessed forever.

112:3 Wealth and riches shall be in his house: and his righteousness endureth for ever.

The Word of God is the light which drives away the darkness of ignorance and sin; Jesus Christ is the Word and the Light of godliness (John 1 and John 8:12). Our LORD is full of mercy and compassion for the sincerely repentant who wholehearted seek to internalize the righteousness of every Word of God.

112:4 Unto the upright there ariseth light in the darkness: he is gracious, and full of compassion, and righteous.

Our LORD is merciful and blesses his beloved, while rejecting the unrepentant; thereby ruling with wisdom and discretion.

112:5 A good man sheweth favour, and lendeth: he will guide his affairs with discretion.

The righteousness of our LORD is defined by the whole Word of God, which will be wholeheartedly kept by the faithful person forever and ever.

112:6 Surely he shall not be moved [the godly person will never be removed from faithfulness to every Word of God] for ever: the righteous [who live by every Word of God] shall be in everlasting remembrance.

Those who trust in the LORD to live by every Word of God, need not fear even death itself.

112:7 He shall not be afraid of evil tidings: his heart is fixed [on godliness], trusting in the LORD.

Those who internalize and live by every Word of God will see their enemies of Satan, sin and death destroyed.

Jesus Christ is sitting at the right hand of God the Father waiting for the time for him to come to the earth to overwhelm his enemies of Satan and sin.

He gives mercy to the humble and repentant who are poor in the spirit of pride and self-justification. His righteousness is the righteousness of every Word of God and he is exalted forever and ever.

112:8 His heart is established, he shall not be afraid, until he see his desire upon his enemies. **112:9** He hath dispersed, he hath given to the poor; his righteousness endureth for ever; his horn shall be exalted with honour.

The unrepentant wicked will be vexed as they perish, while the righteous whom they have hated will prosper.

112:10 The wicked shall see it, and be grieved; he shall gnash with his teeth, and melt away: the desire of the wicked shall perish.

Psalm 113

Praise to God who delivers his faithful.

Jesus Christ delivered those who obeyed him and who followed him out of bondage in Egypt. If Israel had not obeyed God's Passover instructions, their first born would have died. This was only the beginning of obedience, for they had to follow Christ OUT of bondage of Egypt [a type of bondage to sin]!

The spiritually Called Out from sin, must also obey and follow the Lamb of God sacrificed for us, in order to be delivered from bondage to sin.

Refusing to follow every Word of God, means that we are remaining in sin and that we will face the fate of all sinners.

Let us remember the Mighty Deed of the Creator of the universe in giving up his God-hood to die like a lamb for us. He now sits at the right hand of

God the Father awaiting the appointed time to come and establish the Kingdom of God!

The Father in heaven and the Lamb of God, are Great and Greatly to be Praised!

Remember that where the word "LORD" is all capitals; it refers to YHVH the family of God, including God the Father and the Eternal Creator, the Lamb of God who became Jesus Christ!

113:1 Praise ye the LORD. Praise, O ye servants of the LORD, praise the name of the LORD. **113:2** Blessed be the name of the LORD from this time forth and for evermore.

113:3 From the rising of the sun unto the going down of the same the LORD's name is to be praised. **113:4** The LORD is high above all nations, and his glory above the heavens.

Our marvelous Creator gave up eternity and unlimited power, to be made flesh and give his life for his Creation! Our Creator humbled himself and lowered himself to become flesh, to save us from our own wickedness! How marvelous is his love! He is WORTHY to be praised forever!

113:5 Who is like unto the LORD our God, who dwelleth on high, **113:6** Who humbleth himself to behold the things that are in heaven, and in the earth!

He delivered the poor and downtrodden slaves from physical Egypt, and he delivers the spiritually poor [humble and submissive to God], lifting them up out of the filth and bondage of sin and wickedness, delivering his Called and Chosen to eternal life as princes [Kings, and Priests].

113:7 He raiseth up the poor out of the dust, and lifteth the needy out of the dunghill; **113:8** That he may set him with princes, even with the princes of his people.

Physical Israel was enslaved in Egypt and heavily oppressed having no hope, like a barren woman who has no hope of children. Our Mighty God delivered physical Israel out of Egypt and caused her to rejoice like a barren woman who is freed from her trials and has become the mother of many!

Even so, those spiritually called out of their hopeless bondage to sin, have been called into the freedom of the Word of God; and if they persevere in living by every Word of God, they will be spiritually fruitful and filled with the great joy of spiritual fruitfulness, receiving the promises of God for faithfulness: eternal life and blessings.

113:9 He maketh the barren woman to keep house, and to be a joyful mother of children. Praise ye the LORD.

Psalm 114

God called physical Israel out of Egypt to be his people, his Bride; and he has called out a spiritual Israel to become a part of his collective spiritual Bride. Today the faithful of spiritual Israel who follow the Lamb of God and live by every Word of God; are a spiritual Temple, the sanctuary of God where God dwells through the agency of God's Holy Spirit.

> **1 Corinthians 3:16** Know ye not that ye are the temple of God, and that the Spirit of God dwelleth in you?

Psalm 114:1 When Israel went out of Egypt, the house of Jacob from a people of strange language; **114:2** Judah was his sanctuary, and Israel his dominion.

Before the Might of the Lamb of God the Mighty One of creation; the Red Sea was opened up for physical Israel, the Called Out of Egypt: and later the Jordan in flood was parted!

Before the Presence of the Lamb of God the Mighty One of creation, the graves of God's faithful will be opened and the godly will be resurrected to eternal life.

114:3 The sea saw it, and fled: Jordan was driven back.

Before the power of the Deliverer at his next coming to deliver his spiritual Called Out from the bondage of sin, the mountains and hills shall shake and tremble! And governments small and great will also shake with awe at the greatness of our God, and they will deliver their kingdoms up to HIM!

The graves represented by the Red Sea will open to let the faithful followers of the Mighty God go free! The earth will shiver with mighty earthquakes, and governments will shake greatly and tremble before the Strength of our Mighty One!

114:4 The mountains skipped like rams, and the little hills like lambs. **114:5** What ailed thee, O thou sea, that thou fleddest? thou Jordan, that thou wast driven back **114:6** Ye mountains, that ye skipped like rams; and ye little hills, like lambs?

The earth will shake and tremble exceedingly when the Deliverer of the spiritually called out and faithful comes to gather his chosen Bride; and then returns with his Chosen Elect after the marriage feast before the throne of God (Rev 15, 19)!

114:7 Tremble, thou earth, at the presence of the Lord, at the presence of the God of Jacob;

The Eternal is the Rock and Salvation of all those called and faithful to every Word of God, who follow the Lamb wherever he goes. HE has poured out of himself the water of the Word and Spirit of life eternal!

114:8 Which turned the rock into a standing water, the flint into a fountain of waters.

I hope that our readers begin to see the reason why the Creator inspired the writing of these Psalms and their recital at the Passover; and how much more meaningful they make the Passover service.

Psalm 115

Psalms 115 to 118 were sung at the end of the Passover service

David writes that all glory belongs to God, because God delivers those who cannot deliver themselves.

Physical Israel could not come out of Egypt on their own and spiritual Israel cannot come out of sin on their own. If we do not follow the whole Word of God we cannot get free from sin. For sin is the transgression of any part of the Word of God!

115:1 Not unto us, O LORD, not unto us, but unto thy name give glory, for thy mercy, and for thy truth's sake.

Carnal people look to gods that they can see, like men and corporate institutions! Today all men "say" that they follow God, as they ask what man's teachings do we follow, teaching for doctrine the commandments of men.

> **Mark 7:6** He answered and said unto them, Well hath Esaias prophesied of you hypocrites, as it is written, This people honoureth me with their lips, but their heart is far from me. **7:7** Howbeit in vain

do they worship me, **teaching for doctrines the commandments of men**.

Psalms 115:2 Wherefore should the heathen say, Where is now their God?

The God of the faithful called out is in heaven and does as he pleases being the sum of Wisdom, Truth and Power! In due time God the Father will send his Son to the earth and then the earth will tremble at his presence; for he shall destroy the wickedness of acting contrary to any part of the Word of God in any matter!

115:3 But our God is in the heavens: he hath done whatsoever he hath pleased.

There are many idols made of silver and gold, but today's idols are gold and silver itself, men and corporate institutions, and the false doctrines of men. We cleave to the false traditions of men rather than follow the Word of God. Statues can neither hear nor speak and those who follow their own ways instead of the whole Word of God are ignorant and cannot speak the truth and wisdom of God.

115:4 Their idols are silver and gold, the work of men's hands. **115:5** They have mouths, but they speak not: eyes have they, but they see not: **115:6** They have ears, but they hear not: noses have they, but they smell not: **115:7** They have hands, but they handle not: feet have they, but they walk not: neither speak they through their throat.

Those who do not trust and follow the Lamb of God are like the dumb statues that men make; and every person who trusts in and follows idols of men and the false traditions and corporate edifices of men; is as ignorant as any other idol worshiper.

115:8 They that make them are like unto them; so is every one that trusteth in them.

Let spiritual Israel trust in the Mighty God who can deliver us out of our bondage to sin; and trust no more in our false traditions and idols of men!

115:9 O Israel, trust thou in the LORD: he is their help and their shield.

The physical priesthood of the house of Aaron is a physical allegory to teach us that every single spiritually Called Out early harvest person, has been called to the birthright [IF they endure and overcome and prove themselves faithful and loyal to the Word of God]; of becoming priests of the priesthood of Jesus Christ under God the Father.

Let us trust and live by every Word of God instead of following men and their false traditions.

115:10 O house of Aaron, **trust in the LORD: he is their help and their shield.** **115:11** Ye that fear the LORD, trust in the LORD: he is their help and their shield.

The Eternal is ever mindful of his faithful, and he will bless his New Covenant Called Out who are faithful and put their trust in HIM!

He will bless them most of all in spiritual growth in the knowledge and understanding of his perfect word of wisdom and truth; and he will bless the faithful with life eternal in the perfection of godliness!

115:12 The LORD hath been mindful of us: he will bless us; he will bless the house of Israel; he will bless the house of Aaron.

Those who respect the whole Word of God to learn it and to do it; will be greatly spiritually blessed and will be raised up from the depths of the grave to eternal life as spirit!

115:13 He will bless them that fear the LORD, both small and great.

Once they are resurrected to spirit; the Family of God and our responsibilities as the early harvest will continue to increase forever!

115:14 The LORD shall increase you more and more, you and your children.

Those who follow the Lamb wherever HE goes, and are completely faithful to live by every Word of God, will be greatly blessed of the Eternal; while those who prefer their false traditions and exalt men and corporate entities above the whole Word of God; will be strongly corrected and if they remain unrepentant they will utterly perish.

115:15 Ye are blessed of the LORD which made heaven and earth.

Physical people dwell on the earth and cannot cross the void between heaven and earth; only spirit can cross from earth to heaven and back. Only those who are completely faithful to follow the whole Word of God without any compromise, will be changed to spirit.

115:16 The heaven, even the heavens, are the LORD's: but the earth hath he given to the children of men.

If remain unrepentant and fall in final death in the fire; we will never be able to learn or do anything again forever.

115:17 The dead praise not the LORD, neither any that go down into silence.

The faithful followers of God the Father, Jesus Christ and the whole Word of God; will be changed to spirit and they shall rejoice in their lot for all eternity!

115:18 But we will bless the LORD from this time forth and for evermore.

Praise the Eternal, who by his sacrifice, his Word and his Spirit; has led all that follow him out of the spiritual Egypt of bondage to Satan, sin and death, into the spiritual Promised Land of eternal life!

Praise the LORD.

Psalm 116

When we were yet sinners, Christ died for us; and in due time God the Father convicted us of our sins, revealing the need for repentance and the application of the sacrifice of the Lamb of God to us: Calling us to God the Father through Christ.

Then when the Eternal heard the voice of our repentance and forgave us, applying the blood sacrifice of the Son to us; we realized how much he has done for us, and we were filled with love for him because of the love he has showed for us! Please read this story of sin, repentance and love beginning about Luke 7:37.

> **Luke 7:47** Wherefore I say unto thee, Her sins, which are many, are forgiven; for she loved much: but to whom little is forgiven, the same loveth little.

Psalms 116:1 I love the LORD, because he hath heard my voice and my supplications.

Those who understand the depth of our need to be forgiven and who understand the tremendous sacrifice that the Father and the Son have made in caring for humanity and working out their plan for our salvation; will be utterly faithful to become spiritually ONE with them forever.

The proud and self-righteous will lean to their own ways and their idols of men, organizations and false traditions above the Word of God! They claim to love Christ, but they love him in words only and not in deeds;

they love their false ways more than they love God the Father or Jesus Christ.

116:2 Because he hath inclined his ear unto me, therefore will I call upon him as long as I live.

When we realize our sins and we repent, in the painful knowledge that eternal death has us in its grasp.

116:3 The sorrows of death compassed me, and the pains of hell gat hold upon me: I found trouble and sorrow.

Then we sincerely repent and turn back to serve the Eternal and his Word, throwing ourselves on his mercy.

116:4 Then called I upon the name of the LORD; O LORD, I beseech thee, deliver my soul. **116:5** Gracious is the LORD, and righteous; yea, our God is merciful.

The simple or poor in spirit are those who are poor in the spirit of self-will and pride, and are humble and submissive to every Word of God!

When we sin and then we are brought low and humbled; when we cry out in our sincere humble repentance, committing to go and live by every Word of God forever more; then the Eternal will extend his mercy to us and forgive us, and reconcile us with God the Father, bringing us spiritual peace and rest.

116:6 The LORD preserveth the simple: I was brought low, and he helped me. **116:7** Return unto thy rest, O my soul; for the LORD hath dealt bountifully with thee. **116:8** For thou hast delivered my soul from death, mine eyes from tears, and my feet from falling.

It is better to be subject to the Word of God, which is wisdom and truth; then to cleave to our own ways that bring eternal destruction.

David learned to give up his trust in men, and to trust in the Eternal. We should also learn never to trust in any man, and we should test every word of man by the whole Word of God.

116:9 I will walk before the LORD in the land of the living. **116:10** I believed, therefore have I spoken: I was greatly afflicted: **116:11** I said in my haste, All men are liars.

How can we repay the Eternal for his mercy and his deliverance?

116:12 What shall I render unto the LORD for all his benefits toward me?

By taking of the Passover cup of Salvation, the very cup of Redemption that Jesus blessed with the unleavened bread as a symbol of his shed blood for the redemption of God's people, and we commit ourselves to follow the Lamb of God whithersoever he goeth (Rev 14:4).

We repay the love of the Eternal by loving him back, by committing to obeying and following HIM and living by every Word of God! By trying to please him, and by not listening to anyone who teaches us to compromise or turn away from any part of God's Word!

116:13 I will take the **cup of salvation**, and call upon the name of the LORD.

Our baptismal vow [commitment] of espousal to Christ; is to keep the whole Word of God without any turning aside, or any hint of compromise.

We are to keep our vow of espousal to Christ and we are to be a shining witness to all of the earth, of passionate faithful obedience to the wondrous Word of God!

116:14 I will pay my vows unto the LORD now in the presence of all his people.

The physical death of the faithful Called Out is precious to the Eternal; for they have run their race and have won the victory over all temptations and trials, and have proved themselves to be a fit part of the collective spiritual Bride!

116:15 Precious in the sight of the LORD is the death of his saints.

The faithful Called Out are true servants of their master, their espoused Husband and Deliverer; who has redeemed us from death!

116:16 O LORD, truly I am thy servant; I am thy servant, and the son of thine handmaid: thou hast loosed my bonds.

Let us be grateful for our deliverance and keep our baptismal espousal vows to obey our Husband and his Father in heaven and to follow after NO other!

116:17 I will offer to thee the sacrifice of thanksgiving, and will call upon the name of the LORD. **116:18** I will pay my vows unto the LORD now in the presence of all his people.

Let us always do the will of our Lord as recorded in his Word with all our hearts. Let us keep his Word without compromise or any turning to the right or to the left. Let us continually rejoice in the love and mercy, of our Beloved!

116:19 In the courts of the LORD's house, in the midst of thee, O Jerusalem. Praise ye the LORD.

Psalms 117

God showed great mercy in keeping his promise to Abraham and calling physical Israel out of Egypt. He has shown great mercy in calling an early spiritual harvest out of bondage to sin over the past 6,000 years. God's Word is truth and it will endure and be kept by the faithful forever!

Instead of compromising with and rejecting the truth of God to exalt our own false traditions and idols of men and corporations; we should be rejoicing at our calling out of such sin, and into becoming ONE in complete unity with God the Father and the Son!

117:1 O praise the LORD, all ye nations: praise him, all ye people. **117:2** For his merciful kindness is great toward us: and **the truth of the LORD endureth for ever**. Praise ye the LORD.

Instead of a gluttonous meal and idle gossip, do think on and discuss God's deliverance for the faithful sincere keepers of his Word on the Night to be Much Remembered; picturing the beginning of physical Israel's march of deliverance out of Egypt, and our march of spiritual deliverance out of bondage to Satan and sin.

Psalm 118

118:1 O give thanks unto the LORD; for he is good: because his mercy endureth for ever. **118:2** Let Israel now say, that his mercy endureth for ever. **118:3** Let the house of Aaron now say, that his mercy endureth for ever. **118:4** Let them now that fear the LORD say, that his mercy endureth for ever.

If we love God the Father and Jesus Christ enough to keep the whole Word of God and we sincerely repent of doing our own ways; then God will deliver us into the large place of the spiritual Promised Land of eternal life!

118:5 I called upon the LORD in distress: the LORD answered me, and set me in a large place.

Regardless of what happens to us physically; if we are faithful unto our death we have the Promise of Almighty God to bring us up out of our graves and into his Promised Land of eternal life.

No person, not even an angel or some elder, can separate us from the love of our Mighty One! Only our own sins and our refusal to live by every Word of God can separate us from God; and even then he still loves us and will correct us!

What man or spirit can condemn the faithful when we are faithful to live by every Word of God and our eternal spirit High Priest makes daily intercession for us his beloved?

> **Romans 8:34** Who is he that condemneth? It is Christ that died, yea rather, that is risen again, who is even at the right hand of God, who also maketh intercession for us.
>
> **8:35** Who shall separate us from the love of Christ? shall tribulation, or distress, or persecution, or famine, or nakedness, or peril, or sword?

We will be tempted, tried and even killed for our love for the whole Word of God, just as Jesus was; yet death will have no power to hold us, just like it had no power to hold our Leader!

> **8:36** As it is written, For thy sake we are killed all the day long; we are accounted as sheep for the slaughter. **8:37** Nay, in all these things we are more than conquerors through him that loved us.
>
> **8:38** For I am persuaded, that neither death, nor life, nor angels, nor principalities, nor powers, nor things present, nor things to come, **8:39** Nor height, nor depth, nor any other creature, shall be able to separate us from the love of God, which is in Christ Jesus our Lord.

Be strong and of a good courage and commit ourselves to faithfully live by every Word of God the Father with enthusiastic zeal! Sincerely repent of all past sins and the idolizing of men and their institutions and false traditions.

The Eternal who parted the Red Sea and destroyed the first born of Egypt is on our side; IF we are on HIS side and live by every Word of God to follow him wherever he goes!

Psalm 118:6 The LORD is on my side; I will not fear: what can man do unto me?

The Eternal will take the part of all of those who zealously take HIS part and love him enough to DO what he teaches! The Eternal will correct those who persecute his people and when they eventually repent they will turn to the same kind of zeal to love, learn and keep the whole Word of God that fills God's faithful: Yet the adamantly unrepentant will have their part in the eternal destruction of the lake of fire.

118:7 The LORD taketh my part with them that help me: therefore shall I see my desire upon them that hate me.

Trust in God and his Word more than anything else! Test the words of all men against the whole Word of God and hold fast ONLY to what is good according to the whole Word of God.

118:8 It is better to trust in the LORD than to put confidence in man. **118:9** It is better to trust in the LORD than to put confidence in princes.

All those who attack and persecute the faithfully zealous of God will be corrected and if unrepentant they will be destroyed. Yes, even the many elders of today's spiritual Ekklesia who pressure and persecute the righteous to try and turn them away from their zeal, will be thrown into the correction of great tribulation.

When the Adversary surrounds us with his agents and rises up against us; if we RUN to our God and his Word, we shall be delivered from Satan and sin.

118:10 All nations compassed me about: but in the name of the LORD will I destroy them. **118:11** They compassed me about; yea, they compassed me about: but in the name of the LORD I will destroy them.

In the name of [by the authority of, the command of] the Eternal all the enemies of the righteousness of the Word of God will be destroyed.

118:12 They compassed me about like bees: they are quenched as the fire of thorns: for in the name of the LORD I will destroy them.

The enemy is Satan and bondage of sin, and Satan has worked hard to make us fall away from our zeal for our God. Resist him in the name of the Eternal and victory will be gifted to us by our Deliverer just like he led physical Israel victorious out of physical bondage in Egypt!

118:13 Thou hast thrust sore at me that I might fall: but the LORD helped me.

David now begins to quote the song of Moses (Ex 15, Rev 15) which is to be sung by the resurrected bride at the Marriage of the Lamb before the throne of God the Father in heaven!

Our God is mighty, He is valiant, He is gloriously victorious over all his enemies [Satan and sin]: He is great and greatly to be honored and praised!

118:14 The LORD is my strength and song, and is become my salvation. **118:15** The voice of rejoicing and salvation is in the tabernacles of the righteous: the right hand of the LORD doeth valiantly. **118:16** The right hand of the LORD is exalted: the right hand of the LORD doeth valiantly.

David did die physically, Here he refers to the resurrection to eternal life after which he will eternally declare the mighty works of YHVH, the Eternal.

118:17 I shall not die, but live, and declare the works of the LORD.

God will correct his people who go astray, in order to bring them back to him, but God will not give up on those he has called, or willingly give us over to the flames. Only we can choose the eternal death of fire by our adamant refusal to repent from our departure from living by every Word of God.

118:18 The LORD hath chastened me sore: but he hath not given me over unto death.

God is righteousness; and the Word of God defines the righteousness of God!

118:19 Open to me the gates of righteousness: I will go into them, and I will praise the LORD: **118:20** This gate of the LORD, into which the righteous shall enter.

God hears our sincere repentance and he gives us his merciful salvation, by applying the sacrifice of the Lamb of God to us.

118:21 I will praise thee: for thou hast heard me, and art become my salvation.

David prophesies of Jesus Christ the Lamb of God and how he would be rejected for a time. David prophesies of the day of salvation, speaking of the Passover when the Lamb of God was sacrificed for the salvation of all sincerely repentant people.

118:22 The stone which the builders refused is become the head stone of the corner. **118:23** This is the LORD's doing; it is marvellous in our eyes. **118:24** This is the day which the LORD hath made [the Passover which God has ordained]; we will rejoice and be glad in it. **118:25** Save now, I beseech thee, O LORD: O LORD, I beseech thee, send now prosperity.

Blessed are all those who are faithful in their complete submission to live by every Word of God.

118:26 Blessed be he that cometh in the name of the LORD: we have blessed you out of the house of the LORD.

The Lamb of God, Jesus Christ in the flesh, brought the light of spiritual understanding; and he was bound by his promise to die for the sins of humanity like the sacrifices were bound on the altar.

118:27 God is the LORD, which hath shewed us light: bind the sacrifice with cords, even unto the horns of the altar.

Here we have a most fitting end to the Passover service; a praise of God for his eternal mercies for his creation!

118:28 Thou art my God, and I will praise thee: thou art my God, I will exalt thee. **118:29** O give thanks unto the LORD; for he is good: for his mercy endureth for ever.

Psalm 119

Introduction

King James Version (KJV)

The Law of Moses

Many teach that we must keep the commandments, and by that they mean the Ten Commandments only.

Many make a huge error is in holding a distinction between the Law which God gave to Moses and the New Covenant, which they claim requires the Ten Commandments only.

Be on guard for this deception!

In fact Moses NEVER imagined a body of law and rules which he placed on the people as their leader. Moses only taught the people all that God had taught him! The term Law of Moses comes from the fact that Moses was the mediator who passed God's Law on to the people.

Indeed the laws of God were NOT a part of the Mosaic Covenant, which Covenant was only obedience by the people in exchange for care and blessings from God. The people agreed to live by every Word of God (Mat 4:4) and after that Marriage Covenant God revealed how God [not Moses] wanted the people to live.

God thundered out the Ten Commandments from Sinai and wrote them out on a stone [representative of the stony hearts of the people] giving them directly to the people; however GOD also gave all the other laws, statutes, ordinances, precepts and judgments to Moses to be taught to the people!

> **Deuteronomy 5:30-31** "Go say to them, Get you into your tents again. But as for thee, stand thou here by me, and **I will speak unto thee all the commandments, and the statutes, and the judgments, which thou shalt teach them**, that they may do [them] in the land which I give them to possess it."

Notice also the concluding verse of the book of Leviticus which says:

> **Leviticus 27:34** "These [are] the commandments, **which the LORD commanded Moses** for the children of Israel in mount Sinai."

Obviously the book of Leviticus talks about a lot more than just "THE TEN," and all these instructions are also called God's commandments.

There is no such thing as any Law of Moses, separate from the Law of God: Moses taught the people the Law of God, which God gave to him to be kept by God's people!

This is why Paul wrote:

> **2 Timothy 3:16** All scripture is given by inspiration of God, and is profitable for doctrine, for reproof, for correction, for instruction in righteousness:

We are to keep everything that is written in scripture and that includes the so called: Law of Moses! Because ALL of Holy Scripture was inspired by God and represents the WILL of God regarding what God wants us to do!

Jesus taught:

> **Matthew 4:4** But he answered and said, It is written, Man shall not live by bread alone, but **by every word that proceedeth out of the mouth of God.**

> **Matthew 4:10** Then saith Jesus unto him, Get thee hence, Satan: for it is written, **Thou shalt worship the Lord thy God, and him only shalt thou serve.**

ALL of Holy Scripture was inspired by God and represents the WILL of God for us.

The Law of Moses IS the Law of God!

Beware of this falsehood of placing a difference between the God's laws, to deceive men into rejecting a major part of God's law by simply labeling some of God's laws as the Law of Moses and then rejecting it.

Paul writes to Timothy:

> **2 Timothy 3:15** And that from a child thou hast known the holy scriptures, which are able to make thee wise unto salvation through faith which is in Christ Jesus.

What scriptures existed when Timothy was a child? Genesis to Malachi, but not the New Testament!

Continuing Paul says:

> **2 Timothy 3:16** All scripture [the entire "Old Testament" including the Law of Moses, to which the New Testament was canonized and added many years AFTER this letter to Timothy] is given by inspiration of God, and is profitable for doctrine, for reproof, for correction, for instruction in righteousness: **3:17** That the man of God may be perfect, thoroughly furnished unto all good works.

Psalm 119 is an acrostic poem in the Hebrew

This means that the first eight verses begin with the first letter of the Hebrew alphabet "Aleph", and the next eight verses begin with the second letter of the alphabet, and so on, right to the last eight verses which begin with the last letter of the Hebrew alphabet.

Psalm 119 (Greek numbering: **Psalm 118**) is the longest psalm as well as the longest chapter in the Bible. It is referred to in Hebrew by its opening words, "Ashrei temimei derech" ("happy are those whose way is perfect"). It is the prayer of a true faithful Called Out person who delights in and lives by every Word of God.

Psalm 119 has 176 verses which are divided into twenty-two stanzas, one stanza for each letter of the Hebrew alphabet; within each stanza, each of the eight verses begins (in Hebrew) with that letter. The name of God (YHVH) appears twenty-four times.

I will add the English lettering of the Hebrrew alphabet letter to each stanza.

Employed in almost (but not quite) every verse of the Psalms is a synonym for the Holy Scriptures, such as dabar ("word, promise") mishpatim ("rulings"), etc.

Psalm 119 is intended to present man's complete duty to God as declared in:

> **Ecclesiastes 12:13** Let us hear the conclusion of the whole matter: **Fear God, and keep his commandments: for this is the whole duty of man. 12:14** For God shall bring every work into judgment, with every secret thing, whether it be good, or whether it be evil.

Now just imagine the temple service with a group of Levites thousands strong, singing out a verse and then another choir on the other side of the temple, singing out the next verse. Can you imaging the teaching effect as the words of a Psalm thunder over the people on the Feast of Pentecost, or some other High Day when all the people are to be assembled at the temple?

The lyrical nature of the psalms in the Hebrew, has been somewhat diluted by translation.

The psalms are a teaching tool, as well as praise.

King James Version (KJV)

Psalm 119

Aleph

Psalm 119:1 Blessed are the undefiled [those not defiled by sin] in the way, who walk in the law of the Lord.

119:2 Blessed are they that keep his testimonies [example of godliness], and that seek him [seek to be like God through living by every Word of God] with the whole heart [fully and enthusiastically].

119:3 They also do no iniquity [sin]: they walk in his ways [living by every Word of God].

119:4 Thou hast commanded us to keep thy precepts [the teachings of God] diligently.

We should long for the wisdom to keep every detail of God's Word.

119:5 O that my ways were directed to keep thy statutes! [to live by every Word of God, even the points some might consider less important]

If we live by every Word of God right down to the smallest points including the spirit and the intent of the Law, we shall not be ashamed in the day of judgment when God will chose his faithful. But those who teach tolerance for sin and lukewarmness to live by every Word of God shall indeed be ashamed.

119:6 Then shall I not be ashamed, when I have respect unto all thy commandments.

119:7 I will praise thee with uprightness [sincerity] of heart, when I shall have learned thy righteous judgments [judgments are about how to apply the law in various circumstances].

119:8 I will keep thy statutes: O forsake me not utterly.

How can we be cleansed from sin? By sincerely repenting of all PAST sin and committing to STOP sinning in future, and becoming passionately zealous to live by every Word of God.

Beth

119:9 Wherewithal shall a young man cleanse his way? by taking heed thereto according to thy word.

To be righteous one must seek God with a complete total passionate wholehearted love for living by every Word of God, which defines God's very nature.

We are to take every Word of God to heart and love it exceedingly so that we may avoid sin.

119:10 With my whole heart have I sought thee: O let me not wander from thy commandments.

119:11 Thy word have I hid in mine heart, that I might not sin against thee.

We are to diligently seek to learn every Word of God and we are to live accordingly, and also teach others the wisdom of God's Word.

119:12 Blessed art thou, O Lord: teach me thy statutes.

119:13 With my lips have I declared all the judgments of thy mouth.

The deeds of Abraham, Noah and Elijah are testimonies for our instruction, as are the deeds of Christ in bringing Israel out of Egypt and his many other deeds. The testimonies of God are the words of scripture recorded for our example and instruction. That is why the scripture is called the testament of God.

119:14 I have rejoiced in the way of thy testimonies [the scriptural examples recorded for our instruction], as much as in all riches.

119:15 I will meditate in thy precepts [teachings], and have respect unto thy ways [Word].

119:16 I will delight myself in thy statutes [statutes are regulations]: I will not forget thy word.

Right now Satan hates and persecutes the zealous for God and his Word; yet Christ will soon give us total victory over the spiritual god-king of this society when he raises us up our of the Sea of Death to be rewarded bountifully in eternal life at peace with God.

Gimel

119:17 Deal bountifully with thy servant, that I may live, and keep thy word.

We should appeal to God for understanding with a deep desire to understand and live by the wisdom of God.

119:18 Open thou mine eyes, that I may behold wondrous things out of thy law.

The lovers of God are like strangers to today's wicked world, in but not part of this evil society, passing through it on the way to a better place.

119:19 I am a stranger in the earth: hide not thy commandments from me.

119:20 My soul breaketh [the godly long for every Word of God] for the longing that it hath unto thy judgments at all times.

It is pride that brings many to exalt their own ways against the Word of God; all those who compromise with God's Word will be corrected by God.

119:21 Thou hast rebuked the proud that are cursed, which do err from thy commandments.

God will save all those who diligently live by every Word of God and learn from his testimonies [the scriptural examples recorded for our instruction].

119:22 Remove from me reproach and contempt; for I have kept thy testimonies.

God's Word, and even the least of God's laws are far greater than all the rulers of this earth or of any corporate church organization: they are the DELIGHT of the true and faithful godly.

119:23 Princes also did sit and speak against me: but thy servant did meditate in thy statutes.

119:24 Thy testimonies [are instructional examples of righteousness, and examples of false ways to be avoided] also are my delight and my counselors [teachers].

Daleth

God will raise his faithful up from the dust of the grave.

119:25 My soul cleaveth unto the dust [the grave]: quicken [resurrect] thou me according to thy word.

God will teach his Word to the sincerely repentant who seek him and the wisdom of every Word of God.

119:26 I have declared my ways [sincerely repented before God], and thou heardest me: teach me thy statutes [laws].

119:27 Make me to understand the way of thy precepts [instructions]: so shall I talk of thy wondrous works.

God's Word and Law strengthen and deliver us from the heaviness of slavery to sin.

119:28 My soul melteth for heaviness [we must sincerely repent of all sin]: strengthen thou me [deliver me according to God's promises for the repentant] according unto thy word.

119:29 Remove from me the way of lying [sin and falsehood]: and grant me thy law [write your law on my heart Jeremiah 31:33] graciously.

Those called to God the Father through Jesus Christ; must choose to respond positively to that call, and to turn to Christ and God the Father and STOP all sin and rebellion.

They must choose to remove all sin and to internalize the very nature of God, through the passionate enthusiastic keeping of God's Word and the DOING of the Father's Will (Mat 6:10, Mat 4:4).

119:30 I have chosen the way of truth: thy judgments have I laid before me

The faithful choose to study and learn God's Word, wisdom and just decisions, and to learn to discern between good and evil and how to decide justly according to the Word of God.

We need to study the testimonies of scripture and the examples written for our instruction, so that we may learn the difference between right and wrong.

Those who stand on every Word of God will not be ashamed in the Day of Judgment.

119:31 I have stuck unto thy testimonies: O Lord, put me not to shame.

If we live by Word of God, God's Word will enlarge our understanding and fill us with the wisdom of God.

119:32 I will run [live by God's Word] the way of thy commandments, when thou shalt enlarge my heart [prolong life; with the gift of eternal life].

Let us finish the race we have started, and run to the very end; delighting in the law, statutes, precepts, judgments and testimonies of God at all times. Let us trust in them and their author at all times; let us wrap ourselves in them, even if it means suffering and persecution in this physical life.

He

Seek to learn and understand the Word of God with diligence, asking God to teach us His ways.

119:33 Teach me, O Lord, the way of thy statutes; and I shall keep it unto the end.

Seek understanding in prayer; so that we learn, properly understand and keep every Word and the whole Will of God with all our hearts.

The faithful delight in every Word of God and would NEVER reject any part of God's Word to try to justify clinging to past errors and false traditions.

119:34 Give me understanding, and I shall keep thy law; yea, I shall observe it with my whole heart. **119:35** Make me to go in the path of thy commandments; for therein do I delight.

May God keep us from coveting the wealth and pleasures of this world.

119:36 Incline my heart unto thy testimonies, and not to covetousness.

119:37 Turn away mine eyes from beholding vanity [nothing of this world is of any value; except to love God and do his will, Ecc 12:13]; and quicken thou me in thy way.

Let us pray that God establishes and writes his Word on the hearts of those who are devoted to him in deep respect and love to DO his will [Jer 31:33].

119:38 Stablish thy word unto thy servant, who is devoted to thy fear [the faithful are diligently devoted to respect God and do his will].

We should be loath to displease God our Father and our collective espoused Husband Jesus Christ far more than to fear any man, no matter what title they claim. Let us be wholehearted to please our God and he will cleanse the reproach of our sins.

119:39 Turn away my reproach which I fear: for thy judgments are good.

Let us long for the things of God to do them, so that we may become like our Mighty One. Let us become alive to godliness and fill ourselves with the righteousness of every Word of God.

119:40 Behold, I have longed after thy precepts [teachings]: quicken me [raise us up from the water of baptism and the death of the old sinful self; to a new life of godliness] in thy righteousness.

God is merciful to the sincerely repentant and will save them; IF they continue in his Word.

Vau

119:41 Let thy mercies come also unto me, O Lord, even thy salvation, according to thy word.

May God fill the sincerely repentant with his wisdom so that they may answer the wicked according to the will of God (Matthew 10:19).

119:42 So shall I have wherewith [the knowledge] to answer him that reproacheth me: for I trust in thy word.

The hope of the godly is in God and his Word, therefore let his Spirit of Truth remain in us all our days.

119:43 And take not the word of truth utterly out of my mouth; for I have hoped in thy judgments.

God's faithful live by every Word of God continually and without compromise, as long as they live.

119:44 So shall I keep thy law continually for ever and ever.

119:45 And I will walk at liberty [free from bondage to sin and death]: for I seek thy precepts [to live by God's teachings and will].

Some of us shall testify before kings and rulers and it will not be a photo op to discuss opera in exchange for a large monetary donation as some do.

The time is soon coming when the REAL Gospel will be presented to the great of this earth as a witness against their wickedness. The true children of God will NOT be ashamed when they are brought before judges and rulers (Mark 8:38).

119:46 I will speak of thy testimonies also before kings, and will not be ashamed.

The true children of God will delight in his Word and will not be ashamed to be enthusiastically zealous for the Word and Law of our Mighty One!

119:47 And I will delight myself in thy commandments, which I have loved.

119:48 My hands also will I lift up [to keep] unto thy commandments, which I have loved; and I will meditate in thy statutes.

Zain

The only hope for humanity is in the Word of God. God's Word brings LIFE to the afflicted, if they are faithful in loving and keeping all of God's Word to the very end.

119:49 Remember the word unto thy servant, upon which thou hast caused me to hope.

119:50 This [God's Word] is my comfort in my affliction: for thy word hath quickened [gives us life] me.

The zealous to live by every Word of God are despised by the rebellious and the lukewarm, yet the faithful continue in the ways of God.

119:51 The proud have had me greatly in derision: yet have I not declined from thy law.

Those who love God in truth remember all of God's Word and all of his judgments, for God's Spirit brings these things to continual remembrance.

119:52 I remembered thy judgments of old, O Lord; and have comforted myself.

The zealous for the wisdom of God are horrified by the lukewarm compromising of Laodicea, today's Church of God, and the wickedness of the nations.

119:53 Horror hath taken hold upon me because of the wicked that forsake thy law.

In our physical lives of pilgrimage on this earth God's laws and statutes are our chief joy and we sing [rejoice in] of them in our hearts always.

119:54 Thy statutes have been my songs in the house of my pilgrimage.

Let the faithful always remember the Law Giver and keep his wondrous law.

119:55 I have remembered thy name, O Lord, in the night, and have kept thy law.

Those who diligently live by God's law and his teachings always, will rejoice in the wisdom of God's Word.

119:56 This I had, because I kept thy precepts.

Cheth

The godly have cast their lot with the Eternal, just like a faithful wife has bonded herself to her loving husband, and we shall never be moved from keeping his Word. We give ourselves with all our hearts to live by every Word of God, seeking the compassion of our Lord.

119:57 Thou art my portion, O Lord: I have said [made a commitment to live by God's Word] that I would keep thy words.

119:58 I intreated thy favour with my whole heart: be merciful unto me according to thy word.

The wise considered their own ways and rejected the evil, sincerely repenting and them turning ourselves to the teachings and examples of righteousness of every Word of God.

Let us make haste to obey our Master who has bought us at great price.

> **1 Corinthians 6:19** What? know ye not that your body is the temple of the Holy Ghost which is in you, which ye have of God, and ye are not your own? **6:20** For ye are bought with a price: therefore glorify God in your body, and in your spirit, which are God's.

Psalm 119:59 I thought on my [own] ways, and [repented of them to turn to the ways of God] turned my feet unto thy testimonies. **119:60** I made haste, and delayed not to keep thy commandments.

Our espousal to the Lamb is [like all marriages] for rich or poor, in good and bad times, and is an eternal commitment of marriage to the Mighty One of Jacob!

119:61 The bands of the wicked have robbed me: but I have not forgotten thy law.

Day and night we are grateful to our LORD for his mercies, wisdom and righteous judgments.

119:62 At midnight I will rise to give thanks unto thee because of thy righteous judgments.

We should associate whenever possible with those who are zealous for our Lord like ourselves.

119:63 I am a companion of all them that fear thee, and of them that keep thy precepts.

119:64 The earth, O Lord, is full of thy mercy: teach me thy statutes.

Teth

God is faithful to his Word and he will keep all of his promises; therefore we seek to learn and internalize every Word of God.

119:65 Thou hast dealt well with thy servant, O Lord, according unto thy word. **119:66** Teach me good judgment and knowledge: for I have believed thy commandments.

When we went astray God corrected and saved us; and now we burn with love for every Word of God.

> Very soon now God will correct his straying flock in the affliction of great tribulation so that by afflicting the flesh the spirit can be saved.

119:67 Before I was afflicted [corrected] I went astray: but now have I [because of God's merciful correction he straying brethren will sincerely repent and they will turn to live by every Word of God forever] kept thy word.

God is good and the Word of God is holy and just and true (Romans 7:12).

119:68 Thou art good, and doest good; teach me thy statutes.

The proud and wicked persecute the zealous, for their love and Christ-like zeal for every Word of God.

119:69 The proud have forged a lie against me: but I will keep thy precepts with my whole heart.

The wicked prosper in physical things, but the godly delight in God's Word and will not be tempted or bribed to do evil.

119:70 Their heart is as fat as grease; but I delight in thy law.

Rejoice in trials (Rom 5:3) for they mold us into whatever the Master Potter desires us to become.

119:71 It is good for me that I have been afflicted [corrected]; that I might [repent from every false way; to learn the Word of God] learn thy statutes.

God's Word brings life eternal in peace and harmony with God and man. That is of far more value than any transitory wealth or position in this evil world.

119:72 The law of thy mouth is better unto me than thousands of gold and silver.

Jod

We were made by God and we NEED God to teach us the way to live, God loves us and he has given us the wisdom of his Word and Law to direct us into the way that brings eternal life. We need to seek understanding from the one who made us.

119:73 Thy hands have made me and fashioned me: give me understanding, that I may learn thy commandments.

Those dedicated to God will rejoice when God teaches them the Word of life eternal. The zealous will also rejoice when they have leaders and elders who are filled with enthusiasm for God and his Word; and teach God's Word to the faithful.

The job of an elder is to teach zeal for all of God's Word including God's commandments, teachings, precepts, doctrine, and judgments; and NOT to organize sports events or even the Feast; organizing events is a job for deacons, so that elders will have time for study and meditation on God and his Word!

119:74 They that fear thee will be glad when they see me; because I have hoped in thy word.

God's correction is just and is for the purpose of saving the spirit by afflicting the flesh.

This thinking that a terrible Assyria or enemy is to attack us because we are so righteous is just plain garbage. Yes, they are evil, as all men are sinful; but we are NOT righteous, except in our own eyes.

God is all powerful and he will allow us to be corrected for our own wickedness, and to make that absolutely plain God is giving a solid warning and then he will ask us to make our choice to heed the warning or face correction.

If any of the Ekklesia is in the tribulation, it will be OUR OWN FAULT; because we have been thoroughly warned.

If we are so afflicted, let us rejoice in that affliction, because it means that God loves us and is working to save us and bring us to repentance and a true zeal for God and respect for his judgments.

119:75 I know, O Lord, that thy judgments are right, and that thou in faithfulness hast afflicted [corrected] me.

When we have learned our lesson and have sincerely repented, be merciful to us oh LORD.

119:76 Let, I pray thee, thy merciful kindness be for my comfort, according to thy word unto thy servant.

119:77 Let thy tender mercies come unto me, that I may live: for thy law is my delight.

Let those who are too proud to repent and who afflict the faithful, be ashamed of their works which will come to nothing. Let the faithful meditate on the teachings of God's Word always and be zealous for God with all our beings.

119:78 Let the proud be ashamed; for they dealt perversely with me without a cause: but I will meditate in thy precepts.

Let the hearts of the called out understand the examples of scripture, and be established on every Word of our God.

119:79 Let those that fear thee turn unto me, and those that have known thy testimonies. **119:80** Let my heart be sound [remain always firm] in thy statutes; that I be not ashamed.

Caph

The godly faithful long for deliverance from bondage to Satan, sin and death, and our only hope is in the Word [promises of scripture] of God.

119:81 My soul fainteth for thy salvation: but I hope in thy word.

The godly faithful wait for the Kingdom of God longing for its coming. God will comfort his faithful with the Kingdom of righteousness and ultimately all wickedness will be destroyed from off the earth.

119:82 Mine eyes fail for thy word, saying, When wilt thou comfort me?

In this world God's faithful are distressed by all the evils we see as we wait in anxious expectation for the deliverance of the kingdom of God.

119:83 For I am become like a bottle [burned in the fire] in the smoke [the faithful learn patient persevering godliness through their sufferings]; yet do I not forget thy statutes.

In this life, the zealous for God are persecuted and suffer oppression even in their congregations. When will God complete the process and bring judgment on the wicked and righteousness to all the earth with his Kingdom?

Our lives are very short, deliver us speedily.

119:84 How many are the days of thy servant? when wilt thou execute judgment on them that persecute me?

Those who are not zealous to live by every Word of God dig pits and lay snares for the faithful, to try and turn the zealous away from their wholehearted zeal for godliness; but their persecution only makes the zealous even more zealous and brings them closer to God, while sifting out the faithless.

119:85 The proud have digged pits for me, which are not after thy law.

The zealous will be strong for their God and they will run to their Mighty One to save them in their trials. He will help them and they rejoice continually in God's Word.

119:86 All thy commandments are faithful: they persecute me wrongfully; help thou me.

The faithful of God will never willfully – knowingly, turn from God's Word.

Those enthusiastic for God will almost perish from the earth before the coming of our Lord with his just judgments, yet the faithful will never forsake the Word of God even unto death itself.

119:87 They had almost consumed me upon earth; but I forsook not thy precepts.

The faithfully zealous to live by every Word of God will be quickened to life everlasting, and they will rise up in a change into spirit, and they shall be chosen to rule the nations, teaching the Word and Law of God to all of humanity in the Kingdom of God!

Those who are faithfully zealous for God and ALL his ways throughout the sufferings and persecutions of this life will be qualified to teach these things in the Kingdom: Just as Jesus Christ learned through the things that he suffered; and being faithful to the Father in all things, qualified to be our eternal High Priest and the Ruler of the Kingdom of God on the earth.

119:88 Quicken me after thy lovingkindness; so shall I keep the testimony of thy mouth.

Lamed

The Word of God is forever

119:89 For ever, O Lord, thy word is settled in heaven. **119:90** Thy faithfulness is unto all generations: thou hast established the earth, and it abideth. **119:91** They continue [the heavens and earth remain] this day according to thine ordinances: for all are thy servants [God controls everything].

The godly who enthusiastically delight in God's Word and live by it fully; shall have life eternal.

119:92 Unless thy law had been my delights, I should then have perished in mine affliction. **119:93** I will never forget thy precepts: for with them thou hast quickened [the godly faithful who live by every Word of God will be resurrected to life everlasting] me.

God will save all those who are zealous to live by every Word of God.

119:94 I am thine, save me: for I have sought thy precepts.

The faithful will learn from the examples **and instructions** of scripture and they will overcome the plans of the enemy who seeks to destroy us with persecutions and with temptations to sin.

119:95 The wicked have waited [set an ambush for the godly] for me to destroy me: but I will consider thy testimonies.

All physical things will end, but the Word of God will continue forever.

119:96 I have seen an end of all perfection: but thy commandment is exceeding broad [great, everlasting].

Mem

The righteous love God's Word and law, for God's Word and Law are the sum of righteousness.

119:97 O how love I thy law! it is my meditation all the day.

We should meditate [deeply think on] on God's Word always and keep every Word of God in our hearts forever, the law and Word of God is the delight of the godly, giving the wisdom of God to those who keep it.

119:98 Thou through thy commandments hast made me wiser than mine enemies: for they are ever with me.

God's commandments, teachings, examples and instruction, make men wise; when they are thought out, understood and practiced.

119:99 I have more understanding than all my [than the faithless carnal teachers of the ways of men] teachers: for thy testimonies [every Word of God] are my meditation [consider and think upon]. **119:100** I understand more than the ancients [aged wise men], because I keep thy precepts [the teachings of the Word of God].

We can avoid wickedness through diligently living by every Word of God.

119:101 I have refrained my feet from every evil way, that I might keep thy word.

The faithful called out, will stand solidly on the ROCK of their salvation; and the law, teachings and judgments of The Sum of All Wisdom; God the Father and his Word.

119:102 I have not departed from thy judgments: for thou hast taught me.

The faithful hunger and thirst after the sweetness of God's Word; for it is wisdom, truth and life eternal to all those who live by every Word of God in sincerity and faithful zeal.

119:103 How sweet are thy words unto my taste! yea, sweeter than honey to my mouth!

The truly godly loath all falsehood and any departure from the truth of the Word of God.

119:104 Through thy precepts [teachings] I get understanding: therefore I hate every false way.

Nun

God's Word lights the way to peace and life eternal

119:105 Thy word is a lamp unto my feet, and a light unto my path.

In our baptismal commitment we have dedicated ourselves to obey our LORD and to live by every Word of God; keeping all of his commandments, laws, statutes, precepts, teachings, instructions and judgments.

Baptism is a marriage vow to obey our espoused Husband in all things. Everyone should understand that before considering baptism; baptism is a commitment to become ONE in full unity with Jesus Christ and through Christ with God the Father forever.

119:106 I have sworn, and I will perform it, that I will keep thy righteous judgments.

When we are afflicted, let us humble ourselves before our Mighty One and call upon our only Saviour to teach us what we need to learn from the situation and then to deliver us.

119:107 I am afflicted very much: quicken [revive us, deliver us] me, O Lord, according unto thy word.

The godly ask God to accept their loving faithfulness and teach them the wisdom of God's judgments.

119:108 Accept, I beseech thee, the freewill offerings of my mouth, O Lord, and teach me thy judgments.

Though our physical lives may be continually threatened, yet the faithful will NOT BE MOVED from diligently living by every Word of God.

119:109 My soul is continually in my hand: yet do I not forget thy law.

When we are persecuted or suffer, the faithful will continue to stand on every Word of God.

119:110 The wicked have laid a snare for me: yet I erred not from thy precepts.

The examples of scripture are a golden heritage of instruction that brings rejoicing as we learn and live by the Word of our Mighty One which is Wisdom and Eternal Life.

119:111 Thy testimonies have I taken as an heritage for ever: for they are the rejoicing of my heart.

Let us set ourselves to obey the High Tower of Strength and Wisdom, forever; even into the gates of death. For our LORD will raise up his faithful in that day and we shall serve him forever with rejoicing over his tender mercies, awesome wisdom and great love.

119:112 I have inclined mine heart to perform thy statutes alway, even unto the end.

Samech

The faithful godly hate wicked thoughts [evil concupiscence] and imaginations to do evil. Instead their thoughts dwell on what is good and wholesome; the Word of God.

119:113 I hate vain thoughts: but thy law do I love.

The Almighty One is the defense of his faithful; those who put their trust in HIM will NOT be disappointed.

119:114 Thou art my hiding place and my shield: I hope in thy word.

Be gone you who tempt and teach to do evil and compromise with the Word, commandments and teachings of God; for the godly delight to do his will.

119:115 Depart from me, ye evildoers: for I will keep the commandments of my God.

The hope of the called out is the resurrection from death in this evil world, and into the life eternal of living by the Word, commandments and teachings of God.

Our eternal safety lies in our respect for God, and our living by every Word, commandment, law, statute, teaching and instruction of God.

119:116 Uphold me according unto thy word, that I may live: and let me not be ashamed of my hope. **119:117** Hold thou me up, and I shall be safe: and I will have respect unto thy statutes continually.

Those who compromise with the Word of God and commit willful sin, will be destroyed unless they repent.

119:118 Thou hast trodden down all them that err from thy statutes: for their deceit is falsehood.

The wicked who do not live by every Word of God shall be thrown into the fire and destroyed; the unrepentant shall not be forgiven. Only the repentant zealous faithful shall be saved by the Lamb of God.

119:119 Thou puttest away all the wicked of the earth like dross: therefore I love thy testimonies.

Let us fear God and not what any man or organization can do.

> **Matthew 10:28** And fear not them which kill the body, but are not able to kill the soul [pneuma, spirit]: but rather fear him which is able to destroy both soul [pneuma, spirit] and body in hell.

Psalm 119:120 My flesh trembleth for fear of thee; and I am afraid of [awed by the wisdom of] thy judgments.

Ain

God saves those who diligently live by every Word of God and keep his commandments; if not now then in the resurrection to eternal life at that day.

119:121 I have done judgment and justice: leave me not to mine oppressors.

God guarantees the deliverance of his faithful who live by every Word of God and keep God's commandments and God will save them from the grave and death in a resurrection to eternal life on that day.

God will surely do good for his faithful servants and he will save them.

119:122 Be surety for thy servant for good: let not the proud oppress me.

The godly look steadfastly for the righteousness of God's Word.

119:123 Mine eyes fail for thy salvation, and for the word of thy righteousness.

Father be merciful to us and teach us your Word.

119:124 Deal with thy servant according unto thy mercy, and teach me thy statutes.

A servant obeys his master, and a godly servant seeks to please his Master in heaven by learning and doing all his Master's will.

119:125 I am thy servant; give me understanding, that I may know thy testimonies.

Deliver thy dedicated faithful who live by every Word of God, and correct the lax and lukewarm who make void the practical application of the Word of God; teaching for doctrine the commandments of men.

119:126 It is time for thee, Lord, to work: for they have made void thy law.

Those who have the indwelling Spirit of God and are following its lead, will love God and every Word of God; much more than all the wealth and pleasures of this world.

119:127 Therefore I love thy commandments above gold; yea, above fine gold.

God's Word is TRUTH and every way which is contrary to scripture is false

119:128 Therefore I esteem all thy precepts concerning all things to be right; and I hate every false way.

Pe

The scriptural examples of the Mighty Deeds of our God are awesome, therefore God's faithful put their trust in the Mighty One of Jacob.

119:129 Thy testimonies are wonderful: therefore doth my soul keep them.

The opening of God's Word to our understanding is light, like the rising of the sun; and the darkness of ignorance flees from the light of the majesty of God's Word.

119:130 The entrance of thy words giveth light; it giveth understanding unto the simple.

God will fill those who hunger and thirst after his ways and seek them out to do them, as a dry man in the desert seeks water.

> **Matthew 5:6** Blessed are they which do hunger and thirst after righteousness: for they shall be filled.

Psalm 119:131 I opened my mouth, and panted: for I longed for thy commandments.

God is merciful to all those that love God and his Word; for our God is of a mighty reputation to deliver his faithful from the spiritual Egypt of bondage to sin.

119:132 Look thou upon me, and be merciful unto me, as thou usest to do unto those that love thy name.

Oh my Lord, BREAK the chains of bondage to sin, the chains of the god-king of this evil world, and HELP us to stand on thy law and guide our steps always in thy Word and ways.

119:133 Order my steps in thy word: and let not any iniquity have dominion over me.

Deliver the godly faithful from the oppression of sinful men and enable us to live by every Word of God.

119:134 Deliver me from the oppression of man: so will I keep thy precepts.

Let the light of God [a term for God's Spirit of understanding] shine upon his dedicated servants; so that they may learn and live by God's every Word.

119:135 Make thy face to shine upon thy servant; and teach me thy statutes.

The godly weep for all those that are lukewarm for zeal to live by every Word of God, for they are ignorant and deprived of the light of truth and eternal life.

19:136 Rivers of waters run down mine eyes, because they keep not thy law.

Tzaddi

God's Word, laws, commandments, statutes, precepts, judgments, instructions and teachings are righteousness.

> **Romans 7:12** Wherefore the law is holy, and the commandment holy, and just, and good.

Psalms 119:137 Righteous art thou, O Lord, and upright are thy judgments.

119:138 Thy testimonies that thou hast commanded are righteous and very faithful.

The true called out [true pillars of the faith] are consumed with zeal for every Word of God!

119:139 My zeal hath consumed me, because mine enemies have forgotten thy words.

119:140 Thy word is very pure: therefore thy servant loveth it.

The godly faithful will never forget the teachings of the Eternal, for they are HUMBLE in his sight.

119:141 I am small and despised: yet do not I forget thy precepts.

The Word, law, commandments, statutes, precepts, instructions, judgments and teachings of God are truth for they are the very nature of God; and God is TRUTH and cannot lie:

> **Titus 1:2** In hope of eternal life, which God, that cannot lie, promised before the world began;

Psalm 119:142 Thy righteousness is an everlasting righteousness, and thy law is the truth.

The called out pillars love their beloved espoused Husband and his Father with all their being's, loving everything about him including all God's Word, ways, will, commandments and teachings; in richness or poverty, in affliction or rejoicing .

119:143 Trouble and anguish have taken hold on me: yet thy commandments are my delights.

119:144 The righteousness of thy testimonies [instructional teachings and examples] is everlasting: give me understanding [and living by them brings eternal life], and I shall live.

Koph

The faithful pillars cry out to their Maker with all their beings; dedicating themselves to him forever as their Saviour and Mighty One whose Word and commandments are forever. We dedicate ourselves to God, and to DO all that God desires!

119:145 I cried with my whole heart; hear me, O Lord: I will keep thy statutes. **119:146** I cried unto thee; save me, and I shall keep thy testimonies.

Night and day the faithful pillars of God seek to learn more of their LORD and his Holy Word.

119:147 I prevented [arose BEFORE dawn to consider God's Word] the dawning of the morning, and cried: I hoped in thy word.

119:148 Mine eyes prevent [the zealous meditate on the Word of God day and night] the night watches, that I might meditate in thy word.

God will judge his faithful justly and hear their prayers for their zeal towards him and his Word, and God will resurrect to eternal life those who are wholeheartedly zealous for him to live by every Word of God.

119:149 Hear my voice according unto thy lovingkindness: O Lord, quicken [revive me] me according to thy judgment.

The wicked are very far from God, because they despise any zeal to live by God's Word, teaching compromise with the practical application of God's Word; yet the pillars are enthusiastically zealous to live by every Word of God.

119:150 They draw nigh that follow after mischief: they are far from thy law.

God is close to all those who love his Word enough to KEEP it with passionate zeal, for every Word of God is holy and true.

119:151 Thou art near, O Lord; and all thy commandments are truth.

The scriptural lessons are for those living in the end time as well as over the past millennia, and are instructional examples that will be used to teach people to discern between good and evil for all eternity.

119:152 Concerning thy testimonies, I have known of old that thou hast founded them for ever.

Resh

Only those who are diligent and delight in living by every Word of God, will be judged righteous and raised to eternal life.

In any and all affliction and trial; RUN to our Mighty One who ALONE can save. Those who are ardent for God's Word will be delivered; while God will not hear the prayers of the indifferent, complacent and lethargic for the practical application of God's Word.

Those who are not passionately enthusiastic to live by every Word of God are considered to be among the wicked and unrepentant by the Eternal, therefore they will be rejected by Christ as a part of his bride (Rev 3:14:22), until they repent.

119:153 Consider mine affliction, and deliver me: for I do not forget thy law. **119:154** Plead my cause, and deliver me: quicken me according to thy word.

119:155 Salvation is far from the wicked: for they seek not thy statutes. **119:156** Great are thy tender mercies [for the sincerely repentant], O Lord:

quicken me [God will resurrect to eternal life all those that love God's Word to do it] according to thy judgments.

Many are the trials of the just, yet God delivers his faithful.

119:157 Many are my persecutors and mine enemies; yet do I not decline from thy testimonies.

God's faithful pillars are grieved by the complacency of today's Laodicean Spiritual Israel; and all the abominations of men on the earth.

119:158 I beheld the transgressors, and was grieved; because they kept not thy word.

Those who love and live by every Word of God will never perish, even though they may die in the flesh for a time they will be resurrected to eternal life.

119:159 Consider how I love thy precepts [teachings]: quicken me [give life to your zealous] , O Lord, according to thy lovingkindness.

119:160 Thy word is true from the beginning: and every one of thy righteous judgments endureth for ever.

Shin

Even if rulers of the assemblies [Jesus Christ warned us that the faithful would be driven out of the congregations of the faithless] and the world persecutes us for our zeal for God's Word; God's beloved faithful will not be moved.

God's faithful stand in awe of the wisdom and righteousness of every Word of God forever.

119:161 Princes have persecuted me without a cause: but my heart standeth in awe of thy word.

The Word of God is a pearl of great inestimable value.

119:162 I rejoice at thy word, as one that findeth great spoil.

> **DEFINITION: LYING:** A deliberate, willful and knowing attempt to deceive. Mistakes and misunderstandings are NOT lies, they are mistakes and misunderstandings!
>
> The use of a partial truth to deceive concerning the overall picture is lying, and God abhors such deeds.

Today's Ekklesia is filled with lying leaders who use outright falsehood and partial truths deliberately designed to deceive others.

ALMIGHTY GOD HATES THESE FALSEHOODS AND THEY HAVE CUT US OFF FROM HIM!

119:163 I hate and abhor lying: but thy law do I love.

God is to be praised for the wisdom of his Word and the justice of his judgments.

119:164 Seven times a day do I praise thee because of thy righteous judgments.

Those who trust in God and live by God's Word are given the Spirit of God and the great peace of mind which God's indwelling Spirit provides.

Consider the state of today's spiritual Ekklesia and it is immediately obvious that our disease is that we have quenched God's Spirit in our organizations, and we have done that which was right in our own eyes; NOT KEEPING our Father's Word.

The corporate religious disease is incurable and the corporate Ekklesia are doomed to destruction as organizations, unless they repent and turn back to a zeal for our Mighty One and ALL of God's Word.

Yet God will still hide a few faithful individuals (Ez 4-5), when Christ rejects and corrects the corporate organizations in great tribulation.

> **Galatians 5:22** But the fruit of the Spirit is love, joy, peace, longsuffering, gentleness, goodness, faith, **5:23** Meekness, temperance: against such there is no law.
>
> **5:24** And they that are Christ's have crucified the flesh with the affections and lusts. **5:25** If we live in the Spirit, let us also walk in the Spirit.
>
> **5:26** Let us not be desirous of vain glory, provoking one another, envying one another.

Psalm 119:165 Great peace have they which love thy law: and nothing shall offend them.

The Devoted Godly Faithful make every Word of God their hope, and they shall NOT be disappointed!

119:166 Lord, I have hoped for thy salvation [and the soon coming Kingdom], and done [KEPT] thy commandments.

119:167 My soul hath kept thy testimonies; and I love them exceedingly.

The faithful have learned and internalized the nature of God, through the diligent living by every Word of God; and their future is an open door to God the Father and eternal salvation.

God knows all our doings, and he knows who has been zealous and who is apathetic to live by God's Word.

119:168 I have kept thy precepts and thy testimonies: for all my ways are before thee.

Tau

God will hear the prayer of the faithful fervent KEEPERS of his will, who diligently seek out a good understanding of all the things of God.

God may allow trying and testing, but he will deliver his diligently faithful who pass the testing and endure to the very end, according to his will in their day. And they shall stand in their lot [inheritance] in the Kingdom of God.

119:169 Let my cry come near before thee, O Lord: give me understanding according to thy word. **119:170** Let my supplication come before thee: deliver me according to thy word [God's promises are sure].

God's elect shall praise him for his magnificent Word, and for God's Holy Law.

119:171 My lips shall utter praise, when thou hast taught me thy statutes.

God's commandments, laws, statutes, precepts, judgments and teachings are continually on the minds and in the thoughts of his true servants day and night and they shall speak of these things often.

> **Malachi 3:16** Then they that feared the Lord spake often one to another: and the Lord hearkened, and heard it, and a book of remembrance was written before him for them that feared the Lord, and that thought upon his name.
>
> **3:17** And they shall be mine, saith the Lord of hosts, in that day when I make up my jewels; and I will spare them, as a man spareth his own son that serveth him.

3:18 Then shall ye return, and discern [judge] between the righteous and the wicked, between him that serveth God and him that serveth him not.

Psalm 119:172 My tongue shall speak of thy word: for all thy commandments are righteousness.

God will be a strong help to all those who live by every Word of God.

119:173 Let thine hand help me; for I have chosen thy precepts.

The true faithful do not fear the tribulation; they long for the resurrection and the Kingdom of God when all men will live by every Word of God with diligence.

God's Word is the chief delight of the truly converted and passionately faithful: They praise their God for his Word, his wise commandments and instructions, and they will be resurrected to the salvation of eternal life

119:174 I have longed for thy salvation, O Lord; and thy law is my delight. **119:175** Let my soul live, and it shall praise thee; and let thy judgments help me.

When we go astray and we realize our error; we should never try to justify and excuse our sin; rather let us repent with alacrity and sincerity; and having learned a lesson let us return to the righteousness of living by every Word of God.

Let us all diligently pray that if and when we go astray; our God will seek us out, correct us, and deliver us from our sin; turning us back to him, as a shepherd goes out to seek the sheep that have strayed.

119:176 I have gone astray like a lost sheep; seek thy servant; for I do not forget thy commandments.

Psalms 120 - 129

Psalm 120

David wrote fifteen Psalms of Degrees [Ascents or steps] in preparation for the building of the temple by his son Solomon. Once the temple was dedicated these Psalms were sung by the Levitical choir as they stood on the fifteen steps leading into the temple courtyard. Each psalm represents a step closer to God in the Most Holy Place and spiritually these Psalms are about progressively drawing closer to God.

In Psalms 120-124, there is constant reference to trouble and danger; Psalms 125-129 is about confidence in God; and Psalms 130-134, is about the development of a direct and close relationship with God

Psalm 120

Humbled by distress and crying out to God for deliverance

Psalm 120:1 In my distress I cried unto the LORD, and he heard me. **120:2** Deliver my soul, O LORD, from lying lips, and from a deceitful tongue.

David in his distress seeks help and asks to be saved from deceit and lies. This refers to those false things said about him, and is also a request that God keep him free from committing this evil himself.

David asks how the tongue can be controlled; for it seems beyond control: and says that the wicked tongue shall be destroyed.

120:3 What shall be given unto thee [deceitful tongue]? or what shall be done unto thee, thou false tongue? **120:4** Sharp arrows of the mighty, with coals of juniper.

David speaks of dwelling in Arabia [Meshek and Kedar] as a euphemism for being far from the Ark of God at Jerusalem.

120:5 Woe is me, that I sojourn in Mesech, that I dwell in the tents of Kedar!

Dwelling far from God and godliness is about the sin which separates us from God and dwelling very far from peace with God.

120:6 My soul hath long dwelt with him that hateth peace [right now the godly are strangers living among the wicked on this earth]. **120:7** I am for peace [godliness]: but when I speak, they are for war [rebellion against God].

Psalm 121

The distressed may seek help from men and their own resources until they realize that their only hope of deliverance comes from God

Psalm 121:1 I will lift up mine eyes unto the hills, from whence cometh my help.

121:2 My help cometh from the LORD, which made heaven and earth.

121:3 He will not suffer thy foot to be moved: he that keepeth thee will not slumber.

David looks all about him and sees no help for him anywhere on the earth; therefore he seeks the help of the Almighty; who saves his faithful, never resting from delivering those who live by every Word of God.

121:4 Behold, he that keepeth Israel shall neither slumber nor sleep. **121:5** The LORD is thy keeper: the LORD is thy shade upon thy right hand. **121:6** The sun shall not smite thee by day, nor the moon by night.

Ultimately, after the faithful are harvested from the grave by our Mighty Deliverer; the souls [lives] of the faithful will be preserved forever more.

121:7 The LORD shall preserve thee from all evil: he shall preserve thy soul. **121:8** The LORD shall preserve thy going out and thy coming in from this time [the resurrection to spirit and eternal life] forth, and **even for evermore.**

Psalm 122

Distressed people will find relief and joy in sincere repentance and the deliverance of God

Psalm 122:1 I was glad when they said unto me, Let us go into the house of the LORD.

Going up to the house of the LORD is an allegory of sincere repentance and the wholehearted seeking of God to live by every Word of God.

122:2 Our feet shall stand within thy gates, O Jerusalem. **122:3** Jerusalem is builded as a city that is compact [united] together:

Jerusalem where the Ark was moved in David's day and where God had Solomon build the Temple, will be the capital city of the Mighty Redeemer the King of kings over all the earth in the near future. Jerusalem was chosen by God as his city and the seat of the King of kings will be there: Going up to Jerusalem is an analogy of going to seek unity with God.

The tribes of Israel went up to Jerusalem to worship in ancient times, and very soon all nations will flow to Jerusalem to seek the Eternal and to learn his Word

122:4 Whither the tribes go up, the tribes of the LORD, unto the testimony [the Ark of the Covenant] of Israel, to give thanks [to worship] unto the name of the LORD.

When Messiah comes with his resurrected chosen, David will again bring justice to Jerusalem, and Messiah shall bring justice to the whole earth.

122:5 For there are set thrones of judgment, the thrones of the house of David.

122:6 Pray for the peace of Jerusalem: they shall prosper that love thee. **122:7** Peace be within thy walls, and prosperity within thy palaces. **122:8** For my brethren and companions' sakes, I will now say, Peace be within thee.

122:9 Because of the house of the LORD our God I will seek thy good.

When Christ comes he will build the Ezekiel Temple and Christ will dwell and rule from Jerusalem, and all nations shall flow to Jerusalem year by year to keep the Feasts of the LORD! (Zec 14:16). Then God's Spirit will be poured out on all flesh (Joel 2:28) and all people will serve the LORD with wholehearted zeal to live by every Word of God!

Psalm 123

Those who have been been delivered by the Might of God, will look to him and put their trust in him forever

Psalm 123:1 Unto thee lift I up mine eyes, O thou that dwellest in the heavens.

The faithful look up to God in awe and wonder like a maid looks up to her mistress and a young child its parents.

123:2 Behold, as the eyes of servants look unto the hand of their masters, and as the eyes of a maiden unto the hand of her mistress; so our eyes wait upon the LORD our God, until that he have mercy upon us.

123:3 Have mercy upon us, O LORD, have mercy upon us: for we are exceedingly filled with contempt. **123:4** Our soul is exceedingly filled with the scorning of those that are at ease, and with the contempt of the proud.

Those who are passionately faithful to live by every Word of God are despised and held in contempt by the wicked for our love of God and his Word.

Therefore our God will have mercy upon us and he will reward those who are faithful in this life, with a double reward as the first born to spirit [after Christ] to lead and help bring in the latter day main harvest of humanity.

Isaiah 61:6 But ye shall be named the Priests of the LORD: men shall call you the Ministers of our God: ye shall eat the riches of the Gentiles, and in their glory shall ye boast yourselves.

Spiritual AND physical Israel will have a double portion; because of the persecution that they have endured.

61:7 For your shame ye shall have double; and for confusion they shall rejoice in their portion: therefore in their land they shall possess the double: everlasting joy shall be unto them.

Jesus Christ loves fairness, justice and the sound judgment of the whole Word of God; he hates spiritual extortion of offerings by the ministry. The people should give offerings as they can afford and as they have been blessed, not because they are talked into giving more than they can afford.

God will direct the work of the zealous for his Word, in the truth of the whole Word of God. The New Covenant of marriage between Christ and his resurrected chosen is an everlasting Covenant; but the unrepentant wicked will be cast into the fire.

61:8 For I the LORD love judgment, I hate robbery for burnt offering; and I will direct their work in truth, and I will make an everlasting covenant with them.

Repentant physical Israel will be blessed, and a repentant and zealous spiritual Israel shall be greatly blessed; but the unrepentant shall pass into nothingness.

61:9 And their seed shall be known among the Gentiles, and their offspring among the people: all that see them shall acknowledge them, that they are the seed which the LORD hath blessed.

The whole Word of God with all its teachings [doctrine] and wisdom is beautiful!

61:10 I will greatly rejoice in the LORD, my soul shall be joyful in my God; for he hath clothed me with the garments of salvation [which are the learning and the keeping of the whole Word of God], he hath covered me with the robe of righteousness, as a bridegroom decketh himself with ornaments, and as a bride adorneth herself with her jewels.

61:11 For as the earth bringeth forth her bud, and as the garden causeth the things that are sown in it to spring forth; so the Lord

GOD will cause righteousness and praise to spring forth before all the nations.

Psalm 124

Gratitude to God for his deliverance

Psalm 124:1 If it had not been the LORD who was on our side, now may Israel say; **124:2** If it had not been the LORD who was on our side, when men rose up against us: **124:3** Then they had swallowed us up quick, when their wrath was kindled against us: **124:4** Then the waters had overwhelmed us, the stream had gone over our soul: **124:5** Then the proud waters had gone over our soul.

God is on our side when we are on his side to follow him and to live by every Word of God. David speaking of the Red Sea says that it was Almighty God who delivered Israel in a way that no man could. God's deliverance out of the Red Sea is symbolic of God's deliverance out of the grave for all those who faithfully follow him and live by every Word of God!

124:6 Blessed be the LORD, who hath not given us as a prey to their teeth. **124:7** Our soul is escaped as a bird out of the snare of the fowlers: the snare is broken, and we are escaped.

God delivered physical Israel from bondage in Egypt and saved them from the Egyptians and the waters of the Red Sea: Blessed is the LORD God who saves his faithful out of bondage to Satan and sin and delivers them from death out of the mouth of the grave!

124:8 Our help is in the name of the LORD, who made heaven and earth.

Be always faithful to follow the Lamb whithersoever he goeth (Rev 14:4) and to live by every Word of God (Mat 4:4), for God alone can save man from death and the grave, and bring men into the harvest of eternal life!

Psalm 125

A declaration of absolute trust in God to live by every Word of God, and confidence that those who do so will remain unmoved forever

Psalm 125:1 They that trust in the LORD shall be as mount Zion, which cannot be removed, but abideth for ever.

All those who put their trust in the Eternal to live by every Word of God, will be raised from the grave in the resurrection harvest to spirit and they will live in God's righteousness forever

125:2 As the mountains are round about Jerusalem, so the LORD is round about his people from henceforth even for ever.

God will forever surround his resurrected to spirit faithful, and he will be their defense; and the wicked will never again vex them. True righteousness is to live by every Word of God and God's faithful chosen will never again put their hand to iniquity but will be wholeheartedly faithful forever.

125:3 For the rod of the wicked shall not rest [strike against] upon the lot of the righteous; lest the righteous put forth their hands unto iniquity.

God will bless all those who live by every Word of God and God will harvest them into eternal life and he will do good to them for all eternity.

125:4 Do good, O LORD, unto those that be good, and to them that are upright in their hearts.

But all those who do wickedly and refuse to live by every Word of God; who follow evil and false ways and refuse to sincerely repent; will receive the reward of the sinful in the second death in the fire of damnation.

125:5 As for such as turn aside unto their crooked ways, the LORD shall lead them forth [to destruction] with the workers of iniquity: but peace shall be upon Israel.

The sincerely repentant of all nations will have peace with God and they will be grafted into a spiritual Israel (Jer 31:31).

> **Isaiah 49:6** And he said, It is a light thing that thou shouldest be my servant to raise up the tribes of Jacob, and to restore the preserved of Israel: **I will also give thee for a light to the Gentiles, that thou mayest be my salvation unto the end of the earth.**

Those who are full of the righteousness of God; which is to wholeheartedly live by every Word of God and to faithfully follow the Lamb; will be raised to spirit and eternal life to live and be blessed forever more!

Psalm 126

An expression of awe and wonder at God's deliverance

Psalm 126:1 When the LORD turned again the captivity of Zion, we were like them that dream.

When Messiah comes the resurrection from the dead and then coming with them to deliver the remaining people; will be so awesome that the reality of the incredible deliverance will seem like a dream!!

Then when these overwhelming events are understood, the people will break forth in spontaneous irrepressible rejoicing at the marvelous mighty deeds of God, the Awesome Almighty Salvation.

126:2 Then was our mouth filled with laughter, and our tongue with singing: then said they among the heathen, The LORD hath done great things for them. **126:3** The LORD hath done great things for us; whereof we are glad.

God delivered physical Israel from captivity in Egypt and God will deliver humanity in these latter days with even mightier deeds, delivering mankind from the captivity of bondage of sin and from the grave itself!

Our God is awesome and MIGHTY TO SAVE!

> **Revelation 15:4** Who shall not fear thee, O Lord, and glorify thy name? for thou only art holy: for all nations shall come and worship before thee; for thy judgments are made manifest.

Psalm 126:4 Turn again our captivity [deliver us], O LORD, as [bring us to flow out of captivity like waters flow in the streams] the streams in the south.

126:5 They that sow in tears shall reap in joy. **126:6** He that goeth forth and weepeth, bearing precious seed, shall doubtless come again with rejoicing, bringing his sheaves with him.

Then he that sows in the sorrow of deep repentance over sin, shall reap the abundant blessings of the LORD with great rejoicing; and the sowing of the Word will bring forth abundant spiritual fruit in the harvests of mankind into the family of the LORD

Psalm 127

Everything that we do is transitory and temporary because all physical things will perish; the only lasting permanent things are the Word of God and godliness which will last forever.

Therefore nothing that we build physically will long endure; but if we build the nature of God in us through a passionate diligent internalizing and keeping of the Word of God, we shall become a spiritual house of God that will last forever!

Psalm 127:1 Except the LORD build the house, they labour in vain that build it: except the LORD keep the city, the watchman waketh but in vain.

The LORD is building an eternal spiritual House [Temple] in his people for the Spirit of God to reside in forever.

> **2 Corinthians 6:16** and what agreement hath the temple of God with idols? **for ye are the temple of the living God; as God hath said, I will dwell in them, and walk in them; and I will be their God, and they shall be my people.**

Psalm 127:2 It is vain for you to rise up early, to sit up late, to eat the bread of sorrows: for so he giveth his beloved sleep.

That spiritual House is the House that will last forever, while our physical houses will decay and fall over time.

127:3 Lo, children are an heritage of the LORD: and the fruit of the womb is his reward. **127:4** As arrows are in the hand of a mighty man; so are children of the youth. **127:5** Happy is the man that hath his quiver full of them: they shall not be ashamed, but they shall speak with the enemies in the gate.

Many loyal children make for a strong and powerful family. During the spiritual harvests pictured by the Biblical Festivals, God the Father will ultimately bring billions of faithful children into his spirit family.

Psalm 128

A declaration that all those who live by every Word of God will be blessed forever

Psalm 128:1 Blessed is every one that feareth the LORD; that walketh in his ways [all those who live by every Word of God]. **128:2** For thou shalt eat the labour of thine hands [receive the gift of eternal life for our enduring]: happy shalt thou be, and it shall be well with thee.

We may be tested and we may suffer in this, life but if we overcome all adversity and make living by every Word of God our chief delight; we shall receive the reward of our labors and we will be resurrected to spirit and many eternal blessings.

128:3 Thy wife shall be as a fruitful vine by the sides of thine house: thy children like olive plants [full of the oil of God's Spirit] round about thy table.

128:4 Behold, that thus shall the man be blessed that feareth the LORD. **128:5** The LORD shall bless thee out of Zion: and thou shalt see the good of Jerusalem [the New Jerusalem where God the Father will dwell] all the days of thy life [the eternity of eternal life] . **128:6** Yea, thou shalt see thy children's children [Being given eternal life, those who live by every Word of God shall see their children's children and their descendants as well; indeed we shall see our father's fathers as they are resurrected in the harvests of the LORD.], and peace upon Israel.

All nations will be grafted into spiritual Israel, and they will all be at peace with God and with one another.

Psalm 129

> **James 1:2-8** My brethren, count it all joy when ye fall into divers temptations; Knowing this, that the trying of your faith worketh patience. But let patience have her perfect work, that ye may be perfect and entire, wanting [lacking nothing spiritually] nothing.

God uses various tools to correct and mold us so that we may become like him

Psalm 129:1 Many a time have they afflicted me from my youth, may Israel now say: **129:2** Many a time have they afflicted me from my youth: yet they have not prevailed against me.

God has allowed physical Israel to be corrected and they have and will suffer at the hands of their enemies to teach us to be faithful to God, but in the end God will deliver his repentant people and cut the cords of bondage to our adversaries; and extend to us and to them the New Covenant of Jeremiah 31 and Ezekiel 11; and all Israel shall be saved.

Spiritually throughout the past six thousand years God has called out a kind of spiritual Israel and they have been tested and have often cruelly suffered for their zeal to live by every Word of God. At the resurrection to spirit Messiah the Christ will cut the cords of persecution and death, and will deliver his faithful from the Adversary and from the very grave itself.

129:3 The plowers plowed upon my back: they made long their furrows.

A bold metaphor for cruel maltreatment; the persecuted are thrown prostrate upon the ground, while the merciless foe drives the plough over her. The use of the metaphor may be intended to suggest the thought of the slave's back torn and furrowed by the lash (Isaiah 50:6). They threw me down and trod me under foot, and cruelly wounded, mangled, and tormented me.

129:4 The LORD is righteous: he hath cut asunder the cords [God has broken the cords of our bondage to sin and to the Adversary] of the wicked.

129:5 Let them all be confounded and turned back that hate Zion. **129:6** Let them be as the grass upon the housetops, which withereth afore it groweth up: **129:7** Wherewith the mower filleth not his hand; nor he that bindeth sheaves his bosom. **129:8** Neither do they which go by say, The blessing of the LORD be upon you: we bless you in the name of the LORD.

The Adversary himself will finally be judged and destroyed on a future Day of Atonement, and ultimately all the unrepentant wicked will also perish in the second death.

Psalms 130 - 140

Psalm 130

A Psalm of Repentance; read on the Day of Atonement by the early Ekklesia

Psalm 130:1 Out of the depths have I cried unto thee, O LORD.

David cries out in repentance out of the depth of his despair over sin, as an example for us that we should also sincerely repent and wholeheartedly turn to the Eternal.

130:2 Lord, hear my voice: let thine ears be attentive to the voice of my supplications. **130:3** If thou, LORD, shouldest mark iniquities, O Lord, who shall stand? **130:4** But there is forgiveness with thee, that thou mayest be feared.

Let us all sincerely repent and seek our God with all of our hearts, let us all beg our merciful LORD to remember our sins no more and to forgive us so that we may serve him and live by his every Word from henceforth and forever more!

130:5 I wait for the LORD, my soul doth wait, and in his word do I hope. **130:6** My soul waiteth [longs] for the Lord more than they that watch for the morning: I say, more than they that watch for the morning.

Let us sincerely repent and long for the Eternal's merciful redemption; so that we may serve him with wholehearted diligence, now and forever more!

130:7 Let Israel hope in the LORD: for with the LORD there is mercy, and with him is plenteous redemption. **130:8** And he shall redeem Israel from all his iniquities.

Messiah has paid the penalty for our iniquity with his own life as the Lamb of God; redeeming the sincerely repentant who fully commit to: "Go and sin no more" (John 8:11, and "To live by every Word of God" (Matthew 4:4).

Psalm 131

The godly are humble before God their Father to learn the wisdom of godliness

Psalm 131:1 Lord, my heart is not haughty, nor mine eyes lofty: neither do I exercise myself in great matters, or in things too high for me.

Those who are humble before God, who have quieted the spirit of self-will in sincere repentance, will receive mercy. The proud and self-willed will be corrected and humbled to contrition and their pride in their own ways will be crushed to powder.

131:2 Surely I have behaved and quieted myself, as a child that is weaned of his mother: my soul is even as a weaned child.

A child is weaned from its mother never to return to her breast again; so the proud and self-willed lovers of their own ways who exalt idols of men, will be weaned from their pride and self-will never again to return to that error.

131:3 Let Israel hope in the LORD from henceforth and for ever.

When our pride in our own ways, false traditions and idols of men is crushed to powder; we shall turn to put our trust in the LORD forever and ever more!

Psalm 132

A prophecy of blessings for God's faithful

David asks God to remember him for his zeal for God's House and his dedication to live by every Word of God. Yes, David sinned, but whenever he found himself in sin he Sincerely Repented and STOPPED sinning! We are to also STOP sinning and we must never justify ourselves or use excuses to continue in our sin.

Proverbs 24:16 For a just man falleth seven times, and riseth up again [quickly repents]: but the wicked shall fall into mischief [be destroyed for not repenting from his sin].

Psalm 132:1 Lord, remember David, and all his afflictions: **132:2** How he sware unto the LORD, and vowed unto the mighty God of Jacob; **132:3** Surely I will not come into the tabernacle of my house, nor go up into my bed; **132:4** I will not give sleep to mine eyes, or slumber to mine eyelids, **132:5** Until I find out a place for the LORD, an habitation for the mighty God of Jacob.

This speaks of seeking the Eternal and the things of God with all our hearts, to build ourselves into a fitting Temple for God's Spirit; through internalizing the very nature of God through living by every Word of God.

132:6 Lo, we heard of it at Ephratah: we found it in the fields of the wood. **132:7 We will go into his tabernacles: we will worship at his footstool**. **132:8** Arise, O LORD, into thy rest; thou, and the ark of thy strength.

Let the priests [especially the New Covenant called out] and children of God be faithful, clothed with the righteousness of living by every Word of God; let them rejoice in the LORD forever more!

132:9 Let thy priests be clothed with righteousness; and let thy saints shout for joy.

132:10 For thy servant David's sake turn not away [do not reject] the face of thine anointed.

God promised David that his children will also rule. Spiritually, just as people of faith and the works of faith are the children of Abraham (Gal 3:7), the sincerely repentant who are people after God's own heart are the spiritual children of David.

132:11 The LORD hath sworn in truth unto David; he will not turn from it; Of the fruit of thy body will I set upon thy throne. **132:12 If thy children will keep my covenant and my testimony that I shall teach them, their children shall also sit upon thy throne for evermore.**

This is a promise that those who faithfully live by every Word of God will live forever.

God Chooses Jerusalem

132:13 For **the LORD hath chosen Zion; he hath desired it for his habitation. 132:14 This is my rest for ever: here will I dwell; for I have desired it. 132:15** I will abundantly bless her provision: I will satisfy her poor with bread. **132:16** I will also clothe her priests with salvation: and her saints shall shout aloud for joy.

David will be raised up and he will rule all Israel forever, because of his continual repentance and love to live by every Word of God

132:17 There will I make the horn of David to bud: I have ordained a lamp for mine anointed. **132:18** His enemies will I clothe with shame: but upon himself shall his crown flourish.

Psalm 133

Those who make it their life's work to live by every Word of God, internalizing the very nature of God, shall be at one in complete unity with God forever; and they shall be anointed with the oil [the Holy Spirit] of eternal life

Psalm 133:1 Behold, how good and how pleasant it is for brethren to dwell together in unity! **133:2** It is like the precious ointment upon the head [the anointing oil representing the Holy Spirit], that ran down upon the beard, even Aaron's beard: that went down to the skirts of his garments;

This speaks of unity with God; and every person who is fully united with God is also united with all other persons who are fully united with God; and they will receive the gift of eternal life.

Those who turn away from unity with God for unity with others, will not receive the gift of eternal life.

The godly who have the courage to take a stand and to live by every Word of God even if that means being ostracized by others, are the people who will receive eternal life for their love of God.

133:3 As the dew of Hermon, and as the dew that descended upon the mountains of Zion: for there the LORD commanded the blessing, **even life for evermore.**

Compromising with the Word of God for supposed organizational unity brings damnation. Yes. God is the author of division between good and evil, and between those who truly serve him and those who do not live by every Word of God.

> **Malachi 3:16** Then they that feared the Lord spake often one to another: and the Lord hearkened, and heard it, and a book of remembrance was written before him **for them that feared the Lord, and that thought upon his name.**
>
> **3:17** And they shall be mine, saith the Lord of hosts, in that day when I make up my jewels; and I will spare them, as a man spareth his own son that serveth him.
>
> **3:18** Then shall ye return, and discern between the righteous and the wicked, between him that serveth God and him that serveth him not.
>
> **Matthew 10:32** Whosoever therefore shall confess me before men, him will I confess also before my Father which is in heaven.
>
> **10:33** But whosoever shall deny me before men, him will I also deny before my Father which is in heaven.
>
> **10:34** Think not that I am come to send peace on earth: I came not to send peace, but a sword.
>
> **10:35** For I am come to set a man at variance against his father, and the daughter against her mother, and the daughter in law against her mother in law.
>
> **10:36** And a man's foes shall be they of his own household.

10:37 He that loveth father or mother more than me is not worthy of me: and he that loveth son or daughter more than me is not worthy of me.

Psalm 134

God our Creator and Deliverer; is worthy of praise forever more

While the "Hour of Prayer" began the preparations for the evening sacrifice in the afternoon, the evening sacrifice was killed and prepared before the sun set, but was not offered [burned on the altar] until sunset.

Psalm 134:1 Behold, bless [Serve, Obey and Glorify] ye the LORD [YHVH], all ye servants of the LORD, **which by night stand in the house of the LORD** [offering the evening sacrifice]. **134:2** Lift up your hands in the sanctuary, and bless the LORD.

God will bless all those that faithfully serve him and live by every Word of God

134:3 The LORD that made heaven and earth bless thee [God will bless all his faithful who live by every Word of God to Serve, Please, Praise and Glorify HIM with the works of faith!] out of Zion.

Psalm 135

Psalm 135:1 Praise ye the LORD [YHVH]. Praise ye the name [praise the reputation and glory of God, which is what God's name represents] of the LORD; praise him, O ye servants of the LORD.

Standing in the House of the LORD, the physical Temple; is an allegory of all those who are the house of God's indwelling Spirit. All of God's people will praise him and rejoice over all the mighty works of God in delivering us from bondage to Satan, sin and death.

135:2 Ye that stand in the house of the LORD, in the courts of the house of our God. **135:3** Praise the LORD; for the LORD is good: sing praises unto his name; for it is pleasant.

135:4 For the LORD hath chosen Jacob [God chose and called physical Israel out of Egypt, as a type of God also calling a New Covenant spiritual Israel out from bondage to sin.] unto himself, and [physical Israel as a type of a spiritual Israel (Jer 31:31) into which all nations will be ultimately be grafted] Israel for his peculiar treasure.

God is Great in his Mercy and Power to deliver, and he will save spiritual Israel from bondage to Satan and sin [and death itself] with the might of his power, just as he saved physical Israel from bondage in Egypt.

135:5 For I know that the LORD is great, and that our Lord is above all gods.

God the Creator designed and made all things and sustains them by His glorious power. The LORD [YHVH] is glorious and mighty, having the power to do whatever he wills, and he wills deliverance and abundant mercy for His sincerely repentant creation of humanity.

135:6 Whatsoever the LORD pleased, that did he in heaven, and in earth, in the seas, and all deep places. **135:7** He causeth the vapours to ascend from the ends of the earth; he maketh lightnings for the rain; he bringeth the wind out of his treasuries.

The God of Mighty Wonders who delivered physical Israel from Egypt in His mercy, will ultimately deliver all humanity by bringing them to sincere repentance and grafting them into a New Covenant spiritual Israel (Jer 31:31). Even the ancient dead will be resurrected and given an opportunity for salvation (Ezekiel 37).

135:8 Who smote the firstborn of Egypt, both of man and beast. **135:9** Who sent tokens and wonders into the midst of thee, O Egypt, upon Pharaoh, and upon all his servants. **135:10** Who smote great nations, and slew mighty kings; **135:11** Sihon king of the Amorites, and Og king of Bashan, and all the kingdoms of Canaan: **135:12** And gave their land for an heritage, an heritage unto Israel his people.

135:13 Thy name [the name represents the Being and his reputation], O LORD, endureth for ever; and thy memorial, O LORD, throughout all generations.

In due time God will deliver His people from wickedness, sin and bondage to Satan, sin and death, and God will destroy every false god and every false way out of the earth.

135:14 For the LORD will judge [Messiah the Christ will come to rule the people as King of all kings on the earth] his people, and he will repent himself concerning his servants.

135:15 The idols of the heathen are silver and gold, the work of men's hands. **135:16** They have mouths, but they speak not; eyes have they, but they see not; **135:17** They have ears, but they hear not; neither is there any breath in their mouths.

Idols can be more than just images, anything the comes between a person and his faithfully zealous living by every Word of God is an idol.

The makers of false gods are just as ignorant as the false gods they make.

135:18 They that make them are like unto them: so is every one that trusteth in them.

The day will come when all Israel will turn to zealously live by every Word of God and will bless the LORD which brings them into a New Covenant, delivering them from bondage to Satan, sin and death.

The physical house of Israel is an allegory of a spiritual New Covenant Israel, into which all nations will ultimately be grafted. The LORD [YHVH] will come as King of kings and will dwell in Jerusalem.

135:19 Bless the LORD, O house of Israel: bless the LORD, O house of Aaron: **135:20** Bless the LORD, O house of Levi: ye that fear the LORD, bless the LORD. **135:21** Blessed be the LORD out of Zion, which dwelleth at Jerusalem.

Praise ye the LORD.

Psalm 136

A Passover Psalm of Deliverance; written by David

As we read this Psalm think of the physical and spiritual deliverance of the Called Out from the bondage of sin; and praise our God for his tender manifold mercies to us individually as well as his mercies to his creation.

Psalm 136 is a psalm of praise to God for his great love and mercy in delivering his physically Called Out from physical bondage in Egypt; and for delivering his spiritually Called Out from bondage to Satan and sin; by giving his own life as the Lamb of God for his spiritually Called Out bride; into which collective bride all humanity will ultimately be called.

Psalm 136 Opens the Passover Service

Gratitude and praise exalting the goodness and greatness of the Eternal

Psalm 136:1 O give thanks unto the LORD; for he is good: for his mercy endureth for ever. **136:2** O give thanks unto the God of gods: for his mercy endureth for ever. **136:3** O give thanks to the Lord of lords: for his mercy endureth for ever.

Acknowledging the wisdom and might of the Eternal

136:4 To him who alone doeth great wonders: for his mercy endureth for ever. **136:5** To him that by wisdom made the heavens: for his mercy endureth for ever. **136:6** To him that stretched out the earth above the waters: for his mercy endureth for ever. **136:7** To him that made great lights [the sun and moon]: for his mercy endureth for ever: **136:8** The sun to rule by day: for his mercy endureth for ever: **136:9** The moon and stars to rule by night: for his mercy endureth for ever.

Acknowledging the Eternal's power to deliver us from bondage to sin

136:10 To him that smote Egypt [Pharaoh was a type of Satan, and Egypt was a type of bondage to sin.] in their firstborn: for his mercy endureth for ever: **136:11** And brought out Israel from among them: for his mercy endureth for ever: **136:12** With a strong hand, and with a stretched out arm: for his mercy endureth for ever.

God has called men from bondage to Satan and sin, and he will deliver his faithful from the grave typified by the Red Sea.

136:13 To him which divided the Red sea into parts [A type of the baptismal commitment and of God's ultimate opening of the graves of resurrection.]: for his mercy endureth for ever:

136:14 And made Israel to pass through the midst of it: for his mercy endureth for ever:

Those who live by every Word of God will rise up to eternal life, changed to spirit. The wicked shall be destroyed.

136:15 But overthrew Pharaoh and his host in the Red sea [The wicked will be destroyed but those faithful to their baptismal commitment to faithfully keep the whole Word of God will be resurrected to life eternal.]: for his mercy endureth for ever.

136:16 To him which led his people through the wilderness [God leads those who follow him through the spiritual wilderness.]: for his mercy endureth for ever.

136:17 To him which smote great kings: for his mercy endureth for ever:

136:18 And slew famous kings [God will destroy all unrepentant sinners] for his mercy endureth for ever:

136:19 Sihon king of the Amorites: for his mercy endureth for ever:

136:20 And Og the king of Bashan [these Canaanite kings were used as types of unrepentant sinners]: for his mercy endureth for ever:

136:21 And gave their land for an heritage [the wicked will be destroyed from off the earth; and the universe will be given to the faithful]: for his mercy endureth for ever:

136:22 Even an heritage unto Israel his servant: for his mercy endureth for ever.

136:23 Who remembered us in our low estate {God remembered us in our bondage and delivered us]: for his mercy endureth for ever:

136:24 And hath redeemed us from our enemies [spiritually, Satan the Adversary of God]: for his mercy endureth for ever.

136:25 Who giveth food to all flesh [in addition to physical food, God feeds his faithful with the spiritual food of the Word of God]: for his mercy endureth for ever.

136:26 O give thanks unto the God of heaven: for his mercy endureth for ever.

Psalm 137

A prophecy of a future - from David's time - captivity in Babylon, and of sincere repentance and longing for Jerusalem the city of God the Almighty during that captivity.

Longing for Jerusalem or the temple is an allegory of sincere repentance and longing for the God who chose that city.

The ancient Babylonian captivity is a type of one last and final captivity to the now rising Babylon the Great of the New Federal Europe, which is the feet of Daniel 2 and the last heir of the Babylonian Mysteries System.

Psalm 137:1 By the rivers of Babylon, there we sat down, yea, we wept [in repentance and longing for God], when we remembered Zion. **137:2** We hanged our harps upon the willows in the midst thereof. **137:3** For there they that carried us away captive required of us a song; and they that wasted us required of us mirth, saying, Sing us one of the songs of Zion.

How can we sing in rejoicing when we are in heavy correction for all our sins?

137:4 How shall we sing the LORD's song in a strange land?

We cannot sing in rejoicing in our correction; instead we must remember the city of God and our Mighty God and turn to him in sincere repentance

137:5 If I forget thee, O Jerusalem, let my right hand forget her cunning. **137:6** If I do not remember thee, let my tongue cleave to the roof of my mouth; if I prefer not Jerusalem above my chief joy.

During the soon coming correction of greater Israel by the New Federal Europe, Edom [Edom and or Seir migrated north into Turkmenistan and then into modern Turkey] will aid Europe and will rejoice at the calamity of Israel (Psalm 83). Therefore Christ will destroy Turkey from being n independent nation when he comes, as the prophets have written (See Obadiah).

137:7 Remember, O LORD, the children of Edom in the day of Jerusalem; who said, Rase it, rase it, even to the foundation thereof.

Daniel 2 records a prophecy of the history of Babylon the Great which will have its final revival in the now Rising New Federal Europe and which will be destroyed by Jesus Christ at his coming.

Verse 8 is a prophecy of the end of Babylon, the church state religious system of the Babylonian Mysteries, and her many daughter religions.

Babylon is the ancient Babylonian Empire and its religion of the Babylonian Mysteries, having many daughter religions and riding the nations as their supposed ultimate moral authority.

137:8 O daughter of Babylon [the latter day descendant of the Babylonian Empire and religious system of Daniel 2, which will be revived in a soon coming New Federal Europe], who art to be destroyed; happy shall he be, that rewardeth thee as thou hast served us. **137:9** Happy shall he be, that taketh and dasheth thy little ones [her daughter religions which came out of her will also be destroyed] against the stones.

Psalm 138

A prophetic song of repentance at the coming of Christ

Messiah will deliver humanity from the Babylonian Mysteries and will destroy all false gods and religions at his coming. Then God the Father and Jesus Christ will be exalted above all the false gods of men.

Psalm 138:1 I will praise thee with my whole heart: before [Messiah and God the Father will be exalted above all authorities (Strong's lexicon 430 Elohim, all mighty ones on the earth including rulers of men as well as every false god)] the gods will I sing praise unto thee.

David will be raised to life in the resurrection to spirit and he as well as all people will look to God the Father and Messiah the Christ at the new Ezekiel Temple in Jerusalem. All humanity will be grafted into a Spiritual New Covenant [Jer 31:31, Joel 2:28) and will live by every Word of God.

138:2 I will worship toward thy holy temple, and praise thy name for thy lovingkindness and for thy truth: for thou hast magnified thy word above all thy name.

Messiah will come and will deliver humanity. then Israel and the nations will sincerely repent and turn to diligently live by every Word of God, Then Jesus Christ the Messiah Deliverer will rule all nations and rulers as King of Kings over all the earth from Jerusalem.

138:3 In the day when I cried thou answeredst me, and strengthenedst me with strength in my soul. **138:4 All the kings of the earth** shall praise thee, O LORD, when they hear the words of thy mouth. **138:5** Yea, they shall sing in the ways of the LORD: for great is the glory of the LORD.

God knows the proud even though they are far away, and he will correct them; but God delivers all those who are humble before Him.

138:6 Though the LORD be high, yet hath he respect unto the lowly: but the proud he knoweth afar off.

In the hour of trial that is soon coming on this earth we will sincerely repent of our wickedness and the Eternal will deliver us.

138:7 Though I walk in the midst of trouble, thou wilt revive me: thou shalt stretch forth thine hand against the wrath of mine enemies, and thy right hand shall save me.

God's correction is merciful; God removes wickedness and sin to bring the wicked to sincere repentance so that he can give the gift of life everlasting.

138:8 The LORD will perfect that which concerneth me: thy mercy, O LORD, endureth for ever: forsake not the works of thine own hands.

Psalm 139

God knows all things, he knows our every thought and deed, and if we are faithful he will know it and deliver us; and if we stray, God will know it and he will deliver us with his loving correction.

Psalm 139:1 O lord, thou hast searched me, and known me. **139:2** Thou knowest my downsitting and mine uprising, thou understandest my thought afar off. **139:3** Thou compassest my path and my lying down, and art acquainted with all my ways. **139:4** For there is not a word in my tongue, but, lo, O LORD, thou knowest it altogether. **139:5** Thou hast beset me behind and before, and laid thine hand upon me.

Man cannot flee from God, or hide anything from Him; man cannot justify himself before God.

139:6 Such knowledge is too wonderful for me; it is high, I cannot attain [no man can understand the magnificence of God] unto it. **139:7** Whither shall I go from thy spirit? or whither shall I flee from thy presence? **139:8** If I ascend up into heaven, thou art there: if I make my bed in hell, behold, thou art there. **139:9** If I take the wings of the morning, and dwell in the uttermost parts of the sea; **139:10** Even there shall thy hand lead me, and thy right hand shall hold me.

Nothing is kept secret or hidden from God

139:11 If I say, Surely the darkness shall cover me; even the night shall be light about me. **139:12** Yea, the darkness hideth not from thee; but the night shineth as the day: the darkness and the light are both alike to thee. **139:13** For thou hast possessed [knowest] my reins [kidney's or sensitive secret things]: thou hast covered [seen and known] me in my mother's womb.

God is to be praised for His greatness and for His wisdom in making man and all the wonderful creation.

139:14 I will praise thee; for I am fearfully and wonderfully made: marvellous are thy works; and that my soul knoweth right well.

God even knows what flesh is made of and how it is made and how it lives; for God is the Maker thereof.

139:15 My substance [composition] was not hid from thee, when I was made in secret, and curiously wrought [created] in the lowest parts of the earth [Strong's lexicon H 8482 in the pit of the womb].

God designed all the parts of the body and wrote out a plan before he made us.

139:16 Thine eyes did see my substance, yet being unperfect; and in thy book all my members were written, which in continuance were fashioned, when as yet there was none of them.

God loves mankind His created children, and God's thoughts and plans are for the ultimate good of humanity.

139:17 How precious also are thy thoughts unto me, O God! how great is the sum of them!**139:18** If I should count them, they are more in number than the sand: when I awake, I am still with thee.

The ultimately unrepentant wicked will perish, in order that the sincerely repentant may live; free from all evil for everlasting eternity.

139:19 Surely thou wilt slay the wicked, O God: depart from me therefore, ye bloody [wicked] men.

The wicked rebel against God and refuse to live by every Word of God; God will reject the unrepentant wicked. Those who love God will hate every evil way. and they will hate the deeds of the wicked.

139:20 For they [the unrepentant wicked] speak against thee wickedly, and thine enemies take thy name in vain. **139:21** Do not I hate them, O LORD, that hate thee? and am not I grieved with those that rise up against thee? **139:22** I hate them with perfect hatred: I count them mine enemies.

The wicked hate correction but the godly want God to reveal and correct their faults so that they may grow ever closer to our Beloved Father.

139:23 Search me, O God, and know my heart: try me, and know my thoughts: **139:24** And see if there be any wicked way in me, and lead me [away from wickedness into the way to life eternal] in the way everlasting.

Psalm 140

God allows many trials on the righteous, to teach them and make them into the people that he wants them to be. Consider that our trials are the education of kings who are being trained to wisely rule eternal kingdoms. We are being taught to loath wickedness and to reject every wicked way in ourselves and to execute justice for others.

Psalm 140:1 Deliver me, O LORD, from the evil man: preserve me from the violent man; **140:2** Which imagine mischiefs in their heart; continually are they gathered together for war. **140:3** They have sharpened their tongues like a serpent; adders' poison is under their lips. Selah.

140:4 Keep me, O LORD, from the hands of the wicked; preserve me from the violent man; who have purposed to overthrow my goings. **140:5** The proud have hid a snare for me, and cords; they have spread a net by the wayside; they have set gins for me. Selah.

We must also learn to completely TRUST in our righteous God to deliver us from all wickedness

140:6 I said unto the LORD, Thou art my God: hear the voice of my supplications, O LORD. **140:7** O GOD the Lord, the strength of my salvation, thou hast covered my head [God delivers the faithful godly in the battle against Satan and sin.] in the day of battle.

God will resist the wicked who refuse to live by every Word of God and he will deliver all those who turn to Him.

140:8 Grant not, O LORD, the desires of the wicked: further not his wicked device; lest they exalt themselves. Selah.

The evil counsels of the wicked will not prosper: evil men will be caught in their own snares and deceitful words.

140:9 As for the head of those that compass me about, let the mischief of their own lips cover them.

The wicked who do not sincerely repent and turn to live by every Word of God, will ultimately be cast into the lake of fire.

140:10 Let burning coals fall upon them: let them be cast into the fire; into deep pits, that they rise not up again.

Evil teachers will ultimately come to nothing and will fall into severe correction and ultimate destruction if they will not repent of their wickedness.

140:11 Let not an evil speaker be established in the earth: evil [The sorrows of God's severe correction will come upon those who teach contrary to the Word of God]. shall hunt the violent man to overthrow him.

God allows trials of his faithful to teach them godly wisdom, so that in His good time they can be resurrected to rule the nations with godly righteousness. Those who live by every Word of God will be delivered and resurrected to eternal life, even if they are afflicted by the wicked for a time.

140:12 I know that the LORD will maintain the cause of the afflicted, and the right of the poor. **140:13** Surely the righteous shall give thanks unto thy name: the upright shall dwell in thy presence.

Psalms 141 – 150

Psalm 141

The godly put their trust and hope in the LORD their Deliverer

Psalm 141:1 Lord, I cry unto thee: make haste unto me; give ear unto my voice, when I cry unto thee.

The prayers of the repentant and faithful are likened to incense which rises up to heaven as a sweet perfume to God.

141:2 Let my **prayer be set forth before thee as incense;** and the lifting up of my hands as the evening sacrifice.

The godly will seek help from God to learn and live by every Word of God and they will speak and teach righteousness.

141:3 Set a watch, O LORD, before my mouth; keep the door of my lips. **141:4** Incline not my heart to any evil thing, to practise wicked works with men that work iniquity: and let me not eat of their dainties.

Flattery brings destruction and death, but correction to godliness is deeply appreciated by God's faithful, because such correction purges out evil and brings life everlasting.

141:5 Let the righteous smite me; it shall be a kindness: and let him reprove me; it shall be an excellent oil, which shall not break my head: for yet my prayer also shall be [The godly will thank those who rightly correct them.] in their calamities.

When the wicked are overthrown at the coming of Messiah, the people will turn live by every Word of God.

141:6 When their [wicked rulers] judges are overthrown in stony places, they shall hear my [the words of godliness] words; for they are sweet.

Godly people will be afflicted by the wicked and they will die like all men, but God will give them victory over death and raise His faithful to eternal life.

141:7 Our bones are scattered at the grave's mouth, as when one cutteth and cleaveth wood upon the earth. **141:8** But mine eyes are unto thee, O GOD the Lord: in thee is my trust; leave not my soul destitute. **141:9** Keep me from the snares which they have laid for me, and the gins of the workers of iniquity.

The unrepentant wicked will perish, and those who live by every Word of God will be delivered to everlasting life.

141:10 Let the wicked fall into their own nets, whilst that I withal escape.

Psalm 142

In all our troubles we are to put our trust in the Almighty and cry out in sincere repentance to God for our deliverance.

Psalm 142:1 I cried unto the LORD with my voice; with my voice unto the LORD did I make my supplication. **142:2** I poured out my complaint before him; I shewed before him my trouble.

We are not to put our trust in men who cannot even deliver themselves, we are to trust in the Mighty God of our salvation, and we are to live by every Word of God.

142:3 When my spirit was overwhelmed within me, then thou knewest my path. In the way wherein I walked have they privily laid a snare for me. **142:4** I looked on my right hand, and beheld, but there was no man that would know me [help me]: refuge failed me; no man cared for my soul.

The godly faithful will trust and live by every Word of God; and they will cry out to God for deliverance: and if they stray they will quickly repent when they are corrected.

142:5 I cried unto thee, O LORD: I said, Thou art my refuge and my portion in the land of the living. **142:6** Attend unto my cry; for I am brought very low: deliver me from my persecutors; for they are stronger than I.

142:7 Bring my soul out of prison [God will deliver His faithful out of bondage to Satan, sin and death], that I may praise thy name [the name represents the Being, so this means to praise God who is our Deliverer]: the righteous shall compass me about; for thou shalt deal bountifully with me.

Psalm 143

When we find ourselves in times of trouble and we wonder what to do and where we should go; there is only one answer. We must turn to God and immerse ourselves in the Word of God. We must humble ourselves before God and diligently seek Him with a whole heart.

We must sincerely repent of trusting in any unscriptural false words of men, to turn to and to live by every Word of God. Only then can we expectantly call on God for His mercy and deliverance; and the Eternal Deliverer will hear us and accept us as His own.

Psalm 143:1 Hear my prayer, O LORD, give ear to my supplications: in thy faithfulness answer me, and in thy righteousness. **143:2** And enter not into judgment with thy servant: for in thy sight shall no man living be justified.

If the godly fall away becoming proud and self- justifying, full of our own ways and our own high opinions of our own righteousness; God will correct us, crushing our arrogance to contrition and humbling us before Him.

143:3 For the enemy hath persecuted my soul; he hath smitten my life down to the ground; he hath made me to dwell in darkness, as those that have been long dead. **143:4** Therefore is my spirit overwhelmed within me; my heart within me is desolate.

When our pride has been purged and turned to humility before God, then we will turn in sincere repentance to remember and to study the Word of God to learn it, and internalize it and to live by every Word of God.

143:5 I remember the days of old; I meditate on all thy works; I muse on the work of thy hands. **143:6** I stretch forth my hands unto thee: my soul thirsteth after thee, as a thirsty land. Selah.

Then with our wholehearted turning to the Eternal, He will deliver his people from bondage to Satan, sin and the grave in the resurrection.

143:7 Hear me speedily, O LORD: my spirit faileth: hide not thy face from me, lest I be like unto them that go down into the pit. **143:8** Cause me to hear thy lovingkindness in the morning; for in thee do I trust: cause me to know the way wherein I should walk; for I lift up my soul unto thee.

143:9 Deliver me, O LORD, from mine enemies [our true enemies are spiritual; Satan, sin and the grave]: I flee unto thee to hide me. **143:10** Teach me to do thy will; for thou art my God: thy spirit is good; lead me into the land of uprightness [the upright live by every Word of God].

143:11 Quicken [make alive, give life, resurrect] me, O LORD, for thy name's sake: for thy righteousness' sake bring my soul out of trouble.

A faithful servant obeys his master; therefore we are the servants of those we obey. Either doing what we want - which is sin - to our own destruction; or obeying and living by every Word of God, and receiving God's Gift of Eternal Life.

143:12 And of thy mercy cut off mine enemies, and destroy all them that afflict my soul [our enemies are spiritual; Satan, sin and the grave]: for I am thy servant.

Psalm 144

God's faithful are strengthened by the Almighty to fight all evil and sin; and God goes before those who diligently live by every Word of God to deliver them and give them victory over Satan, sin and the grave itself.

Praise God our Deliverer who is Worthy to be Praised! Let us Rejoice in Him forever!

Psalm 144:1 Blessed be the LORD my strength which teacheth my hands to war [against evil], and my fingers to fight [against sin]: **144:2** [God is] My goodness, and my fortress; my high tower, and my deliverer; my shield, and he in whom I trust; who subdueth my people under me.

God will grant his faithful eternal life and rule over the nations, just as he has granted David to be resurrected to rulership over all Israel.

God is great and God loves mankind His created children.

144:3 LORD, what is man, that thou takest knowledge of him! or the son of man, that thou makest account of him! **144:4** Man is like to vanity [a wisp of smoke here and gone, compared to God]: his days are as a shadow that passeth away.

A prophecy of the coming of Christ to rule all nations as King of kings

144:5 Bow thy heavens, O LORD, and come down: touch the mountains, and they shall smoke. **144:6** Cast forth lightning, and scatter them [Jesus Christ will crush the enemies of righteousness at His coming.]: shoot out thine arrows, and destroy them.

144:7 Send thine hand from above; rid me [Christ will deliver the godly faithful and crush the enemies of God at His coming.], and deliver me out of great waters [meaning many peoples Rev 17:15], from the hand of strange children; **144:8** Whose mouth speaketh vanity, and their right hand is a right hand of falsehood.

When Christ comes and God's dead are resurrected and given the kingdoms of men, and the enemies of God are destroyed: A new song of the Great Victory will be sung in praise of the Mighty Delivering God!

144:9 I will sing a new song unto thee, O God: upon a psaltery and an instrument of ten strings will I sing praises unto thee.

It is God who will deliver David from death and who will deliver His people from the grave to sit on thrones as kings on the earth.

144:10 It is he that giveth salvation unto kings: who delivereth David his servant from the hurtful sword.

When Christ comes he will deliver his faithful from Satan, sin and death; and the wicked will be vanquished from off the earth: and the Holy Spirit of God will be poured out on a humbled and repentant humanity (Joel 2:28).

144:11 Rid me, and deliver me from the hand of strange [wicked unrepentant people] children, whose mouth speaketh vanity, and their right hand is a right hand of falsehood:

Then the blessings of God will be poured out on the earth; first during the millennium and then forever more.

144:12 That our sons may be as plants grown up in their youth; that our daughters may be as corner stones, polished after the similitude of a palace: **144:13** That our garners may be full, affording all manner of store: that our sheep may bring forth thousands and ten thousands in our streets: **144:14** That our oxen may be strong to labour; that there be no breaking in, nor going out; that there be no complaining in our streets.

144:15 Happy is that people, that is in such a case [living by every Word of God]: yea, happy is that people, whose God is the LORD.

Psalm 145

Psalms 145 to 150 are songs of praise and rejoicing in the LORD by all people then living in the millennium; after Christ comes to deliver mankind from Satan, sin and death.

Yet, these Psalms are mainly about **the Feast of the Eighth Day**, when all peoples and nations will sing the praises of the LORD forevermore after the main harvest of humanity is brought into the Family of God.

God will give every person an opportunity to be delivered from bondage to Satan, sin and death; those who embrace that opportunity will receive the gift of life everlasting while the incorrigible unrepentant wicked will perish and the earth will be cleansed by fire. God the Father will then come down to the earth and His children will inherit the universe under the Father's leadership.

Mankind which has been redeemed and saved from eternal death, to be given the gift of eternal life in peace with no more war, suffering or death, and the gift of a universe to complete and perfect; will praise their Maker and Deliverer and their Father for all His goodness, all His mercy and all His love forevermore!

Revelation 21:4 And God shall wipe away all tears from their eyes; and there shall be no more death, neither sorrow, nor crying, neither shall there be any more pain: for the former things are passed away.

Psalm 145:1 I will extol thee, my God, O king; and I will bless thy name for ever and ever. **145:2** Every day will I bless thee; and I will praise thy name for ever and ever. **145:3** Great is the LORD, and greatly to be praised; and his greatness is unsearchable.

145:4 One generation shall praise thy works to another [every generation will praise God to all others], and shall declare thy mighty acts. **145:5** I will speak of the glorious honour of thy majesty, and of thy wondrous works. **145:6** And men shall speak of the might of thy terrible acts: and I will declare thy greatness. **145:7** They shall abundantly utter the memory of thy great goodness, and shall sing of thy righteousness.

The LORD will yet save humanity!

145:8 The LORD is gracious, and full of compassion; slow to anger, and of great mercy. **145:9** The LORD is good to all: and his tender mercies are over all his works. **145:10** All thy works shall praise thee, O LORD; and thy saints [all sincerely repentant people] shall bless thee.

145:11 They shall speak of the glory of thy kingdom, and talk of thy power; **145:12** To make known to the sons of men his mighty acts, and the glorious majesty of his kingdom. **145:13** Thy kingdom is an everlasting kingdom, and thy dominion endureth throughout all generations.

145:14 The LORD upholdeth all that fall, and raiseth up all those that be bowed down. **145:15** The eyes of all wait upon thee; and thou givest them their meat in due season. **145:16** Thou openest thine hand, and satisfiest the desire of every living thing.

145:17 The LORD is righteous in all his ways, and holy in all his works. **145:18** The LORD is nigh unto all them that call upon him, to all that call upon him in truth. **145:19** He will fulfil the desire of them that fear him: he also will hear their cry, and will save them.

145:20 The LORD preserveth all them that love him [enough to live by every Word of God]: but all the wicked will he destroy.

145:21 My mouth shall speak the praise of the LORD: and let all flesh bless his holy name for ever and ever.

Psalm 146

Psalm 146:1 Praise ye the LORD. Praise the LORD, O my soul. **146:2** While I live [the godly will live forever] will I praise the LORD: I will sing praises unto my God while I have any being.

Do not trust in the words of men but test every word of men by the Word of God, and hold fast only to what is consistent with every Word of God (1 Thess 5:22): No matter what temporal or ecclesiastical title men claim.

146:3 Put not your trust in princes, nor in the son of man, in whom there is no help. **146:4** His breath goeth forth, he returneth to his earth; in that very day his thoughts perish.

No man can save us and no words of men can save us: Only God the Father, King of the Universe and the Creator, can deliver men from Satan, sin, death and the grave.

146:5 Happy is he that hath the God of Jacob for his help, whose hope is in the LORD his God: **146:6** Which made heaven, and earth, the sea, and all that therein is: which keepeth truth for ever: **146:7** Which executeth judgment for the oppressed: which giveth food to the hungry. The LORD looseth the prisoners:

The Eternal will open the eyes of the spiritually blind and will deliver those stooped down in bondage to sin. The righteousness of God is to live by every Word of God.

146:8 The LORD openeth the eyes of the blind: the LORD raiseth them that are bowed down: the LORD loveth the righteous:

The Eternal will save those cast out of the Assemblies for their zeal to live by every Word of God, and God will save those cut off from their physical families for their zeal for godliness.

146:9 The LORD preserveth the strangers; he relieveth the fatherless and widow: but the way of the wicked he turneth upside down.

The Feast of the Eighth Day pictures a humanity changed to spirit, going forward into eternity with God, in the righteousness of living by every Word of God. Eternity as represented by the Feast of the Eighth Day will begin when the New Jerusalem comes down to the earth from heaven.

146:10 The LORD shall reign for ever, even thy God, O Zion, unto all generations. Praise ye the LORD.

Psalm 147

Praises to God for the coming and deliverance of Christ the Messiah, and for the opportunity of eternal salvation!

Psalm 147:1 Praise ye the LORD: for it is good to sing praises unto our God; for it is pleasant; and praise is comely.

When Christ comes, Jerusalem and the third Temple will be built as per Ezekiel 40 - 48 and representative populations of ALL the tribes of Israel will return to the physical Promised Land. Then those who have been humbled and had their pride broken to contrition and sincere repentance will be saved.

147:2 The LORD doth build up Jerusalem: he gathereth together the outcasts of Israel. **147:3** He healeth the broken in heart, and bindeth up their wounds.

God the Father knows every star in the heavens and he knows and loves all those who turn to Him to live by every Word of God. All the sincerely repentant who are meek, submissive and humble before God, turning in sincere repentance to diligently live by every Word of God; will be healed in spirit and delivered from bondage to Satan, sin and death; and the unrepentant wicked will be destroyed.

147:4 He telleth the number of the stars; he calleth them all by their names. **147:5** Great is our Lord, and of great power: his understanding is infinite. **147:6** The LORD lifteth up [delivers] the meek: he casteth the wicked down to the ground.

When Christ comes, a repentant Israel and humanity will sing to God in rejoicing for their deliverance; singing out to the Great God, the Giver of Salvation and all Good Things.

147:7 Sing unto the LORD with thanksgiving; sing praise upon the harp unto our God: **147:8** Who covereth the heaven with clouds, who prepareth rain for the earth, who maketh grass to grow upon the mountains. **147:9** He giveth to the beast his food, and to the young ravens which cry.

God has all power and has no need of the help of horse or man.

147:10 He delighteth not in the strength of the horse: he taketh not pleasure in the legs of a man.

God will save all those who fear to sin and who love and respect God enough to live by every Word of God.

147:11 The LORD taketh pleasure in them that fear him, in those that hope in his mercy.

Jerusalem as the capital, represents all the tribes and people of Israel, and when their Deliverer comes to save then they will all surely rejoice and praise God.

147:12 Praise the LORD, O Jerusalem; praise thy God, O Zion.

God will make Jerusalem the capital of Messiah over the whole earth, and will greatly bless her, placing the Ezekiel Temple of God within her.

147:13 For he hath strengthened the bars of thy gates; he hath blessed thy children within thee. **147:14** He maketh peace in thy borders, and filleth thee with the finest of the wheat.

> **Micah 4:2** And many nations shall come, and say, Come, and let us go up to the mountain of the Lord, and to the house of the God of Jacob; and he will teach us of his ways, and we will walk in his paths [God's ways, Word]: for the law shall go forth of Zion, and the word of the Lord from Jerusalem.

Psalm 147:15 He sendeth forth his commandment upon earth: his word runneth very swiftly.

God the Creator, made all things including the heat and the cold and the seasons of the earth.

God created the beautiful patterns of the night frost, scattering the hoar frost like grey ashes on the ground; and God makes the snows to fall on the mountains in winter and causes them to melt in summer to water the land.

147:16 He giveth snow like wool: he scattereth the hoarfrost like ashes. **147:17** He casteth forth his ice like morsels: who can stand before his cold? **147:18** He sendeth out his word, and melteth them: he causeth his wind to blow, and the waters flow.

In that day, God's Spirit will be poured out on all flesh (Joel 2:28) and all nations which have not known God will be grafted into the New Covenant (Jer 31:31) and a new spiritual Israel.

147:19 He sheweth his word unto Jacob, his statutes and his judgments unto Israel. **147:20** He hath not dealt so with any nation: and as for his judgments, they have not known them. Praise ye the LORD.

Psalm 148

A song of praise to God and Messiah for making all things and for delivering mankind from Satan, sin, death and the grave to eternal salvation.

Let every person and every being praise the Mighty God of Jacob, forever and forever, Amen!

Psalm 148:1 Praise ye the LORD. Praise ye the LORD from the heavens: praise him in the heights.

148:2 Praise ye him, all his angels: praise ye him, all his hosts. **148:3** Praise ye him, sun and moon: praise him, all ye stars of light. **148:4** Praise him, ye heavens of heavens, and ye waters that be above the heavens.

God created all things and is worthy of praise and great glory!

148:5 Let them praise the name of the LORD: for he commanded, and they were created. **148:6** He hath also stablished them for ever and ever: he hath made a decree which shall not pass. **148:7** Praise the LORD from the earth, ye dragons [wild beasts], and all deeps [creatures in the sea]:

All things will be brought into subjection and under control by God the Almighty!

148:8 Fire, and hail; snow, and vapours; stormy wind fulfilling his word: **148:9** Mountains, and all hills; fruitful trees, and all cedars: **148:10** Beasts, and all cattle; creeping things, and flying fowl:

All men will be humbled and offered the gift of Eternal Salvation, and they shall praise the God of their Salvation forever and forever, Amen!

148:11 Kings of the earth, and all people; princes, and all judges of the earth: **148:12** Both young men, and maidens; old men, and children: **148:13** Let them praise the name of the LORD: for his name alone is excellent; his glory is above the earth and heaven.

148:14 He also exalteth the horn [life and strength] of his people, the praise of all his saints [the saints are those who live by every Word of God]; even of the children of [the sincerely repentant from all nations will be grafted into the New Covenant spiritual Israel] Israel, a people [New Covenant spiritual Israel (Jer 31:31) will be a people near unto God and the Word of God will be written in their minds and on their hearts] near unto him. Praise ye the LORD.

Psalm 149

At the coming of Messiah the Christ, the resurrected saints will sing a new song of rejoicing in the deliverance of the Mighty Saviour.

Psalm 149:1 Praise ye the LORD. Sing unto the LORD a new song, and his praise in the congregation of saints.

Just as Israel rejoiced when they came up out of the Red Sea and saw their pursuers destroyed, the saints of spiritual Israel will break out in song and will dance and shout in great rejoicing when the Saviour comes and they are resurrected and delivered from the bondage of death and the grave!

149:2 Let Israel rejoice in him that made him: let the children of Zion be joyful in their King. **149:3** Let them praise his name in the dance: let them sing praises unto him with the timbrel and harp.

The Eternal will save his sincerely repentant people and will give the gift of eternal salvation to those who are meek and teachable before God the Great, the Almighty!

149:4 For the LORD taketh pleasure in his people: he will beautify the meek with salvation.

When Messiah comes with deliverance the resurrected saints will rejoice day and night for their deliverance from bondage to Satan, sin and death.

149:5 Let the saints be joyful in glory: let them sing aloud upon their beds.

The resurrected servants of God will be full of the TRUTH of every Word of God, and the sword of truth will continually be in their mouths to destroy all wickedness and sin from off the earth!

149:6 Let the high praises of God be in their mouth, and a two-edged sword in their hand;

Messiah the Christ and all his resurrected saints - the bride of the New Covenant - will come to rule all nations with the truth and righteousness of every Word of God, and they will correct the unrepentant and cleanse the earth of wickedness and sin.

149:7 To execute vengeance upon the heathen [the unrepentant wicked], and punishments upon the [upon unrepentant wicked people] people;

The king of wickedness is Satan and his kings are his spirit followers who have enslaved the nations; they will be bound and imprisoned for one thousand years and will then be defeated one last time and judged to destruction. See the Fall Festivals studies.

149:8 To bind their kings with chains, and their nobles with fetters of iron;

The resurrected saints will have the honour, with Christ; of executing the judgment of God and destroying Satan and his demonic followers on the Fast of Atonement.

149:9 To execute upon them the judgment written: this honour have all his saints. Praise ye the LORD.

Psalm 150

God our Maker the God of our Salvation will save humanity from bondage to Satan, demons, sin, sorrows, suffering and death; to give the gift of eternal life to all those who live by every Word of God.

Then as pictured by The Feast of The Eighth Day, all sincerely repentant humanity will inherit the entire universe and will go forward in peace and unity with God for everlasting eternity!

Praise God forever and forever; for all that he does for the sins of men!

Psalm 150:1 Praise ye the LORD. Praise God in his sanctuary: praise him in the firmament of his power. **150:2** Praise him for his mighty acts: praise him according to his excellent greatness. **150:3** Praise him with the sound of the trumpet: praise him with the psaltery and harp. **150:4** Praise him with the timbrel and dance: praise him with stringed instruments and organs. **150:5** Praise him upon the loud cymbals: praise him upon the high sounding cymbals. **150:6** Let every thing that hath breath praise the LORD. Praise ye the LORD.

Visit our Website

theshininglight.info

www.ingramcontent.com/pod-product-compliance
Lightning Source LLC
Chambersburg PA
CBHW082109230426
43671CB00015B/2650